THE PRACTICES OF HOPE

The Practices of Hope

Literary Criticism in Disenchanted Times

Christopher Castiglia

NEW YORK UNIVERSITY PRESS
New York

NEW YORK UNIVERSITY PRESS
New York
www.nyupress.org

References to Internet websites (URLs) were accurate at the time of writing. Neither the author nor New York University Press is responsible for URLs that may have expired or changed since the manuscript was prepared.

Library of Congress Cataloging-in-Publication Data
Names: Castiglia, Christopher, author.
Title: The practice of hope : literary critics in disenchanted times / Christopher Castiglia.
Description: New York : New York University Press, c2017. | Includes bibliographical references and index.
Identifiers: LCCN 2017008042| ISBN 978-1-4798-1827-3 (cl : alk. paper) | ISBN 978-1-4798-0355-2 (pb : alk. paper)
Subjects: LCSH: Criticism,
Classification: LCC PN81 .C393 2017 | DDC 801/.95—dc23
LC record available at https://lccn.loc.gov/2017008042

New York University Press books are printed on acid-free paper, and their binding materials are chosen for strength and durability. We strive to use environmentally responsible suppliers and materials to the greatest extent possible in publishing our books.

Manufactured in the United States of America

10 9 8 7 6 5 4 3 2 1

Also available as an ebook

For Robert L. Caserio

CONTENTS

ACKNOWLEDGMENTS

This book began when Gordon Hutner invited me to write an article for *American Literary History* on Newton Arvin. I am deeply grateful to him for that invitation. A version of chapter 2 appeared in the *New Cambridge Companion to Herman Melville*, a section of the fourth chapter appeared in a special issue of *Early American Literature*, and sections of the introductory material appeared in *Turns of Events, Critique and Postcritique*, and a special issue of *English Language Notes*. With these publications I benefited from the thoughtful criticism provided by anonymous readers and from the insight and generous guidance given by their editors, for which I thank Robert S. Levine, Hester Blum, Rita Felski, Elizabeth Anker, Russ Castronovo, David Glimp, Sandra Gustafson, Edward Cahill, and Edward Larkin. I gratefully acknowledge permission to reprint those sections here.

For inviting me to present portions of this book at conferences or at their home institutions, I offer my thanks to Jonathan Arac, Hester Blum, Amanda Claybaugh, Dave Coolin, Nan Da, Jonathan Elmer, Bert Emerson, Carrie Hyde, Eve Keller, Greg Laski, Dominic Mastroianni, Lloyd Pratt, Joseph Rezek, and Leonard Tennenhouse. I also thank audience members at those presentations for helpful questions, comments, and suggestions, especially David J. Alworth, Paul Bové, Ed Cahill, Leigh Gilmore, Nancy Glazener, Christian Haines, Glenn Hendler, Maurice Lee, Heather Love, Joseph Rezek, Augusta Rohrbach, Jack Selzer, and Jordan Stein. My chapter on Richard Chase benefited from several conversations with Bradley King. My deepest thanks go to Donald E. Pease, whose encouragement of and insight into this project since its inception have demonstrated a generosity and a capacious intelligence from which I consistently benefited. He is the interlocutor one both fears and thanks one's stars for.

Much of my thinking for this book happened during a graduate course I taught at Penn State. To the participants of that section of English 597 I owe a large debt. I am also grateful to the graduate students who have continued on that journey with me, especially Ting Chang, Colin Hogan, Lisa McGunigle, Ryan Marks, Eric Norton, Nate Redman, Sarah Salter, Erica Stevens, Tyler Roeger, Eric Vallee, and Nate Windon. Your generosity to me and to each other has been an inspiration. I thank Leslie Joblin for her meticulous help in preparing the manuscript.

Many colleagues and friends have offered commentary, listened patiently, and/or gotten me laughing during the writing of this book, for which I give my hearty thanks to Branka Arsić, Martin Berger, Michael Bérubé, Hester Blum, Joe Bound, Russ Castronovo, David Chinitz, Elizabeth Maddock Dillon, Tom Douthit, Paul Erickson, Eric Hayot, Kate Jensen, Julia Spicher Kasdorf, Kristen Kelly, Bob Levine, Chris Looby, Janet Lyon, Jen Manion, Anne McCarthy, Dana Nelson, Carina Pasquesi, Rick Rodriguez, Ben Schreier, Susan Squier, Matt Tierney, Priscilla Wald, Joyce Wexler, Jim Woodell, and the Rumors crowd (you know who you are). Dana Nelson, my co-editor on *J19*, has been almost every day for the last five years a source of sanity, sensitivity, and laughter. I am enormously grateful to have that in my life.

From my first meeting with Eric Zinner to discuss this book, I knew his sensitivity to its concerns, his capacious understanding of the audience it addresses, and his dry sense of humor as a counter to my rambling enthusiasm all make him the editor I had hoped to find. I am enormously grateful to him for his guidance, support, and patience. I also want to thank Alicia Nadkarni and Alexia Traganas for their cheerful guidance throughout the process.

A Mellon Distinguished Scholar Residency at the American Antiquarian Society and a faculty fellowship at the Penn State Institute for the Arts and Humanities enabled the writing of this book. I am grateful to the staff and directors of the AAS and the IAH. I thank the Columbia University Butler Library Special Collections staff and the Smith College Sophia Smith Collection staff for their guidance through the Richard Chase and Newton Arvin papers, respectively. I would like to thank as well Mark Morrisson for his support as friend, colleague, and department head.

Robert L. Caserio has been a colleague, mentor, friend, dinner companion, and source of inexhaustible knowledge. His generous enthusiasm, his staggering erudition, his unflagging kindness, and his levelheaded professionalism have sustained and guided me throughout the writing of this book. Dedicating it to him is the least I could do to show my gratitude.

This book really has a co-author, Chris Reed, my partner in everything. He read draft after draft, discussed every idea, kept me from going too far off the tracks, and convinced me the book was worth writing when I wasn't so sure. His shrewd intelligence, his impeccable editing, his tough criticism, and his interesting conversation made the book—and me—stronger and kinder. In ways big and small, he is both my hope and its fulfillment.

Introduction

Practices of Hope and Tales of Disenchantment

These are disenchanted times in literary criticism. There are indeed plenty of reasons for anger, despair, and disappointment today. While circumstances can create suffering, however, they do not dictate the dispositions with which those conditions are met. Disenchantment is the disposition that political theorist Jane Bennett describes as arising when the world is pictured as "a place of death and alienation," and when "the very characterization of the world as disenchanted ignores and then discourages affective attachment to that world."[1] Although disenchantment is not the only such disposition, it is the one criticism has most often endorsed, maintaining practices of professionalization in a discipline that—perhaps not coincidentally—finds itself of rapidly decreasing interest to students and broader audiences. We did not invent critical disenchantment, of course. Nearly seven decades ago, Richard Chase complained of his colleagues who sever and reject, fetishize alienated emotions, dismiss previous generations, and "puff our inner righteousness into an image of the universe and annihilate every other image."[2] That long history does not mean, however, that disenchantment is intrinsic to literary critique. Neither Bennett nor Chase questions the need for critique of an unjust world. What they do challenge is the assumption that to be effective, critique must become what Bennett calls a "disenchantment tale," narrowing it to exclude the replenishing experiences of wonder that make the world worth fighting for and encourage resilience when those struggles seem overwhelming; disenchantment tales discourage "affective connections" in contexts where detachment is dangerous.

Recent challenges to critical disenchantment have taken on the label of "postcritique." This movement challenges the knee-jerk suspicion with which critics scrutinize a text's purported depths for ideological wrongdoings (and, less often, subversions thereof) by abstract and clearly distinguishable agents locked in easily schematized struggle.[3] What Jennifer Fleissner characterizes as "the self-aggrandizing tendencies of the moralized ideology critique"[4] rarely acknowledges complexities of complicity or motivation, least of all on the part of the seemingly objective, unimplicated, and superior critic. My sympathies are with this critique of critique. But I want to argue that contemporary criticism comprises at least three versions of critique, not one, and that they require separate considerations. The first version is the most exasperating because of its rote and often cynical predictability, arising from professionalization into a discipline in which a tone of self-congratulatory indignation is taken as the sign of critical acuity and topical relevance imagined to be requisite for publication, job placement, and academic advancement. It is this version of critique that has pushed some to seek methodological alternatives in a desire to move "post" critique.

It is a mistake, however, to abandon critique simply because it has been badly used. Any critical methodology can become grad school *doxa* and eventually grow hackneyed, which does not make it unnecessary. Yet even suspicious critique at its more vigorous—the second version—should not continue unaltered. It arose from a Cold War state epistemology that, maintained melancholically long past the Cold War's end, not only makes critique seem outdated but puts its conservative methodology and progressive content at cross-purposes. Despite its perpetuation of the divisive and disenchanted Cold War disposition, however, I believe a third version of critique is possible. Less belated and more suited to current needs in academia and beyond, the critique I have in mind centers on two terms—"idealism" and "imagination"—that may seem naive or old-fashioned but are essential to making criticism more than a disenchantment tale.

My argument is that critique at its best comprises the analytical challenge of *expressed* idealism. Theodor Adorno insists that every utopian statement is a "determined negation," a critique of the present in the act of articulating a more desirable future.[5] The opposite is also true: every critique is a determined affirmation, an inverted expression of idealism. In offering critiques, we measure the present or the past against ideals, in comparison to which what is or has been seems inadequate and unjust. Without ideals, there would be no critique. But our ideals are effaced by rituals of professionalization in a discipline that regards articulation of idealism as a sign of naïveté, triviality, or bad faith, making idealism cause for embarrassment. A critique that states our ideals, in contrast, would make clear what we are for, demonstrating how idealism is the basis for ethical judgment and encouraging the shaping and expression of ideals necessary to social engagement and change. Affirming our ideals, we claim for critique its greatest and most generous social relevance.

Idealism, always present, implicitly and explicitly, in critique, is not enough. Imagination is what makes idealism a *social* practice. Too often, however, current habits of critique brush aside the ficticity of imaginative literature as mere reflection or obfuscation of something *real* prior to and weightier than fantasy. But literature's *unreality* is what makes it most socially relevant. Imagination guarantees the perpetual unreality of ideals, refusing the imperative "reality" that limits the possible to what is or has been, to precedent and presence. More constructively, imagination shapes ideals into worlds, giving them the look of the social in ways that keep us from abandoning our desire for material consequences, and simultaneously making the *social* into an unreal—and hence reimaginable—possibility. Imagination allows us to express ideals in familiar forms—as a system, a social structure—without accepting as necessary the terms in which that familiarity is currently constituted. When we *acknowledge* imagination as the proper location of the ideal, we infuse the real with inexhaustible wonder. Embracing critical imagination will mean relinquishing our infatuation with fact, evidence, and the supposedly transparent *realness* of history or sociology, the stable and empirical sources of what Rita Felski analyzes as the illusion of "context" and hence of "meanings."[6] What we get in return is the unpredictable and potentially liberating possibility of enchantment, as available to critique as to the literature it analyzes. And that, too, is central to critique's potential for social engagement and change, for there is no significant social change without imagination. "In imagining what is possible, in imagining what does not yet exist," Sara Ahmed writes, "we say yes to . . . the possibility of things not staying as they are, or being as they stay."[7] The same imagination that can make literature a rejection of what is in favor of what might be can turn critique into a radically transformative affirmation. Far from being a disenchantment tale, a critique that embraces that visionary function produces what F. O. Matthiessen calls "imaginative vitality."[8]

As my citations of Chase and Matthiessen suggest, in setting about the work of reimagining critique, we need not start from scratch. Eve Sedgwick suggests that the new life of the discipline lies, paradoxically, in the past, and I agree. The following chapters offer models for a revitalized critique drawn from Cold War era intellectuals. Although often disparaged as apologists for American exceptionalism and the Cold War consensus, these critics, I will show, not only strenuously opposed the conformity and paranoid destructiveness of Cold War America but envisioned more just and humane alternatives. Subject to harassment, arrest, and loss of jobs, they had ample reasons for disenchantment, and some of the most prominent critics of this era suffered from alcoholism, mental breakdowns, and suicide. What is striking, however, is how little disenchantment there is in their criticism. On the contrary, they articulate remarkable wonder at the imaginative possibilities of literature as a source of social critique and, more surprisingly, transformation. How imaginative idealism continued to thrive in their criticism despite the odds and how we might, as they did, turn disenchanted critique into a practice of hope are the subjects of this book.

Hope, as I use the term, is different from optimism or want, its two most common synonyms. Far from implying a cheery faith that all will turn out well, hope, as I will discuss shortly, relies on disappointment and failure. And because ideals are by nature incommensurate with lived conditions, hope is a continuous dissatisfaction; unlike wants, it cannot be satisfied. Instead, hope, as a perpetual openness to the as-yet-untried, is an end in itself. Hope is a disposition toward the imaginative value of dissatisfaction and the social value of illusion, whimsy, vision, reverie, daydreams, all sources of world making trivialized within disciplinary regimes of the "real." Hope is the articulation of the origins of critique in imaginative idealism, self-consciously unachievable standards for living, tested and refined in the context of an as-yet-unreal world, against which real conditions inevitably come up short. Hope is what I would identify as the *literariness* of literature. It is also the thing without which social change is impossible.

Literary critics, persistent in their suspicion, have overlooked the centrality of hope to cultural theorists who have described its socially transformative powers. Hope as a disposition can be central to what Nancy Bentley calls "a collective mood-shift" in contemporary literary studies.[9] Because of its transformative potential as a disposition rather than a prescriptive program, hope may avoid the charges of political complacency that have dogged some other methodologies identified with that shift. At a time when suspicious critique is often taken to be synonymous with politics, challenges to the former can "easily be dismissed as politically quietist, too willing to accept things as they are," as Stephen Best and Sharon Marcus acknowledge, though they refute that charge with the argument that "immersion in texts (without paranoia or suspicion about their merit or value)" may result in an "attentiveness to the artwork as itself a kind of freedom."[10] They speculate that "in relinquishing the freedom dream that accompanies the work of demystification, we might be groping toward some equally valuable, if less glamorous, states of mind."[11]

Although I agree that greater attention to the artwork can generate new freedoms, I worry that a programmatic change (reading a text's surface rather than searching its depths, for example) without a clearly articulated shift in disposition (one can read surfaces as suspiciously as one reads depths) will produce the fallacies John Guillory calls "spontaneous philosophies," which arise from "the assumption that epistemological positions have a *necessary* relation to political positions."[12] Responding to a perceived crisis in the ways we read now, we run the risk of unintentionally replicating some of critique's least salutary features: the binary logics, the self-righteously unambiguous and unambivalent presentation of rote conclusions, the lack of critical self-contextualization, the denial of inheritances from earlier critical movements we imagine we have surpassed in sophistication and ethical commitment. If we simply make critique into the object of suspicious scrutiny, feeling superior to and unimplicated in what we would move "post," all we are likely to produce is critique *après la lettre*. I believe, however, that a critical disposition toward hope can play a social role without suspicion or objectivity. Hope, as a dispositional alternative, promises an approach to social engagement that revises, rather than relinquishes, criticism's "freedom dream" in at least three ways.

First, hope challenges present social conditions insofar as they fail to live up to a reader's ideals. Hopeful analysis does not stop with the critique of what is, however, but works through the damaging consequences of those conditions to arrive at constructive—although not naively utopian—alternatives. As Julia Kristeva asserts, "It is only by traversing our grief that there can be any possibility of hope."[13] Maintaining historical specificity through critique of existing circumstances, hope nevertheless does not confine its ideals to historiographical definitions of the real that limit the scope of the possible. Hope retains a trace of material history through the terms of critique while denying, in its ideals of the possible, the imperative precedents of history or the limits on possibility imposed by truth claims grounded in empirical appeals to material "reality." This is the second function of hope: to open to the imagination abstract values, suggesting new applications for venerable concepts in ways that bring us together in public acts of deliberation. And last and most important, hope engages readers in the speculative world making it models and inspires.

Understood in this way, hope is socially transformative, although not in the narrowest sense "political." Hopeful ideals generate social engagement, as I have suggested, by providing the standards against which the already existing world is measured. That function can rely on individual ideals, but the work of social transformation requires collective deliberation at least as much as individual critique. To that end, ideals in their fullness generate critique, but as a means of collective deliberation they must be evacuated of any fixed content. They must be recognizable by a group as the placeholder of meanings that are not predetermined and are, therefore, subject to deliberative participation. "Democracy," for example, is perceived by many as an ideal worthy of collective consideration, yet the definition of that term is subject to collective (but not necessarily consensual) meaning making, which in turn not only defines but becomes democratic. An ideal thus becomes a practice of hope because of its emptiness, which is not an absence of meaning but an availability of multiple (but not limitless) meanings. Describing this seeming paradox as a practice he calls hope, Ernesto Laclau observes that hope registers an unfulfilling present, being "always related to something which is lacking."[14] He describes how "empty signifiers"[15] allow groups with diverse demands to converge under the umbrella of an "empty" ideal, forming what he calls "a political frontier."[16] Such frontiers strengthen hope by allowing those who make demands to feel part of a larger—even a universal—collectivity that also gives specificity to abstractions that become anchored, through particular wants, to historical contingencies.[17] The exchange between universals and particularities generates what Laclau calls "a moment of hope," the occasion for a practice by which demands collect to form a political force and are given ethical extension.[18]

The process Laclau describes is a perpetual struggle, evacuating ideals even as it strives to reconceive them. Such perpetual yearning for alternative presents is hope as a passion and hence as politics. This is where the quality of imagination joins with evacuated ideals to form what Chantal Mouffe calls a "kind of place-holder for all those things that cannot be reduced to interest or rationality," among which she includes "all those things that a rationalist approach is unable to understand in the very construction of human subjectivity and identity."[19] For Mouffe, political progress comes out of hope's perpetually unfinished business, or what she calls "the *radical impossibility* of democracy."[20] Arguing that democracy "is something that will always need to be a *project* which we are going to fight for, but knowing that we will never be able to reach it," Mouffe concludes that "there is no final goal—*democracy is a process*."[21]

The democratic project arising from evacuated signifiers takes specific shape if we assume, for example, that "race" is not a fixed position but a dis-position, an evacuated sign that allows the imaginative construction of new "postrace" narratives. This is the case made by Ramón Saldívar, who writes that "postrace" novels "perform the critical work of symbolic action, denoting the public work of the private imagination." Saldívar insists that such imaginings are enacted not from a fixed social position but "through the pathway of fantasy in the service of the profoundly unsymbolic racialized imagination." The "historical fantasy" is thus released from symbolic representation, giving rise not to a subject determined by established life narratives, as the "racial" subject, but to an actor in the collective invention of what Saldívar calls "new political destinies." Understood in this way, fantasy is not "merely phantasmal depiction of deep ideological mystifications"—a description that sounds like many literary critics' concept of a text's narrative as an obfuscation of "deeper" ideological meanings—but the basis for understanding and joining in the making of new social "destinies we may witness taking shape among diasporic groups in the US today."[22] "Race," evacuated of given significances, becomes a dynamic basis for new "political frontiers." And it is Saldívar's own inventive ideal of a relationship between narrative and history in which the latter does not overdetermine the former that makes his a critical practice of hope.

The terms central to these contemporary critics' various definitions of hope—"loss," "emptiness," "evacuation," and "dissatisfaction"—may seem strange synonyms for a concept usually associated with optimism. But these terms describe states of unsettlement and dissatisfaction—crisis and disappointment—central to any practice of hope. That practice welcomes, even instigates, what Gayatri Spivak calls "bring[ing] to crisis." At the heart of both crisis and hope, Spivak says, is "that moment which you cannot plan for," which forces "something inherited" to "jump into something other, and fix onto something that is opposed." Shaken loose from the stranglehold of precedent and convention, an unanticipated moment can rearrange the social landscape, generating possibilities that require, in Spivak's words, "not the leap of faith, which hope brings *into* crisis, but rather the leap of hope."[23] Describing a disturbance of the known akin to Spivak's crisis, Ernst Bloch articulates hope's refusal to "make peace with the existing world," which denies the change and chance that, for Bloch, frustrate any assertions of finality, predictability, or satisfaction. The affective response to hope's refusal of "the existing world" is what Bloch calls disappointment, which is not the sign of despair but the productive proof that hope is doing its work, that people are being propelled beyond the limits of complacency. According to Bloch, we know "*well-founded* hope, mediated, guiding hope," because, unlike wants with predefined satisfactions, it is almost certainly accompanied by disappointment, without which "*it would not be hope.*"[24]

In Bloch's view, disappointment—the affective condition of crises in the known—is therefore the metric of critique's ethical judgments. For Bloch, power runs like a current through assemblages of fact, which are versions of experience told from positions of dominance, discrediting competing accounts as naïveté, ignorance, or triviality. But those accounts represent *someone's* (often a collective someone's) ideal realness, and when these versions rub together, hope is the friction. Discerning that "so-called facts are not standing still, but are circulating and developing," Bloch contends that hope attains the right—the *obligation*—not only to reveal but to *judge* the tendencies of the real. It is that act of judgment that makes critique a social force. Similarly, activism, for Rebecca Solnit, is a practice of hope, springing from the belief that "another world might be possible, not promised, not guaranteed, but made."[25] Such making is only possible, however, with the simultaneous evacuation—the putting into crisis—of the real accompanied by the imaginative idealism of hope. As Solnit notes, the common feature of transformative social movements "is that they begin in the imagination, in hope."[26]

The irony is that imagination is often what leads to dismissals of hope as trivial, but imagination constitutes hope's reparative capacity. Such derogations are common in a society where the humanities in general and literary studies in particular are seen as impractical luxuries and wastes of time (who would want an imaginative, much less an idealistic, workforce?). But literature, for Bloch, has an essential social function as the site of what he calls "anticipatory illuminations," which represent what "has not yet become, that which has still not been accomplished, but which has not been thwarted in existence."[27] For Bloch, anticipatory illuminations constitute what Michael Taussig calls "the half-awake world" in which "free-floating attention" generates hope.[28] Emerging from such states does not mean, for Taussig, "awakening from a period of inertia to one of action," but rather engaging an imaginative "demystification and re-enchantment" of the real that gives hope "an electrifying role to play."[29]

Thus conceived, hope arises from what the midcentury American literary critic Newton Arvin names "the marvelous, the picturesque, the half-incredible," all of which he attributes to imaginative literature.[30] In making that claim, Arvin is the heir to Ralph Waldo Emerson, who endorses a belief in "the Unattainable, the flying Perfect."[31] For Emerson, literature imagines into being "a point outside of our hodiernal circle through which a new one may be described"; it "afford[s] us a platform whence we may command a view of our present life, a purchase by which we may move it."[32] Or, as Arvin writes of Whitman, "Wonder and reverence and a mystical faith that based itself upon them, this—and not respect for demonstrable fact"—is the desirable state of mind for approaching literature.[33] Arvin's reference to wonder anticipates Jane

Bennett's description of an "ethic for a disenchanted world," which requires "the exercise of imagination. Though not quite an imperative, imagination is an interior 'injunction,' a 'weakly messianic' urge to exercise one's capacity to see things as otherwise than they are. Imagination energizes us with alternatives, with the power of the new and startling and wonderful. The burden of this task falls to imagination now that, unfortunately, the outside, everyday world—disenchanted of spirit—is utterly unable to inspire and enliven us."[34]

It may be difficult to believe that hope holds these possibilities, since political disenchantment in the United States derives in part from too much rhetoric about hope. From Ronald Reagan's "New Day in America" to Barack Obama's "Audacity of Hope," such invocations consistently prove enticements to surrender social imagination to a government that gestures toward inclusion but more typically generates the estranged conditions that lead citizens to grasp at such flimsy promises. Rhetorics of hope coming from mainstream politicians can contribute to disenchantment by promising effortlessly enchanted futures. Yet disenchantment, in political rhetoric as in literary criticism, is subject to revision. If hope, in contemporary political discourse, is a hollow concept, then like all evacuated signifiers it is also an opportunity.

Seizing this opportunity will have profound consequences for the practice of literary criticism, starting with who we imagine literary critics to be. Hand in hand with conventional critical practices that assert as fact claims for what a text is "really" saying beneath its aesthetic distractions or on its surface goes the construction of the critic as objective, disinvested, and terribly serious. Challenging ideology is hard work, and critics may be forgiven impulses to heighten their gravity by disparaging what is trivial, superficial, fantastic, and speculative, all elements of the text's distracting surface. But no critique is complete without the simultaneity of familiarity and wonder, of the real and the anticipatory. Taking hope as a critical disposition may have to start with a change of self-conception by the critic. When I advocate for hopeful reading, then, I am urging us to forsake claims to constant suspicious vigilance and instead heed the "half-awake" nature of literature, its traffic in daydreams, reveries, speculations, intuitions, all sources of imaginative idealism.

Literature is a training ground in the unreal—what Bennett, following Friedrich Schiller, calls an "aesthetic education"—and hence a powerful partner in the work of critique aimed not *at* the text but alongside it.[35] If we see literature not only as the object of criticism but as its best source of restorative wonder, we might again have a critique in the service of what R. W. B. Lewis called "living value," a self-transforming and adaptable willingness to hold vision above necessity.[36] Literature's hopefulness, Newton Arvin tells us, is "accessible as always to those who wish not merely to 'interpret the world variously' (in Marx's phrase) but to change it."[37] Without hope, we have, in Arvin's words, "no more notion of what literature is about than a mole has of astronomy."[38] As literary critics scramble to prove our relevance, instead of selling out our stock-in-trade in exchange for greater market shares in the "real world," we might try showing how the *unreal* world—the realm of idealism and imagination, of hope—is precisely what makes literary study valuable, even necessary. Before making that case, though, we may have to relearn how to approach literature not with suspicion but with what Richard Chase calls "a kind of thought which is bounteous, in the sense that it is open-minded, skeptical, and humanist."[39]

A more bounteous criticism will first require a change in disposition. A frame of mind or orientation, a disposition is less self-conscious than a methodology and more sustained than a mood.[40] Dispositions are neither natural character traits nor simple matters of circumstance (either "he's just born happy" or "if I had what she has I'd be happy too") but what make certain epistemologies feel right, even necessary. The fact that dispositions change, often en masse, suggests that they are historically grounded, as much the product of the times as of the literary texts under scrutiny. To begin to understand—and change—our contemporary critical disposition, then, we should start with its historical sources in the Cold War.

The historian John Lewis Gaddis argues that the Cold War itself was a battle of dispositions in which orientation toward action took the place of action itself. Unlike the world war that proceeded it, which solicited active participation from American civilians (rationing, knitting, factory work, etc.), the Cold War required little except dispositions that could be manipulated for what Gaddis calls "immediate psychological benefits."[41] Citizens underwent exercises like the "duck and cover" drills in American schools, which produced not a rational reassurance of safety during nuclear attack but a perpetual state of *readiness*; citizens were encouraged to understand "politics" not in terms of what the government did or asked them to do but by what dispositions it encouraged them to adopt. Coming of age in that era, early proponents of New Historicism, New Americanism, and other forms of ideology critique not only made their tone a signature feature of literary criticism but turned dispositions into a *sign* of politics: a critic's orientation toward politics came to stand in for an explicit articulation of social or political ideals or positions. So entrenched did this substitution become that, as I observed earlier, a challenge to a critic's disposition is taken as a rejection of her or his politics. Today dispositions of arch knowingness, breathless outrage, or detached condescension render *unnecessary* any clearly articulated political commitment, being a dispositional sign that a critic is *ready* for engagement, even when none ensues.

Among the dispositions encouraged in citizens during the Cold War, none was as powerful as suspicion, which became the epistemological center of the Cold War state's authority. In the Cold War United States, government leaders taught Americans that communists—and their equivalent, homosexuals—could be anywhere, even among friends and family. A citizen's duty was to sniff them out, report them, and feel proud to be an agent in freedom's security, without investigating or imagining alternatives to the imperative logics underlying definitions of "freedom." Convincing citizens that dangerous ideological agents lurked behind surface innocence, the state made suspicion a national disposition. Suspicion thus operated as the dispositional entrance into what Donald Pease calls a "state fantasy" in large part because its objects, being hidden, were potentially ubiquitous, making the realm of state inquiry inexhaustible and its explanatory capacities total.[42] There was no outside to Cold War suspicion; citizens could adopt it as a patriotic disposition or become its object. The world broke into a clear-cut opposition between abstract political philosophies, as absolute attitudinal differences between smugness and shame, suspicion and furtiveness, schematized what might otherwise have been understood as a complex web of complicities and similarities.

The way its critics characterize "critique"—a suspicious peering below a text's surface to reveal the unsavory ideologies concealed below, creating absolute and abstract binary oppositions identified by an unimplicated (and hence superior) critic—suggests its Cold War origins. If it was almost inevitable that suspicion became a predominant critical disposition for baby boomers raised during the height of the Cold War, what is surprising is that criticism, reproducing the epistemological dispositions of the Cold War state, sustains an identification with the same state whose ideological positions that criticism, in its content, frequently opposes. Long past the Cold War's end, in other words, critical disposition and content work at cross-purposes, a condition of belatedness that has given some the impression that critique has, in Bruno Latour's words, run out of steam.[43] By rote reproduction, an already-problematic Cold War disposition has lived on long past its moment, becoming the professionalized combination of suspicion, self-approbation, and indignation that, with a nod to Stephen Colbert, I call *critiquiness*.

As part of his satire of ultraconservative commentary on the televised *Colbert Report*, Colbert coined "truthiness" to describe the *sound* of truthfulness without reference to logic or fact but based solely on what a speaker (usually, for Colbert, a politician) and his or her audience wish to be true. Critiquiness, similarly, names the appearance of critique, of textual politics, that produces expectations about the way the world— and the text—works without reckoning with experiences that vary from or defy those expectations. Like truthiness, with its sanctimonious assertions of facts that seem to prove the ideology that generates them, critiquiness performs self-satisfaction about an agency (an "ideology") locatable in a text's "depth" that is a phantasmatic location of the critic's own beliefs, which, because of their projection onto a text, do not need to be named or defended. Critiquiness, like truthiness, is a disposition that substitutes for the work properly done by the root term ("truth" or "critique"). It is the *sound* of critique without the ethical positioning, the explicit statement of ideals, and the imaginative presentation of alternatives based on those ideals that critique at its best involves.

Critique's optimal disposition is available to us, of course, but it requires deliberate practice, an ongoing movement toward what Jane Bennett describes as "a feeling of being connected in an affirmative way to existence."[44] For Bennett this process, akin to what Michel Foucault calls "the care of the self,"[45] requires three stages: "a set of *exercises* . . . to install the ethical code on the body; a *rationale* for obedience to ethical principles and exercises; and *an ideal of the self* to which the ethical person aspires."[46] These terms offer a template for literary critics whose intensive focus on their object of study can preclude an equally rigorous analysis of their own dispositions. "Exercise" suggests sustained attention to the ethical positions associated with continuous study of literature, taking seriously the effects of literature on ethics and not just the other way around. The second step—rationale—is even more important: as Latour observes, the stale predictability of much recent scholarly critique arises from its lack of self-analysis and its unwillingness to justify disciplinary *doxa*.[47] Finally, "an ideal of the self" may expand to include ideals for the world in and around literature and literary criticism, making dispositional "care" into a practice of hope. Such a process potentially enables greater freedom of speculation, more willingness to locate social engagement in places other than in abstract ideological agencies, renewed faith in the imaginative and unempirical, and deeper respect for the cultural seriousness of seemingly fanciful forms that articulate the *not-yetness* of social experiences vying for public credibility. It would mean understanding critique as a practice of hope.

The following chapters take up a number of mid-twentieth-century American writers on canonic American literature—Granville Hicks, Constance Rourke, Richard Chase, Newton Arvin, Charles Feidelson, Marius Bewley, and Richard Poirier, as well as R. W. B. Lewis, F. O. Matthiessen, C. L. R. James, and Lewis Mumford—who, across the period running from the Great Depression through the first decades of the Cold War to the conflict in Vietnam, wrote criticism advocating for the imaginative idealism of hope. Most of those critics are forgotten or ignored today, or, when they are recalled, they are disparaged as Cold War nationalists of the "myth and symbol" variety. The following chapters will argue, however, that together they form a valuable past for critical practices of hope today. Here one example, drawn from the end of the period under consideration, will suggest the trajectory of the history I trace.

In 1963, the young Indian scholar A. N. Kaul published his prizewinning Yale dissertation as *The American Vision: Actual and Ideal Society in Nineteenth-Century Fiction*. Kaul urged readers to move beyond inevitable reality to embrace the world-making capabilities of the social imagination. There "is a way of regarding social reality," Kaul writes, "which takes into account not only observable social facts but also various aspects of imaginative response to these facts; which considers such things as ideals, or mythic archetypes of thought, to be important if not readily visible components of that reality."[48] For Kaul, critique is not political in the common sense, since it does not suggest "even to the most sanguine mind anything more than a possibility, a suggestion of potential reality."[49] Yet that "possibility" is not without social consequences. While "practical men battled over new political and economic institutions," Kaul writes, nineteenth-century authors sought "the moral values necessary for the regeneration of human society," a search that brought them repeatedly to "the theme of ideal community life."[50] Criticism that neglects the value of such "potential realities" limits itself to what Kaul calls "a mere instrumentality." In contrast, he refers to William James, who understood that an effective social theory would involve "a critical attitude toward the actual society of the time on the one hand and a constant preoccupation with ideal community life on the other."[51] It is this combination that I identify as the practice of hope.

The hardest question one could ask of nineteenth-century American authors, which is also the toughest posed to those advancing the new "mood" in literary criticism today, is, as Kaul knew, "whether they can be said to possess any relevance to that culture's present reality."[52] The answer, he also knew, is yes, especially because in generating his vision of the good society, the nineteenth-century author "had to depart more radically from the imitation of existing reality and rely more heavily instead on the plastic power of his imagination."[53] That imagination, Kaul observes, was uniquely capable of undertaking, as Mark Twain did, "the exploration of a possibility which is totally denied in the world of actuality."[54] Kaul therefore favored Romantic authors, who produced a "body of literature that sought not only to represent the existing social order, but also to confront it with the image of an ideal society."[55] Those authors did not shy away from social critique, but they went beyond to picture the social ideals that motivated their judgments. According to Kaul, they "confronted the society of the time, critically evaluating it and at the same time tending away from it to project, in their distinctive ways, the image of an ideal community or an ideal social order."[56] In that way, Kaul believed, "the actual and the ideal function in a mutual critique."[57] In what Kaul calls "critical times,"[58] imaginative ideals became especially important to Romantic authors not because they were "less concerned with the perfection of human society" but "because they were more so."[59] By imagining worlds "out-of-place and out-of-time for the period,"[60] they gave shape to "a set of values for relationship between individuals," turning flights of fancy into a hopeful social ethics.

Such imaginative idealism, Kaul argues, is central to literature's "continuing vitality."[61] But it is just as important as a reading practice. The plots of Romantic literature, although obviously "not fictional transcripts from existing reality," he insists, "can be called unreal only if by reality we mean the status quo."[62] Yet the social significance of a Romantic plot remains unrecognized, Kaul claims, when a reader "finds it implausible, or, alternatively, recogniz[es] it as something that could not have happened" and therefore "takes it as a dream or a romance and concludes that it can have no possible relevance to real life and its issues."[63] Kaul recognizes the unlikelihood that in his own era "many persons would even remotely entertain such large-scale ideals as the earlier imagination delighted in"[64] and laments that intellectuals in particular "still prefer bearing the weight of the old philosopher's displeasure to facing the uncertain risk of believing in the imminence of paradise."[65] But Kaul also asserts that it "is the fact of paramount importance for the literary critic" that "if there is no place for [Romanticism's idealism] in the given theory of the novel, the task of criticism should be to revise the established assumptions in order to accommodate the new achievement, and not the other way round."[66] To underscore the need for imaginative idealism in critical reading, Kaul concludes with some challenging questions still relevant today: "Is it not erroneous," he inquires, "to suppose that social ideals of such scope can have no relevance to the problems of existing reality? Because history defeated their hopes, is it fair to conclude that it also discredited them irrevocably? Did history not rather discredit itself in the process, and does not America need today, perhaps more than ever before, great myths and visions with which to support history and perhaps even shape it?"[67] Kaul clearly believed America did need those myths and visions, and that literary criticism could create and popularize them as a sustained and vital practice of hope.

When Kaul was writing *The American Vision* in the early 1960s, there were ample reasons to be disenchanted. It was a time when the Berlin Wall, erected in 1961, gave material form to the ideological standoff between the Soviet Union and the United States. In 1962, China attacked Kaul's native India. And evidence of Soviet arms installations off the coast of Florida began what became known as the Cuban Missile Crisis. As the book went to press in 1963, hostilities escalated between China and the Soviet Union; British defense minister John Profumo was charged with leaking classified information to the Kremlin; American newspapers printed photographs of self-immolating South Vietnamese Buddhist monks; 16,300 American troops were stationed in Vietnam; and in November both U.S. president John F. Kennedy and South Vietnamese prime minister Ngo Dinh Diem were assassinated, the latter with support from the CIA. Meanwhile, race relations in the United States were explosively tense. In 1963, civil rights activist Medgar Evans was killed in Mississippi; the 16th Street Baptist Church in Birmingham, Alabama, was bombed, killing four girls; and Martin Luther King Jr. was arrested protesting that bombing, resulting in his famous "Letter from a Birmingham Jail." In August of that year, 25,000 people marched in Washington, DC, and heard King deliver the "I Have a Dream" speech. Publishing about hope and idealism at such a moment might seem quixotic, even irresponsible. Faced with the grave social conditions of the Cold War, literary critics, like the Romantic authors they admired, were vulnerable to, in Kaul's words, "the charge of being escapists, allegorists, day-dreamers, wishful thinkers, fantasy-mongers, romancers."[68] My argument in this book, however, is that the opposite is true: by turning to practices of hope, critics like Kaul developed the pertinent criticism for disenchanted times not by providing an escape from harsh realities but by refusing to let the suspicion, conformity, and techno-practicality vanquish what they perceived as the motivation and finest form of resistance and resilience in American literature.

In the chapters to follow, I turn to critics, as they turned to Hawthorne and Melville, to form a "usable past" for a critical practice of hope. I choose these critics for several reasons. First, I am struck by how profoundly disenchanted their times were. Writing in the period between the end of the Second World War and the antiwar movement of the mid-1960s, critics such as Rourke, Chase, Poirier, and Kaul show that critical hopefulness has a particularly social efficacy in countering the dominant social beliefs that generate disenchantment. They do so, moreover, by showing how critique and idealism operate simultaneously

to the mutual critical benefit of both. In addition to seeing those critics as instantiations of a coherent critical legacy, however, I will analyze
how they mark distinctive moments in a series of imaginative translations. Beginning with 1930s critics Granville Hicks and Constance
Rourke and continuing through to the scholars of literary symbolism
and style Marius Bewley and Richard Poirier, the following chapters explore evolving understandings of the relationship of texts to society in
the changing historical contexts. The years between Hicks and Poirier
did not occasion a turn away from socialist politics toward something
more apolitical or supportive of the Cold War consensus. Rather, they
created a concept of literature that demonstrates an increased awareness
of the function of imagination, idealism, and literary "worlds elsewhere"
in maintaining resilience and motivating hopeful reconstructions in a
world that seems to offer or to tolerate nothing but what already is. Each
of the following chapters focuses on a word—"nation," "liberalism," "humanism," "symbolism"—that characterizes an episode in that series of
translations.

These words draw a good deal of suspicion in literary criticism today,
and that is part of why I chose them. My goal is not to antagonize but
to demonstrate that the same concepts adopted from different critical
dispositions can produce very divergent results from the valences they
are widely assigned today. In other moments in the history of criticism,
these terms became empty signifiers, which imaginative critics filled
with social possibilities. My aim in turning to the critics discussed in the
following chapters is to contend that those possibilities are still available
to literary criticism, that we are another stage in a developing (although
not necessarily progressive) tradition and not the other side of a divide
as extreme as that which characterized Cold War political antagonisms.
The Cold War past, in short, can be our way out of its melancholy reproduction as critical disenchantment, making it again the visionary force
Kaul, like the other critics examined here, knew it could be.

Cold War critics have become, in Matthew Frankel's words, "a bit of
an embarrassment," their belief in "imaginative vitality" considered
"analytically vague and . . . politically suspect."[69] This embarrassment
stems in large part from midcentury criticism's focus on myths and
symbols, often taken as proof of the critics' support for the Cold War

consensus. Such assessments overlook, however, the explicit critiques these critics set forth as the nuclear arms race escalated and Senator Joseph McCarthy's House Un-American Activities Committee (HUAC) wielded tyrannical power. In 1950, Lionel Trilling protested "the proliferation of government by police methods," generating among citizens "the ideal of mere security."[70] Condemning Cold War conformity, R. W. B. Lewis in 1955 opposed a chauvinistic culture that valorized the rigid social normativity, rampant militarism, and xenophobic self-policing of McCarthyism. "Ours is an age of containment," Lewis lamented; "we huddle together and shore up defenses."[71] In Cold War America, Lewis believed, "a sterile awareness of evil uninvigorated by a sense of loss" produced "the expressed belief in achieved hopelessness."[72] Lewis Mumford agreed, arguing that the hardheaded practicality and gray-flannel-suit conventionality of Cold War America had made mandatory what he names "every kind of cowed conformity."[73] Mumford's critique was especially aimed at the science that precipitated the nuclear arms race. Looking back in 1956–1957, in a preface to the thirtieth anniversary reprinting of his study *The Golden Day*, Mumford laments undervaluing Henry Adams's warnings about the "disintegration of Western Civilization"[74] that would result from scientific innovations. "Long before the scientists concerned were sufficiently roused from their sleep-walking routines to realize what they were in fact doing," Mumford writes, Adams "saw, if they did not, that the train of events set in motion by the accidental discovery of the Becquerel rays would, in time, threaten the structure of civilization, making 'morality become police' and creating bombs of 'cosmic violence.'"[75] Reassessing Adams in the context of the Cold War, Mumford praises his capacity to attest "to the meaning of the present crisis in world civilization,"[76] through "the clairvoyance, as well as the scholarly historic insight, of his foreboding mind."[77] Mumford echoes Newton Arvin, who in 1950 claimed in his reading of Adams, "I firmly believe that before many centuries more, science will be the master of man. The engines he will have invented will be beyond his strength to control. Some day science may have the existence of mankind in its power, and the human race commit suicide by blowing up the world."[78]

Far from endorsing a conservative consensus, Trilling, Lewis, Mumford, and Arvin parallel the writing of one of the few midcentury critics credited with political acuity, C. L. R. James. Lewis's concern about a "world civilization" imperiled by the barbarism arising from the contradiction between ideals and state practice echoes James's *American Civilization*, originally composed in 1950, in which he asserts that "the bureaucratization and centralization of social life" had brought about "a state of hopelessness" and had poisoned American ideals.[79] James wrote:

> Liberty, freedom, pursuit of happiness, free individuality had an actuality and a meaning in America which they had nowhere else. The European wrote and theorized about freedom in superb writings. Americans lived it. That tradition is the most vital tradition in the country today. Any idea that it is *merely* a tradition, used by unscrupulous July 4 politicians to deceive the people, destroys any possibility of understanding the crisis in America today. The essential conflict is between these ideals, hopes, aspirations, needs, which are still the essential part of the tradition, and the economic and social realities of present-day America.[80]

James's defense of the principles of American nationhood is all the more remarkable in light of his inhumane imprisonment by "unscrupulous July 4 politicians." Like his contemporaries, however, James *used* those explicitly stated ideals as the basis of stringent critique of their betrayal, not in order to abandon idealism itself.

James and his contemporaries sound even more similar when they offer a vision of the literary imagination as a space of social engagement and a practice of hope. Mumford makes a claim for "the importance of the poet and the artist and the thinker, as a counterbalance to the over-valuation of . . . a civilization plainly threatened by barbarism from within."[81] To counter this barbarism, Lewis argued for "the moral and artistic possibilities of a century ago,"[82] exemplified by the Romantic writers he admired. Like Mumford and Lewis, James gleaned his idealism from Romantic literature in general and Melville in particular. Melville's "clear vision of the future," James writes, taught him the possibilities generated by the literary imagination.[83] Melville's association of outsiders—mariners, renegades, and castaways—with imagination shaped James's assessment of historical figures such as Toussaint Louverture, leader of the revolutionary insurrection in Haiti. In *The Black Jacobins*, James writes, "Firm as was his grasp of reality, old Toussaint looked beyond San Domingo with a boldness of imagination surpassed by no contemporary."[84] That "boldness of imagination" allowed Louverture to see Haiti as it might be, a *not-yet* Haiti, that turned simmering resentment into a revolutionary movement not only *against* racialized subjugation but also *toward* an imagined outcome of revolutionary hope.[85]

James's understanding of the role of imagination in shaping revolutionary ideals is too often ignored in favor of his explicit political analysis, despite the fact that James saw the two as intrinsically related. The same combination of imaginative idealism and social critique is overlooked in critics like Mumford and Lewis, but for the corollary reason: their focus on literary myth renders their criticism, as Frankel observes, "politically suspect." Yet Lewis in particular was an ardent proponent of literature in general and myths in particular as incentives to progressive social change. He understood myth as an aesthetic means for generating a deliberative and self-transforming culture. In *American Adam* (1955), Lewis, introducing his eponymous mythic "figure of heroic innocence and vast potentialities, poised at the start of a new history,"[86] might seem to be celebrating Cold War America's self-image as both "innocent" of ideological intentions and "heroic" in its exceptionalist efforts to safeguard the globe. Yet Lewis observes that any such myth is "crowded with illusion, and the moral posture it seemed to indorse was vulnerable in the extreme."[87] Lewis thus sees myth as imbuing the "moral posture" his myth seems to praise with an "openness to challenge" and a "susceptibility to controversy" that make possible what, following Hegel, Lewis describes as "the unfolding course of a dialogue . . . containing a number of voices."[88] Myth is thus "a collective affair"[89] built not on unity or consensus but on contestation, or what Lewis describes as a "determining debate" that "may be said to *be* the culture."[90] For Lewis, then, myth is a form of critique, showing how a culture "achieves identity not so much through the ascendency of one particular set of convictions" but through "the sometimes bruising contact of opposites."[91] But myth is also, for Lewis, a practice of hope, providing what Laclau calls "empty signifiers." Invoking values that bring a collective together not "simply to settle the terms of discussion" but rather "to provide materials for the creative imagination," myth offers "a comprehensive view of life, in an ideal extension of its present possibilities."[92]

For other critics, such as Richard Chase, discussed in the second chapter, myth was also politicized but in ways that mark a significant change from the practices of the Marxist critics of the 1920s and 1930s. In that period, critics such as Victor Calverton and Vernon Parrington, who urged criticism beyond "the narrow field of *belles letters* alone,"[93] believed that myths romanticize an industrial hegemony that separates the masses and diverts their attention from the consolidation of economic power in the Northeast. Believing that Romanticism drew writers away from clearheaded social realism, Parrington upbraided Hawthorne for his "distortions of the soul under the tyranny of a diseased imagination" and for "delocalizing" the material world.[94] Midcentury critics such as Chase, however, found ideological conformity in realist fiction and political promise in Romantic myth. The very characteristics that, for Calverton and Parrington, made myth politically suspect—its emotionalism, eccentricity, and aesthetic distortions—were what, for Chase and many of his contemporaries, made literature most valuable as a socially engaged practice of hope.

For some critics writing during the Cold War, mythology became politicized through its focus on embodied relationality in the form of sexuality, understood less as the basis for individual identity than as the grounds for unexpected cultural alliances. Almost every midcentury critic treated in the following chapters names D. H. Lawrence as a significant—if problematic—influence. Lawrence's *Studies in Classic American Literature* (1923) famously divides the nineteenth-century canon between followers of the head, who were believers in self-improvement and rational reform, and disciples of the heart and of the erotic unconscious. Favoring the latter, Lawrence opposes textual expressions of the mundane conventionalities of everyday life. Desire, fantasy, affective excess, and unchecked eroticism—these for Lawrence distinguish the greatest American novels. What proved troublesome for Lawrence—hardly surprising to readers of his fiction—was the common association of the unconscious with homoeroticism. In defensive response, Lawrence counterintuitively consigns homosexuality to the realm of conventional experience, thereby removing it from what he claims was most inventive and honest about American literature. In relation to Melville, whom midcentury critics would celebrate for his expressions of same-sex intimacy, Lawrence writes that his "desire for a 'perfect relationship' is just a vicious, unmanly craving," and, as he writes of Hawthorne, "we ought to decide to have done at last with craving."[95]

When midcentury critics took up Lawrence, they accepted his opposition between head and heart, convention and the unconscious, but they reversed his judgments. For them, homosexuality is a critical force opposed to convention and, as a form of social contestation, bridges the gap between the individual unconscious and a politically conscious collective idealism. Homosexuality counters conventions associated with what F. O. Matthiessen calls the "mechanization" of modern society, threatening the "wholeness" of man and leading to the "neurotic strain" in modern life, while for Arvin it represents the "strong intuition of human solidarity as a priceless good," opposed to the "brutality of indiscriminate skepticism."[96] Whether in Richard Poirier's reference to the "sexually irregular," Chase's to the love of comrades, or Mumford's to imaginative possibilities "concentrated on relationships and values" that are "somehow illicit,"[97] homosexuality became, as the third chapter will show, a form of socialist humanism and shaped the symbolist aesthetics of the critics discussed in the final chapter. At a time when homosexuals were reviled in clinical, legal, and political discourse, these critics, making homosexuality the political heart of their mythologies, put it at the center of the emerging field of American literary studies.

The alternative socialities forged through sexuality characterize midcentury criticism's fascination with the broader unpredictable alliances made among the scapegoats of Cold War ideology, figures that Mumford, echoing James, called "outcasts, recluses, exiles."[98] In *The American Novel and Its Tradition* (1957), Chase aligns "aesthetic possibilities" with the "extreme range of experiences" characteristic of those who live "radical forms of alienation, contradiction, and disorder."[99] Within "the borderland of the human mind where the actual and the imaginary intermingle," Chase writes, those outcasts enjoy the "blissful, idyllic, erotic attachment to life and to one's comrades, which is the only promise of happiness."[100] As with Chase's "extreme experiences," for Poirier the habitués of his "world elsewhere" represent "an exercise of consciousness momentarily set free," a condition enjoyed by "the foolish, the preposterous, and the sexually irregular."[101] Restricted within a boundaried "consciousness" that was the interior equivalent of the defensively bordered nation, the citizen of the world of imagination becomes "a law unto himself," ignoring "all outward allegiance, whether to nature or society."[102] These outcasts experience what Lionel Trilling called the "lively sense of contingency and possibility, and of those exceptions to the rule which may be the beginning of the end of the rule."[103] The kind of "sense" Trilling had in mind became his own critical ideal, what he called simply "the imagination of love."[104]

For the critics discussed in the following chapters, visions such as Chase's, Trilling's, and Poirier's were refusals of disenchantment, or what Lewis calls the "new hopelessness" that, he claims, "is, paradoxically, as simple-minded as innocence."[105] Like his contemporaries discussed here, Lewis knew that we cannot abandon critique, which "contains many remarkable and even irreversible psychological, sociological, and political insights" amounting to "the picture most clearly warranted by public and private experience in our time." But he also knew that the disenchanted criticism in his day seemed "curiously frozen in outline," offering "no opposite possibilities on which to feed and fatten."[106] That nourishment, for Lewis, was still possible in literature and literary criticism, which, he claims, "can pose anew, in the classic way of illumination as it did in the American nineteenth century, the picture of what might be against the knowledge of what is."[107] A criticism that uses imaginative idealism to confront "what is" with "what might be" is a practice of hope. But its "illumination" is dimmed when "a habit of forgetfulness" leads to "the sheer dullness of unconscious repetition."[108]

We have largely forgotten—or diminished—our critical past, and the result is the "unconscious repetition" of a malnourished critique. But we might reencounter the past and once again begin to think the no longer thinkable. When midcentury critics turned to Melville and Whitman, they sought a revival not only of the nineteenth-century past but also of the living possibilities available to them as critics. As Mumford acknowledges, "It was precisely my sense of the present promise that made the past so vividly alive to me."[109] Mumford anticipates Michael Taussig's claim that "an incandescent present" requires the survival of the past in order to generate "a space of no time" and "dismantle the institutions of the present and then presumably build them anew."[110] Just as midcentury critics looked back a century for an "incandescent present," so might we look to our critical past to find an alternative to exhausted critique, refusing, in Bruno Latour's words, to let "a prestigious critical tradition . . . die away."[111] In what Rita Felski calls "the current climate of retrospection," as we "reassess methods of reading that have come to seem stale and unsurprising,"[112] we might reassess the dispositions shaped by critics who offer remarkably *un*suspicious critiques centered on the socially transformative power that Chase calls the moral imagination. In so doing, we, too, might come to seem less "stale and unsurprising."

In 1955, R. W. B. Lewis claimed, "We stand in need of more stirring impulsions, of greater perspectives and more penetrating controversies," invigorating the sense of "unbounded possibility."[113] The answer was certainly not to be found in the version of critique described four years later by Newton Arvin, who wrote, "We hug our negations, our doubts, our disbeliefs to our chests, as if our moral and intellectual dignity depended on them."[114] Even earlier, Van Wyck Brooks inquired, "Where are we going to get the new ideals, the finer attitudes, that we must get if we are ever to emerge from our existing travesty of a civilization?"[115] Their frustration can be heard again in our "postcritique" moment. And just as their exasperation led to remarkable acts of critical creativity, so the conversations today enabled by the empty signifier "critique" should be an exhilarating possibility, not a melancholy loss. We again have an opportunity to redefine critique, infusing it with the imagination and idealism that, in Arvin's words, are "accessible as always to those who wish not merely to 'interpret the world variously' (in Marx's phrase) but to change it."[116] If the "greater impulsions" called for by Lewis and the "finer attitudes" Brooks desired are, for us, "unbounded possibilities," then we can make critique, as they did, less a disenchantment tale and more a practice of hope.

1

Nation

I Like America

I begin this chapter with two counterintuitive propositions. First, we are only now, nearly three decades after the nominal end of the Cold War, beginning to move past its influence on literary criticism, a belatedness that may be in large part responsible for our apparent uselessness in the contemporary world. And second, the influence of the Cold War is most strongly felt, paradoxically, when our critiques are aimed at the ideologies, particularly national exceptionalism, endorsed by the Cold War state. To put the case more sharply: we are reproducing Cold War state epistemologies even (especially) when Cold War ideology is our nominal object of critique. In making these claims, I do not mean to minimize or assign cynical motives to the sustained and incisive critique of Cold War ideologies undertaken by critics of literature and culture in the past three decades. My aim here is not to argue for abandoning ideology critique but rather to strengthen it, although not in its current form. My contention is that we need alternatives to our currently ubiquitous methodologies for critique because their dispositions—if not their explicit content—draw unintentionally upon Cold War epistemologies that, in a post–Cold War world, are no longer effective for countering the social inequalities we most typically oppose. More important, we need alternative methodologies for *sustaining the ideals central to criticism's social engagement.*

Throughout the Cold War, the self-contained and superior national image was haunted by a persistent insecurity, the most obvious symptom of which was the hysteria personified by Joseph McCarthy, whose insistence that communists and homosexuals lurked everywhere, poised to subvert "our way of life" from within, suggests fears about the permeability of America and the instability of a way of life ready to collapse from internal fissures. The response to that anxiety was the cultivation of suspicion, the capacity to detect dangerous ideologies lurking beneath surfaces that appeared innocent, even pleasurable. Suspicion as a Cold War prophylactic had several destructive consequences. For one, it required endlessly renewed anxiety. Suspicion could never be resolved but took on an ever-shifting variety of objects, making everything a potential source of ideological treachery. For another, it attempted to forestall self-criticism, thwarting inquiry into whether threats to American democracy might not be coming from the U.S. government itself, *especially* in its perpetuation of suspicions. Finally, the conservative impulse of preservation ("keeping safe") encouraged citizens to hold dear a good-enough democracy, preventing them from imagining and instituting *better* versions of everyday life, much less governmental structure. Whether the "way of life" lived by most citizens was worth preserving, in other words, was a question forestalled by the imperative protectivism generated by supposedly imminent threat. Suspicion encouraged citizens to believe that there is no need for any activity except to suspect and expose. Certainly the state epistemology of suspicion implied there was no need for—indeed, there were a great number of incentives against—imagining better versions of America.

We can hear the echoes of these state strategies in contemporary critical methodologies if we turn to the account of critique offered by one of its fiercest challengers. In 2004, Bruno Latour asked if we are not exhausted by the predictability and belatedness of critiques that, going too far with too little self-analysis, have become unduly suspicious.[1] In the process of "trying to detect the real prejudices hidden behind the appearance of objective statements," critique produces "an excessive *distrust* of good matters of fact disguised as bad ideological biases!"[2] Latour here echoes Eve Kosofsky Sedgwick's skepticism about the "binarized, highly moralistic allegories of the subversive versus the hegemonic, resistance versus power" that characterize contemporary practices of critique.[3] Becoming its own version of conspiracy theory, critique, claims Latour, has made itself "suspicious of everything people say because of course we all know that they live in the thralls of a complete *illusio* of their real motives."[4] Critique thus enacts what Sedgwick calls the "moralistic hygiene by which any reader of today is unchallengeably entitled to condescend to the thought of any moment in the past (maybe especially the recent past)," an entitlement that "is globally available to anyone who masters the application of two or three discrediting questions."[5] Unmaking the naive fetishes of a desperate and docile populace, critique, as Latour mockingly contends, leaves only "the courageous critic, who alone remains aware and attentive, who never sleeps, and turns those false objects into fetishes that are supposed to be nothing but mere empty white screens on which is projected the power of society, domination, whatever."[6] One of Latour's key insights is that scholars criticizing networks of power often re-create them in ways that uncannily resemble conspiracy theories. Readers of disguised subtexts and draconian schemes, Latour claims, make "the same appeal to powerful agents hidden in the dark acting always consistently, continuously, relentlessly."[7] Academics differ from conspiracy theorists only in the former's use of more abstract and metaphoric agents: "society, discourse, knowledge-slash-power, fields of forces, empires, capitalism."[8] Those abstract "appeals to powerful agents hidden in the dark" unmask everyone except academic critics themselves, who remain "intimately certain that the things really close to our hearts" are—and should be—immune to conspiratorial examination.[9]

As is clear, Latour believes such explanatory suspicion has outlived its usefulness and "deteriorated to the point of now feeding the most gullible sort of critique."[10] Unlike "military experts" who "constantly revise their strategic doctrines, their contingency plans, the size, direction, and technology of their projectiles, their smart bombs, their missiles," critics, Latour maintains, have resisted the need "to prepare ourselves for new threats, new dangers, new tasks, new target," leading him to query, would it really be surprising "if intellectuals were also one war late, one critique late?"[11] It is not that such critiques are invalid, Latour acknowledges, "but simply that history changes quickly and that there is no greater intellectual crime than to address with the equipment of an older period the challenges of the present one."[12] Outmoded critical artillery keeps buffeting equally obsolete enemies, which Latour describes as the "big totalities" that "like the Soviet empire . . . have feet of clay."[13] The challenge becomes discerning and devising what resources are needed for the struggle at hand. "The practical problem we face," Latour asserts, "if we try to go that new route, is to associate the word *criticism* with a whole set of new positive metaphors, gestures, attitudes, knee-jerk reactions, habits of thoughts."[14] Today, critiques take for granted that nefarious ideologies lurk beneath a text's seemingly innocuous surface and must be unmasked by an unimplicated critic who assumes no responsibility *but* to unmask. It is hard to miss the echoes, in this description, of life during the Cold War, especially when Latour invokes the abstract agencies attributed to the Soviet empire.[15]

That such echoes should arise from methodologies forged by scholars who came of age in the Cold War is hardly surprising. What *is* surprising is the decades-long shelf life of those methodologies *after* the Cold War's end, the belatedness observed by Latour. The intellectual popularization of ideological critique began, after all, not *during* the Cold War but at its end, with the rise of New Historicism in the mid-1980s and, in American literary studies particularly, with reassessments such as *The American Renaissance Reconsidered, Reconstructing American Literary History, Ideology and Classic American Literature, Sensational Designs,* and *Beneath the American Renaissance,* the first published in 1985, the next three in 1986, and the last in 1988, the exact span of the Reagan-Gorbachev negotiations that ended in the Malta Summit and the Cold War's nominal end.[16] Of course, the social and literary reevaluations associated with New Historicism owe a great deal to the political commitments of the civil rights, antiwar, and feminist movements of the 1960s and 1970s, which have their own complicated relationships to Cold War politics. I have no wish to undervalue those movements or to diminish the importance of the scholarly work they generated. What I do want to point out is a significant tension between the socially engaged intentions of that work and its methodological assumptions and consequent practices. While the former brought to light and productively analyzed structures of cultural and political power, the latter, despite those intentions, worked at cross-purposes by reproducing the state-sponsored epistemological strategies that made critical resistance necessary in the first place. Taking the Cold War state to be the origin of diffused suspicion, abstract ideological enemies, and totalizing explanations, we can see how the kinds of critique disparaged by Latour register not only opposition to but also *identification with* the Cold War state, the unquestioned and totalizing explanatory powers of which began to diminish exactly as ideology critique took hold in the academy. Faced with the loss at the end of the Cold War of the state's compelling explanatory power, critics both repudiated and replicated those explanatory strategies. The perseverance of a Cold War-inflected methodology enacted the ambivalent introjections central to what Freud called melancholy, and to what, in this particular cultural context, I am calling Cold War melancholy.

Let me offer two influential examples that helped establish the tone and strategies of what became the New Americanism, a branch of ideology critique inflected by New Historicism and directed again the Cold War American state.[17] I choose these essays not because they are particularly egregious in their Cold War melancholy but because their Cold War roots are closer to the surface than in most other examples of critical suspicion and therefore acknowledge to some degree the Cold War source of the methodologies they helped make academic *doxa*. The first, Donald E. Pease's "*Moby Dick* and the Cold War" (1985), shows how the U.S.-Soviet antagonism absorbed "everyday life into a 'battlefield' arena" in which "the complications, doubts, and conflicts of modern existence get a single opposition that then clears up the whole mess and puts everybody back to work."[18] Given the will to get "back to work" without any work to do, Americans during the Cold War fell prey not to Soviet attack but to what Pease calls *boredom*. We required someone else's decisive action to relieve our boredom, yet the destructive consequences of action on the Cold War battlefield made inaction seem like adequate *opposition to* catastrophe, a heroism without heroics. Supporting this thesis through *Moby-Dick*, Pease reminds us that Ishmael's boredom, which sets the novel in motion, is cured by the epic conflict between Ahab and Leviathan that absorbs all other doubts and conflicts. Ishmael not only finds in Ahab relief for his boredom but also *creates* Ahab to rationalize his inactivity, which becomes heroic simply by *not* replicating Ahab's murderous acts. Indecision thereby becomes an opposition without any need to oppose.

In this brilliant analysis Pease, critiquing the Cold War state, constructs the critic *as* that state, even as he frames his essay as a corrective to the ideologically implicated misinterpretations put forward by what he names as the composite "Cold War critics," for whom Ishmael, the model American, heroically opposes the totalitarian (Soviet) Ahab. For Pease, however, there are no heroes, only fatal action and bored inaction. Melville alone comes out well, having unmasked modernity's ideological stratagems, in which he presumably is not implicated. But this is not Melville's drama. Setting out to contest the axioms of Cold War critics, Pease renders himself as Ishmael opposing the tyrannical power of an absolute Other, whose dangerous acts of misinterpretation rationalize what can be understood as *Pease's* boredom. In this battle of Pease versus Cold War critics, in other words, the terms are reversed (Pease now represents *antiexceptionalism* while Cold War critics represent American hegemony), but the structure of the reading he critiques—heroic individual versus an ideologically tyrannical state "other"—remains intact, replicating what Pease identifies as the mythological rationale for the Cold War state consensus. By Pease's own interpretation, furthermore, just as Ishmael *creates* Ahab, so Pease creates the category "Cold War critics" to rationalize the brave posture of his critical boredom: by unmasking ideologically suspect misreadings, Pease makes *un*misreading a triumphant, if (because) inactive, opposition, while *our* boredom, our interpretive inactivity in the face of Pease's spectacularly tight and comprehensive reading, seemingly disappears on the battlefield where New Americanists, armed with bored suspicion, confront Cold War critics, armed only with a weak exceptionalism. Replicating the oppositional inactivity he criticizes as *the* Cold War ideological structure, the New Americanist becomes an exemplary Cold War citizen.

The ways the Cold War inflects methodologies in ways at odds with critical intentions are clear if we compare "*Moby Dick* and the Cold War" with the introductory chapter of Pease's *Visionary Compacts* (1987). In that chapter, Pease writes that nineteenth-century Romantic authors should be studied not in order to critique, through them, the nation and its founding ideologies but because those writers kept the unfinished promise of the Revolution alive *despite* their discouraging ideological contexts:

> None of these writers disclaimed the founding principles as merely ideological. Each of them envisioned the founding principles as well as the covenant of relations as unfulfilled promises in need of the renewal that visionary compact could effect. In fulfilling these promises, they developed new faculties, like self-reliance and the collective memory, capable of converting founding principles into motivating forces rather than past ideals. Instead of opposing the nation's principles, in an age of political compromise, these writers found those principles to be vital moral and political energies.[19]

For Pease, fictions by Hawthorne and Melville express "an as yet unrealized vision" and draw attention to the past's "ongoing power to renegotiate the terms of the covenant binding Americans to one another."[20] Pease states, "A nation can lose its soul the same way an individual can, by compromising on its principles," so writers must "establish an enabling context for overcoming the divisions of cultural life at work in our own time."[21]

These are stirring statements, striking in their explicit articulation of the idealism I attribute to practices of hope, and Pease is singular among New Americanists for demonstrating the mutually constituting relationship of visionary ideals and incisive critique. But Pease's statement of these ideals came at the beginning of the period marked by Cold War melancholy, before its full influence took hold. When Pease turned to his reading of *Moby-Dick* in relation to the Cold War, however, idealism became suspicion and inaction, while idealism's unfinished business turned into settled ideological oppositions, and the desire to unify Americans through a constructive statement of ideals became the opposition to abstract enemies Pease calls "negative freedom." I am not insinuating that Pease changed his mind or was anything but sincere in his stated endorsement of *positive* freedom; rather, I want to underscore how Cold War melancholy, as it took shape as the New Americanism, supplanted articulation of critical ideals, privileging instead a suspicious critique that functions as what Pease calls negative freedom, "the desire merely to be free *from* a variety of constraints" rather than to work constructively toward a "commonwealth of freedom."[22] Methodology and intent, in other words, began to work at cross-purposes.

While my second example, Walter Benn Michaels's "Romance and Real Estate," would seem to work from the ideal of an economic commons, no explicit statement of such an ideal can be found. As with Pease's essay, it is not that there is no ideal but rather that explicit idealism has become closeted in favor of the state-inflected methodologies that make "negative freedom" the only visible motivation. In that essay, Michaels discovers in *The House of the Seven Gables* Nathaniel Hawthorne's efforts to protect property from a wildly fluctuating market by making real estate immaterial.[23] Faced with the fact that one in four young speculators failed financially in the mid-nineteenth century, Hawthorne, according to Michaels, attempted to stabilize capital by making success reliant not on labor, investment, or inheritance but on "character." Thus the daguerreotypist Holgrave attains property through a marriage guaranteed by his supposedly consistent and creditable character. Michaels argues, however, that Alice Pyncheon is doomed by her fatally mistaken belief in such inalienable integrity of character, which enslaves her to her family's hereditary enemy embodied by the man who mesmerizes her, Matthew Maule.

Although persuasive, this interpretation rests on several sleights of hand by which the "Hawthorne" who desires a market-stabilizing personhood is distinguished from "Alice," who, although created by Hawthorne, thwarts his intentions by showing "character" to be as unstable as the basis of speculation as capital. To acknowledge that Hawthorne imagined both the narrator (identified as "Hawthorne") *and* Alice would challenge Michaels's oppositional logic with a less dualistic acknowledgment of Hawthorne's ambivalence. A second but related assumption: Holgrave's belief in consistent character makes him "master" over Phoebe Pyncheon, becoming in the process an owner. Yet the same belief makes Alice Pyncheon the object of exchange, a slave to Matthew Maule's hypnosis. It is unclear why (apart from the not insignificant operations of gender inequality, which Michaels replicates without analyzing) belief in integral character makes one a master and another a slave, one an owner and another a commodity. Is Phoebe's independence at the end, moreover, a result of Holgrave's noblesse oblige, as Michaels suggests, or of her participation in the life of a community of support, unlike the lonesome Alice? What makes Michaels believe that Phoebe *wants* "individuality," that Holgrave is giving it to her rather than attempting to force it upon her and failing?

Michaels's critique avoids such questions. To finish where he does—with Phoebe beholden to Holgrave, Alice enslaved to Maule, Holgrave betrayed by the detachment of character from property while Maule is betrayed by *not* detaching them, and above all Hawthorne betrayed by his naive efforts to raise the romance above market capitalism—Michaels must leave no one's resistance effective. If individuality, collectivity, and ambivalence threaten to frustrate that conclusion, Michaels ignores them to arrive at his conclusion: resistance of any kind is futile, since capitalism is synonymous with selfhood, all attempts at agency shaped and managed by the force they seek to oppose. As Michaels puts it, "The slave cannot resist her master because the slave is her master."[24]

Capitalism's immunity from challenge is, of course, a Cold War fiction, in which American "free market enterprise" would incontrovertibly overcome Soviet communism (the collectivism denied to Phoebe by Michaels's reading?). Whether one feels exhilarated or disgusted by that inevitability makes no difference once capitalism comes loose from its human agents to become unassailable because abstract and hence both ubiquitous and absent. Only the critic seems able to detect and reveal capitalism's treachery from within, an ironic conclusion given Michaels's explicit distancing, at one point, of the Cold War mindset from his own critical methodology. Like Pease, Michaels opposes a misreading that asserts that Hawthorne romanticized individuality even though "the specter of 'treachery within' cannot be so easily laid to rest."[25] Here Michaels entertains the possibility of an interpretation that imagines, wrongly, that Alice's story demonstrates a heroic conflict between an individual and a market that has already gained a foothold within that individual. Such a reading, Michaels concludes, smacks of "the McCarthyesque imagination of conspiracy."[26] In Michaels's reading, by contrast, "Alice is ultimately betrayed not only by her father's desire but by the very claim to individual identity that made her imagine herself immune to betrayal."[27] The enemy cannot be repulsed by heroic action because the enemy creates the agent of that action *as* an "individual" capable of independent and oppositional action, ensuring the self-division that renders Alice—and everyone else in the novel (and outside it)—a slave to capital's vicissitudes. While McCarthy claimed to find enemies victimizing the innocent, Michaels finds no innocents and hence no opposition, necessitating suspicion not only between citizens but *as* subjectivity, which becomes a perpetual surveillance of its own unconscious formations, endlessly frustrating any project of conscious ideological opposition.

In this airtight interpretation of Hawthorne, however, the critic is similarly divided between intention and methodology: seeking to counter McCarthy's hermeneutics of suspicion, Michaels replicates *and increases* McCarthy's power to incite that disposition, making the opponent on the battlefield more powerful *and* less visible by self-dividing what might, to the unschooled, appear unified (the subject who acts). More to the point, the hermetic logic of Michaels's interpretation gives the impression, despite the strategic occlusions discussed earlier, that dissent—either within or against Michaels's reading—is futile. Contra his own claims, the *critic* is allowed an oppositional stance as especially astute (i.e., suspicious), becoming the agent that, supposedly, capitalism disallows, as Michaels's explanatory power and its suspicion-inducing effects become as totalizing as those of the Cold War state, epitomized by McCarthy's House Un-American Activities Committee. The irony is that Michaels's essay was published in 1985, the year Mikhail Gorbachev's appointment as general secretary of the Soviet Union set in motion events that led to the end of the Cold War. This is not to make the absurd claim that Michaels would want the Cold War to continue. But his essay's oppositional logic and ideological suspicions maintain the Cold War state melancholically, even as the political efficacy of those state strategies began to erode.

The worst consequence of Cold War melancholy, as my reading of Michaels's essay suggests, is not its belatedness, however, but how it figures social agency. In Pease's book *The New American Exceptionalism* (2009), "state fantasy" becomes as debilitatingly internalized (and hence both ubiquitous and invisible) as capitalism is for Michaels. Analyzing "state fantasy" as "the dominant structure of desire out of which U.S. citizens imagine their national identity," Pease writes, "Rather than associating fantasy with a delusion that requires critique, I align my discussion of state fantasy with Jacqueline Rose's insight 'that fantasy—far from being the antagonist of public, social being—plays a central, constitutive role in the modern world of states and nations.'"[28] The totalizing ubiquity of the "system" of state fantasy becomes clear when Pease asserts, "A state fantasy should not be construed as a specific, restricted instrument of governance. It sustains the continued symbolic efficacy of the entire order it legislates."[29] By making governmentality a "system" rather than "a specific, restricted instrument," Pease undervalues resistance to any particular site of national exceptionalism. The problem is that although state "efficacy" involves its invulnerability to the kinds of critique that can be leveled against specific "instruments," Pease *is* offering a critique of that efficacy. That paradox opens two possibilities: either "state fantasy" is itself a delusion, or the critic is an exception to the state's exceptionalism and therefore not *all* citizens are constituted within state fantasy.

Pease opens the possibilities only to close them. Although he acknowledges the "rifts" in civil society made evident by movements for social justice, such movements, for Pease, are *part* of the state fantasy, diverting attention from the truly devastating deployment of state exceptionalism: the Cold War itself. Foreclosing the possibility of efficacious civic transgression constituted apart from state fantasy, Pease contends that the latter "simultaneously gives expression to the agency of the law and to the desire seeking to transgress that very law. Identification with this desire involves the state's subjects in an ambivalent process whereby they simultaneously identify with the authority of the state's laws and with the illicit desires that would transgress the law." Because of the Cold War American government's construction of the Soviet Union, citizens "could not articulate criticism of U.S. imperialism without feeling as if they had spoken on behalf of the imperial enemy with which they were also fantasmatically identified."[30]

Could not? Apparently not, for when Pease invokes collective social movements—the civil rights, feminist, or farmworkers' movements, for example—he quickly turns each movement into a *leader* (Martin Luther King Jr., Betty Friedan, Cesar Chavez). Only two movements are represented as leaderless: gay liberation following the 1969 Stonewall uprising and prison reform after the 1971 uprising at Attica.[31] But even these are quickly defanged. "Each of these extrastate social movements," Pease reports, "resulted in legislation that changed the political standing of the group's members," but in achieving that legislation these groups "harnessed their petitions to the utopian demands organizing their national fantasies. None of these groups, according to Pease, "inaugurated a state fantasy to reconfigure the social order."[32] Pease's analysis may be right. What is troubling, however, is its insistence on an unambiguous truth, the assertion of which requires certain manipulations that, if resisted locally, nevertheless confirm the explanatory power of their abstract logic. Once movements turn into leaders, once their goal becomes "legislation," once groups (such as the Stonewall rioters) that are without identifiable leaders and that produced *no* legislation and contested the validity of existing laws and modes of state surveillance are dropped from this account, once social struggle is reduced to "utopian demands," then it is easy to subordinate affiliative movements for social change to "state fantasy." Just as the exceptionalist state has "decided what historical events they would allow representation within the historical record," so has the exceptional critic.[33] In seeing through national exceptionalism, the critic *becomes* exceptional and therefore, not surprisingly, assumes the strategies and powers of that state, translated now to critical methodology. In the act of criticizing the Cold War state, in other words, the critic melancholically occupies the vacated space of that state, perpetuating his exceptionalism by repeatedly appropriating the state's powers to select, abstract, and reveal a disembodied enemy against which all agency— except the seemingly unimplicated critical power to expose—is useless. And because of the absolute and totalizing nature of revelations (capitalism is everywhere already, state fantasy absorbs all opposition, differing opinions reveal complicity), readers are put in the position of absolute choice: accept the reading in its totality or none of it. New Americanism: love it or leave it.

It will not have escaped notice that in the preceding analysis I have attempted to "reveal" the ideological motives hidden behind the interpretations offered by Pease and Michaels. In so doing, I replicate what I criticize them for doing with Hawthorne and Melville. Such critiques come so easily to literary critics of my generation because they have been done so often, so well, and with such compelling conviction by critics such as Pease and Michaels. But it is precisely that influence that makes it all the more necessary to reexamine critically not only their work but, more important, the myriad critical projects that work has inspired and schooled. I have focused on only two critics, but I trust that the elements of Cold War melancholy I have identified—the focus on "hidden" ideologies, the abstraction of opposed forces, the totalizing of explanations, the placement of the critic beyond implication—are familiar to most who read literary and cultural criticism today, and that is the problem. Despite the political commitments that animated (and in some cases continue to animate) such work, its methodological assumptions have become so naturalized *as* acuity that they can—indeed, must—be replicated without challenge, a fact that makes critique often seem rote, predictable, and unmotivated.

Yet we would be making a mistake, I believe, to dismiss critique wholesale, as some have encouraged us to do. The Cold War may be over, but the need for astute and impassioned social analysis is not. At the same time, however, we should not uncritically replicate a methodology that has outlived its sources, commitments, and usefulness. Unconscious repetition risks losing not only academic vitality but also the connections between academic criticism (or critical reading in general) and the forces of imagination and idealism that motivate the social changes for which we so often purport to advocate. An articulation as content and as methodology of these ideals would open the way for debate, if nothing more, making the reading of criticism as much a creative and participatory event as the writing of it. In the chapters that follow, I will argue that the kinds of imaginative idealism—hopefulness—I am suggesting here existed in criticism throughout the Cold War, and that we might do well to return to those critics who wrote during that period to learn, paradoxically, how to overcome our Cold War melancholy. To begin that analysis, however, I start with two critics, Granville Hicks and Constance Rourke, who wrote before the start of the Cold War and whose primary concerns—nationalism, exceptionalism, and activism— were precisely those most often targeted by New Americanists (and New Historicists in general).

Anticipating by thirty years the "America: Love It or Leave It" bumper stickers aimed at critics of U.S. involvement in the Vietnam War, the literary critic Granville Hicks in 1938 recalled a hostile interlocutor asking him, "'If you don't like this country, why don't you go back where you came from?'"[34] Hicks's response—"I do like this country"—might surprise readers today, when the social critique associated with his Marxist politics and affection for the United States have come to seem mutually exclusive.[35] Hicks's quarrel was not with America, however, but with an economic bloc that maintains its class privileges in the name of patriotism at the expense of the economically disadvantaged majority, who are further weakened by being denied access to national belonging.[36] Making class position explicit, Hicks tells the accuser he addresses ironically as "that certain patriot," "We belong to the same class—what a sociologist friend of mine calls the middle middle class."[37] Hicks then suggests the power that comes with wielding the nation's name and what staunch defenders of "patriotism" are actually trying to protect: "This class constitutes rather less than ten percent of the American population, with more than eighty percent, as far as incomes are concerned, below it, and less than ten percent above."[38] When men like his accuser speak of "America," they mean a relatively small number of people who control most of the wealth, and *that* is the nation Hicks dislikes. But Hicks believed the *other* America, living with economic inequality and therefore social and legal injustice, deserves affectionate advocacy. That affection, moreover, is bestowed *in the name of the nation* because "America" thus becomes, as it was in Hicks's landmark literary history *The Great Tradition*, a weapon of the weak and a vision of a just society that, for Hicks, was the fulfillment of proclaimed national values.

Severing the idea of America from the control of elite economic interests, Hicks offers a definition of patriotism at odds with the values that became known as the Cold War consensus. "My kind of patriotism," he tells his accuser, is an ideal of change that is "more closely akin than yours to the patriotism of the men who fought in the American revolution, of the abolitionists, of the westward-moving pioneers."[39] This, he says, is the "patriotism that believes in change." Hicks demonstrates that Americans living with an exploitative economic system sanctioned and protected by the legal operations of the state can and *should* claim patriotism as a means of oppositional organization, public deliberation, and self-definition. Hicks writes about the 80 percent of Americans living below the middle class that they would not become patriots by "forcing them to sing 'The Star-Spangled Banner' and take oaths of allegiance."[40] Claiming, "Even if they haven't much of a stake in America as it is, they have a tremendous stake in America as it might be," Hicks concludes, "I think they will become patriots if they understand my kind of patriotism."[41]

Expressing patriotism for "America as it might be" makes one a citizen whose allegiances are not to the government of the United States but to something closer to what Lauren Berlant describes as "scenes of *substantive* citizenship" available in civil society.[42] Within that sphere— what is often called "the commons"—may arise "a discussion among various collective interest groups struggling over the core norms, practices, and mentalities of a putatively general U.S. population."[43] Berlant argues that "citizenship may be best thought of as an intricate scene where competing forces, definitions, and geographies of freedom and liberty are lived concretely,"[44] making citizenship "an aspirational concept in discussions of diverse communities, real and imagined."[45] Hicks, in his semiautobiographical *Small Town*, imagines local communities as sites where national values can be debated, reformulated, and "lived concretely." Giving lived shape to Berlant's concept of interactive citizenship, Hicks demonstrates that alienation is not the only possible outcome of what Berlant describes as "the contradiction between the sovereignty of abstract citizens and the everyday lives of embodied subjects."[46] Unlike Berlant, however, Hicks conceives of citizenship not as a subcultural practice that challenges the norms of mainstream society but rather as cooperation *within* that society to ensure that the opportunities available to some are available to all. It was important to Hicks that the civil sphere not be exiled from the mainstream; his goal was to reclaim national belonging not for those who reject or condescend to America, such as "artists and writers . . . who flatter their own weaknesses by expressing contempt for their native land,"[47] but for the underprivileged majority prevented by capitalism from claiming national belonging. Within a truly functional civil sphere, Hicks believed, such belonging is possible.

But should we call such scenes of substantive citizenship and complex possibility "America"? For decades now, scholars have urged against it, citing nationalism's ties to neoliberalism, systemic racism, military violence, colonization, imperial appropriation, and global control of populations, among other charges leveled against nation-states in general and the United States in particular. As Alan Trachtenberg puts the case:

> The day has long passed when any hint of national celebration has appeared in discourse associated with American studies. To the contrary, the concept of nation has been virtually exorcised as incongruous in an age of globalism. To confine a field of studies to the boundaries of a nation-state has come to seem deliberate blindness. . . . The quest for cultural nationality has been almost entirely surpassed by a quest for transnational and postnational identities and prospects.[48]

Without minimizing the importance of those challenges, however, we might consider the value of Hicks's argument not just for his day but for ours. For Hicks, the challenge was to show disaffected citizens what stake they might have in claiming national belonging as a means to social change. Today, the problem is different, although related. When economic elites orchestrate patriotism to increase and justify their own profits, they do something even more dangerous than leaving citizens feeling alienated from America; they lead citizens to feel patriotism for a version of America that goes against their own interests. Whereas Hicks sought to inspire patriotism for a progressive America, our challenge is to make the case for bringing it back to a version similar to Hicks's, a task that requires less knee-jerk antagonism and more understanding of the affections and ideals that make Americans (and not only Americans) *want* to be part of something larger than their local identifications. To acknowledge attachment to the ideals associated with national belonging is not necessarily to shirk the responsibility of critiquing either the nation or its claims to exceptionalism. At the inception of American studies, scholars understood the simultaneity of idealism and critique. As Trachtenberg reports, American studies "took from Emerson, Whitman, Brooks, and their followers the idea of America as a yet unrealized ideal, an idea necessary as motive and goal to the practice of historical cultural criticism."[49] The figures on Trachtenberg's list of nineteenth-century reformers claimed and redefined national belonging, wedding critique and idealism in ways that we often miss today by focusing exclusively on the former at the expense of the latter. Turning those figures into wielders of critique unmotivated by indispensable ideals—especially ideals expressed in the name of the nation—we turn them into versions of ourselves. In so doing, we not only distort their motivations but lose for our own advocacies the balance that gave theirs weight and appeal. Our critiques of the often cataclysmic violence nationalism has justified are of vital importance (leading us, for example, to be rightly suspicious of idealizations such as Hicks's of "westward-moving pioneers" whom we now recognize as the agents of settler colonialism). But if the nation is doing something for people who would like progressive change but need courage and motivation, we might think twice before yanking it away, both because we will lose that audience and because we might not have any viable alternative for performing the same work. *I Like America* became a popular success because, I would argue, Hicks took seriously and worked with peoples' professed beliefs rather than dismissing them as intrinsically corrupt and violent. Patriotism, Hicks discovered, also has the potential to become what James Scott calls a weapon of the weak, serving progressive as well as conservative ends. Following his lead may help us to understand what "America" does not only *to* but also *for* the economically and socially disadvantaged.

To explore the progressive benefits of national belonging without suspending our critique of nationalism, we might consider, as I believe Hicks and Constance Rourke did, "America" as something like what Ernesto Laclau calls an empty signifier, which allows citizens to define, support, and organize themselves locally under the rubric of the nation. When "America" functions as an empty signifier, national belonging allows groups with diverse aspirations, pleasures, and demands to converge under the umbrella of an "empty" ideal, forming what Laclau calls "a political frontier."[50] Such frontiers strengthen creative resolve by allowing those engaged in local struggles to feel part of a larger— even a universal—collectivity. At the same time, local collectivities give specificity to abstractions that become anchored, through particular demands, to historical contingencies.[51] The exchange between abstractions and localities generates what Laclau calls "a moment of hope," during which disparate individuals collect to form a political force and are given ethical extension.[52] Laclau's account helps explain the affective attachment to the sign "America" that Hicks professes and Rourke, as I show later, no less strongly implies. That affection works for both scholars to disperse national unity into disparate pieces that become visible as local communities while simultaneously maintaining a connection to a larger civil society within which disputes and convergences take on political import. The empty signifier "America" thus serves as what Berlant describes as "a crucial bridge between the legal and the substantive domains of U.S. citizenship."[53]

The challenge becomes one of balance: if taking away nationhood leaves people with only local and particular identifications, losing those leaves them with abstractions so vast that they create little else than homogeneous empty time. This is where Constance Rourke's work becomes important. She not only demonstrates a valuable methodological balance between local particularity and national abstraction but also accommodates "America" to the transnational movements of culture scholars are more likely to credit today. Hemispheric, transnational, and postnational critics have challenged assumptions concerning the autonomous sovereignty and unified population of the United States and therefore might well challenge Hicks's containment of civil debate within the borders of the United States. Kirsten Silva Gruesz, for example, discussing the different claims on the name "America," suggests that "a consensual understanding of shared values" is troubled from the start "by multiple ambiguities about the extent of the territory it delineates, as well as about its deeper connotations."[54] In light of these challenges, this chapter augments Hicks's efforts to recuperate American nationalism with Rourke's scholarship on folk culture, which also presents the nation as an empty signifier valuable for progressive social change. Finding a civil sphere that accounts both for the everyday lives of embodied subjects and for the transnational flows of culture that Hicks overlooks, Rourke integrates regional identity and transnationalism with national belonging. As I will discuss at greater length later, Rourke saw "American" culture as intrinsically transnational, involved in the movements of European cultural traditions to the United States. The needs and aspirations of particular local communities *within* the United States produced hybrid cultural forms that, in time, became absorbed into "American" culture without relinquishing either their European or their regional pasts. Without denying the function of the sign "America," Rourke implicitly uses both the diversity of communities within and the flows of culture from without national borders to redefine nationhood in ways that instantiate Hicks's impulse in *I Like America* to include recent immigrants—albeit only from Europe—as well as Yankees like himself in his vision of America.[55]

In destabilizing "America," scholars of transnationalism sometimes pose ever-larger and more abstract entities ("contact zones," "the hemisphere") that not only are granted a stability and sovereignty denied the United States (a critical gesture Gruesz warns against) but that also occasions what Berlant calls "the delocalization of citizenship," which "has not made the world simply postnational" but has given conceptual legitimacy to corporations that function "like empires."[56] As Berlant warns, "transnationality" can be conflated with capitalism as readily as nationalism was in Hicks's era, as "national standards of conduct" are reshaped, not transcended or replaced.[57] In this regard, too, Rourke's nationalism offers a valuable corrective. For her, "America" works against such "delocalization." Attention to the regional folk cultures of the United States was a way to resist any idea of a unified, univocal nation without retreating to a more abstract or similarly unified alternative.

Suggesting that one can like America without loving *or* leaving it, or can like aspects of America without therefore liking *everything* about it, or can like parts of it without assuming their exceptionality, or can like it without definitively defining what "it" is, Hicks and Rourke deconstruct the Manichaean terms on which a good deal of criticism depends today (freedom/bondage, national/transnational, opposition/complicity, good intentions/bad faith, etc.). The opposition they most importantly challenge is that between critique and idealism. Both Rourke and Hicks were idealists. Their ideals were expressed through their concept of nationhood. But they were no less critical of the society they lived in for that. By the time the Cold War made the bombastic imperative to love America or leave it a mass-produced commodity, the changes Hicks called for, premised on the separation of "America" from capitalism, or Rourke's belief that the flow of cultures across borders did not threaten but strengthened national identity, had become almost unthinkable. Ultimately, Hicks, as I will show in the final section of this chapter, was undone by the conflations of capitalism with claims to make the world "safe for democracy" and of communism with threats to the "American way of life." In that climate, where the differences within that made civil society function became reimagined as enemies threatening that society, suspicion, not idealism, became the order of the day, and the "case for change" fell on deaf ears.

We need not go on replicating in literary criticism, however, the polarizations of Cold War rhetorics, in which suspicion is still a mandatory disposition. Too often, the continuance of midcentury state epistemologies as contemporary critical methodology—what I have called Cold War melancholy—has made critique and idealism even less compatible than they appeared to be in the 1950s. I do not mean to suggest there is no cause for suspicion today or that there is less need for social critique than in the past. But we might learn from Hicks and Rourke that critique does not need to work *against* ideals but arises *from* and can serve to strengthen them. The idealism underlying our critiques needs articulation, especially when we discuss citizenship and the meaning of America. If we do not start claiming "America" for our social aspirations, others will. "Our enemy speaks our language," Jodi Dean warns. "And because our enemy has adopted our language, our ideals, we lack the ability to say what we want. Our present values thus become horrific realizations of their opposites, entrapping us in psychotic politics."[58] If it is true that the civil sphere has become, as Berlant contends, "an ordinary space of activity that many people occupy without thinking much about it, as the administration of citizenship usually delegated to the political sphere and only periodically worried over during exceptional crises or the election season," then literary critics need to rethink our mission.[59] But first we need to rethink our dispositions. There are reasons to be skeptical of much that Hicks and Rourke wrote, and my point in this chapter is not that we should adopt their theories or their ideals. My point, rather, is that they offer different ways to think about dispositional possibilities, and in so doing may give us a way beyond our critiques of national belonging and, therefore, beyond our Cold War melancholy.

On one level, *I Like America*, presenting itself as a programmatic response to "the cruel choices that poverty forces upon millions," is, as Hicks later acknowledged, a work of communist propaganda.[60] Resisting the prescriptions of entrepreneurial individualism that predominated—then as now—in conservative responses to poverty, Hicks argued, "What the privileged minority mean when they talk about individualism is perfectly clear: they mean their personal right to make a profit."[61] Like other American communists, Hicks deployed patriotism as a prophylactic against fascism, although he stands out by laying claim to patriotism as something other than an endorsement of nationalism.[62] With Germany and Italy as reference points, Hicks warns that "when the masses of the people have learned to use their government for their purposes, big business" will find a demagogue to march on Washington "in the name of American rights and liberties, and, though it will be Fascism, it will be called something else."[63] "Whatever it is called," he says, it "stirs up race prejudice, crushes labor unions, persecutes religious groups, tortures political opponents, and destroys culture; not only because it thrives on nationalism and leads inevitably to war, but also because it is a plan for scarcity instead of a plan for abundance."[64] Hicks insists, "Our pride . . . ought not to include hatred and contempt for other peoples," adding, "You will meet people who talk about Kikes and Wops and Hunkies. These people will call themselves patriots. But do not let them make you think that patriotism is a bad thing. Their narrow-mindedness is not patriotism."[65]

Hicks was animated by his belief that the American government supports the interests only of the wealthy, fostering false hopes for upward mobility and economic equality in order to prevent clear-sighted revolution. At a moment when many Americans revered Franklin Delano Roosevelt and his New Deal response to the Great Depression, Hicks argued strenuously that Roosevelt's initiatives rescued the economically privileged in the guise of saving the poor. In a chapter titled "Nobody Starves—Much," he documents the misery of Americans barely subsisting on government relief. Arguing that "recovery inevitably leads to depression," Hicks challenges the long-term viability of an economy founded on consumerism, which, he believed, will require repeated and increasingly disastrous bailouts to sustain. "It takes a stronger and stronger stimulus to start the producer-goods industries going," Hicks contends, "and it is easy to imagine that some day we will not find a stimulus of the required strength."[66] In the meantime, recovery takes on increasingly destructive forms, including "war, sometimes the opening of new territory."[67] Hicks's parody of an economic elite who rely on government rescue might well sound familiar to those of us reading after the government bailouts following the mortgage loan crisis of 2007–2008: "'They know that finance capitalism . . . has got to clean house. And they're going to do it! Give us another chance! Give us time! Give us twenty-five more years!'"[68] In the face of disingenuous mea culpas and cynically reluctant government acquiescence, he warns that "if we ever hear businessmen talking about a planned capitalism, we had better watch out. At the moment, the very word 'plan' is anathema to them. . . . And their 'plan' would be a desperate scheme to protect their privileges. . . . It would be a Fascist plan to make scarcity permanent."[69] Refuting such claims to inevitable scarcity, Hicks declares, "We have the power in our hands to abolish poverty. Simply by raising the national income to what it perfectly well might be, we could give all the underprivileged at least a decent standard of living."[70] Acknowledging that he "would like America better if its people were decently housed, decently fed, decently cared for," Hicks claims that the means for doing so are available but are withheld. "We can produce food enough, we can build houses enough, we can train doctors enough," but, he argues, meeting the needs of the poor is contrary to the design of government, so poverty continues and indeed worsens.[71]

Given his trenchant critique of government-supported capitalism, one might expect Hicks to agree with the poet he quotes saying, "'I HATE AMERICA,'" and complaining, "'It's such a middle-class nation. Middle-class people are smug and conventional and materialistic. They have no spirit themselves and they crush the spirit in others. They stifle the arts. There's something in the American atmosphere I can't stand."[72] From Hicks's perspective, however, the loss of the middle class was one of the most disastrous effects of the widening gap between wealth and poverty. The middle class "was not afraid to fight for changes that were not only in its own interests but also in the interests of the great masses of people. Much of what you and I cherish in American life today," Hicks says, "we owe to the struggles of our middle-class ancestors."[73] The poet's complacent disdain for the middle class is a cliché, Hicks believed, shared by academics who, in his estimation, had become "smug, narrow-minded, largely indifferent to what was happening off the campus, and extremely timid."[74] Claiming the authority of an intellectual expelled from academia for contravening its capitalist paymasters, Hicks presented himself as the voice of—and for—a diminishing middle class that takes the side of the workers. Middle-class ideals, he argues, "are not lost," insisting, "We can fight for them still, and fight for them all the better because we are part of the working class," "whatever the collar."[75] America is, in his words, "a working-class nation, which is a good reason for liking it." "We are," he asserts, "most of us, honest toilers. The exploiters and the loafers are in a numerically insignificant minority. We of the working ninety-seven percent have made the nation what it is."[76]

Hicks's concept of what makes the nation "what it is" has less to do with abstractions like "liberty" and "equality" than with their local manifestations in the everyday lives of people like his neighbors in rural Grafton, New York.[77] Accounts of life in Grafton are important to *I Like America* and central to Hicks's better-known book *Small Town* (1948). Hicks used what we might call a radical localism to challenge nationalism's insistence on identifications with what Benedict Anderson calls the "spontaneous empty time" generated by the abstract "imagined community" of a purportedly unified nation. Hicks imagines America less in relation to fixed abstractions and more in terms of the vicissitudes of seasonal change and local sites within which, he suggests, social change is possible. "I make no apologies for the way in which my affections are restricted," Hicks declares, adding, "If I knew more of America, as well as I know this part, I would find just as much to admire and rejoice in."[78] Despite his praise for local life—which risks becoming the idealization of an abstract "folk" common among communists in the 1930s—Hicks was well aware that local life is often motivated by self-interest, narrow-mindedness, and greed. Nor did his focus on local life blind him to the oppression and suffering of people throughout the world. In *I Like America*, Hicks tells a story about an artist visited by a demon come to prove that the artist's life is itself a dream. "'Let me tell you what kind of world you live in,'" the demon insists, "'and then you will see that there cannot be the slightest semblance of reality in this Charming Fantasy of painting, hoeing, talking, reading.'" The specter continues:

> Today Japanese troops gathered hundreds of Chinese citizens and shot them down with machine guns. Today two Spanish babies, sleeping in their beds, were blown to bits. Today German secret service agents entered the home of an obscure Protestant pastor, took him from the midst of a family engaged in evening prayers, and dragged him to a concentration camp. Today a spy wrecked a Russian train, and a score of Soviet citizens died. Today a woman, whose husband had been discharged from the W.P.A., murdered her children and committed suicide. Today a Negro boy committed to life imprisonment for a crime he did not commit, was taken from jail by a mob and burned to death. Today police fired upon strikers, killing one and wounding twelve. Today—.[79]

The artist stops the demon, protesting, "I do not forget during all but five minutes of the day what kind of world it is I live in. I could not forget if I wanted to. No dream has to point with mocking finger at the cruelties and absurdities of every day. I want to know what happens in Spain, in China, in Jersey City, for I realize that they are as much part of my life as this study in which I am writing or the field on which I can look."[80] As for himself, Hicks writes, "I am wise enough to rejoice, but I do not therefore ignore the other world, the world of struggling, suffering millions."[81]

It would be easy, at this point, to take the demon's part, accusing Hicks of lamenting the extraordinary violence in the world while focusing on the injustices carried out by the local school board. My point is not to defend Hicks's specific choices, although I believe they are defensible, especially within the practical constraints that, after he was fired from Renssellaer Polytechnic Institute, relegated him and his family to rural life in the mountains east of Troy, New York. But I want to underscore the balance he maintained between national and local citizenship, which offers a model for how to address the nation critically but without a totalizing suspicion. As I argued earlier, a balance of national and local belongings has great potential for organizing community activism carried out under the empty signifier of "America." Fighting an abstraction is impossible (though it is the battle many literary and cultural critics still choose quixotically to wage). By making abstractions local, however, citizens have an object for their actions, while the broader national identification makes those actions feel like part of a larger and more inspiring and sustaining context. By maintaining a balance between local and national belonging, patriotism can lead, as Hicks believed it would, to constructive activism.

Without the kind of balance Hicks maintains, however, those living within national borders are left with two options: either they identify with the nation, thereby opening themselves to charges of naive complicity or intentional malfeasance, or they occupy a metaphysical space *within* but not *of* the United States. No dissenting peoples, in this logic, can be Americans, or the alignment of "America" with its governmental policies (an alignment that too often elides economic analysis) begins to come undone. Little wonder that, when we invoke abstract systemic operations of power, local cultures of resistance often become more identified with peoples *outside* the United States while local struggles within and in the name of America drop from sight. "America: love it or leave it" is still the order of the day. But this paradox arises only if we assume that to like America is to abjure one's capacity to criticize, that criticism and affection are mutually exclusive. It is that assumption that Hicks, separating policy and populace, usefully troubles. The two "patriotisms" invoked in *I Like America* allow Hicks to manifest two critical dispositions, simultaneously. Of patriotism as national capitalism, he offers an incisive critique; of patriotism as collective action, he can express only idealism. What is most remarkable about *I Like America* is that Hicks's critique did not necessitate the suspension of idealism, or vice versa. On the contrary, *I Like America* shows that one is impossible without the other. Rather than deploying critique to debunk ideals, a strategy that makes the corruption of values seem identical to the values themselves, Hicks shows how ideals and critique are two sides of the same coin. Critique, that is, does not arise sui generis but is the result of deeply held ideals violated by practices that produce misery and injustice. Citizen-critics and citizen-idealists are one and the same.

Critics in Hicks's own day failed to see the balance between critique and idealism in his work, focusing as they did on the strident Marxist realism of his works like *The Great Tradition* (1933) and therefore faulting him for his supposed lack of idealism.[82] F. O. Matthiessen, for example, claimed that Hicks ignores the often ecstatic idealism manifested by nineteenth-century American literature. Hicks, Matthiessen charged, is "not fully enough aware of the part which art can actually play in enriching human life."[83] It is not enough, Matthiessen argued, for an author to "take for his material only the surface details of the kind of life with which the reader is most familiar," an assumption that confines "any reader's comprehension of art" to "the realistic novel of his own day and circumstance."[84] Instead, Matthiessen encouraged Hicks to turn to poetry, which expresses

> the strain of affirmation of the ideal . . . sometimes ecstatic, sometimes somber, not necessarily taking form in verse, but running through Jonathan Edwards to Emerson and Emily Dickinson, from John Woolman to Whitman, throbbing at the heart of Thoreau's discoveries in Walden, finding its most tragic voice in the darker passages of Moby Dick, often coming to articulation in only a minor key, but still being our principal expression of the aspiration of the individual spirit.[85]

Seeing only the critique evident in Hicks's Marxism, Matthiessen overlooks the idealism of the former's claims for what "we could accomplish if we work together," striving "to turn the America-that-is into the America-that-might-be."[86]

If Matthiessen found too much critique in Hicks's work and not enough idealism, today we are likely to make the opposite charge, with the same blindness to the efficacious balance Hicks both advocated for and methodologically enacted. Reading *I Like America* nearly eighty years after its publications, I sometimes cringe. Hicks's Marxism is *so* dogmatic, almost comically predictable in places. What makes me most uncomfortable, though, is that I'm not sure whether my discomfort is with his particular ideals or with idealism itself. If the former, then Hicks has done his work, for the point of articulating ideals is to invite public debate over the values and consequences they comprise. But if the latter, it is hard not to feel that I am shirking my responsibility as a critic and a citizen. When articulating ideals—when idealism in and of itself—becomes shameful, synonymous with complicity or ignorance, our critiques do not become more rigorous. On the contrary: if the ideals that *are already at their core* are implicitly turned into an embarrassment, our critiques become rote, even cynical. If we choose to fill the empty signifier "America" by using it to stand in for reprehensible government policies or violent and disenfranchising social forms, are we suppressing an ideal patriotism (a loyalty *to* idealism)? And if we articulated our ideals, might they possibly look like at least some version of America? And would we like that?

Was Hicks an "American exceptionalist"? Sure. Today, that accusation would be all that is necessary to discredit Hicks's views on national belonging and the virtues of an affective attachment to the United States. In literary criticism today "American exceptionalism" is synonymous with a conservative, militaristic, imperial, and exploitative range of political positions on the part of the U.S. government and of earlier critics who established "American" canons and authors, who perpetuated myths of idealized national character, and who translated those policies into cultural narratives. In the logic of American exceptionalism, the United States not only is isolated from the rest of the globe, its culture arising, as Frederick Jackson Turner had it, from the soil of the continent (which, of course, comprises only the United States), but its exceptional qualities render it superior to the rest of the world and therefore justify intervening, economically and militaristically, in international politics. This outgrowth of exceptionalism has been the target of much literary and cultural criticism (as well as historical and political analysis), and rightly so. While the concept of American exceptionalism is often taken to have a self-evident meaning and hence an over-determined politics, however, it, like "America" itself, is an empty signifier, the potential occasion for debate and redefinition, rather than the foreclosure of any such deliberations. As a starting point for such a debate, I would argue that for Hicks and Rourke, American exceptionalism was not synonymous with either isolationism or superiority to other nations or nonstate formations, although both believed there *is* something exceptional—distinctive—about American culture. They might lead us to ask, then: What might be distinctive to U.S. culture and why? Are the politics of American exceptionalism—or of its use as an accusation—as clear-cut as we believe? Do we deny America an exceptional status only to grant it, uncritically, to other geopolitical entities? Finally, might exceptionalism do a socially progressive work akin to what we intend to enable by disavowing the nation?

For Hicks and other American communists of the 1930s, American exceptionalism was a response to the meaning assigned the term in 1929 by its originator, Joseph Stalin, responding to American communists who believed the U.S. proletariat would find ways to overcome capitalism other than through international revolution. More than simply denouncing American communists' divergence from Soviet doctrine, however, Stalin used the phrase to demonize those who opposed police suppression of intellectual freedom and the centralization of state power in government bureaucracy.[87] "American exceptionalism" thus represented ideals of public debate and the right to challenge governments that disguise state oppression as philosophical superiority—the very opposite of what the term became under Cold War American nationalism. While Hicks reversed the use Stalin made of the term, putting it in the service of a Marxist critique of capital, he neglected to analyze what it was about America that made it distinctive, its small towns better suited to functional democracy than villages elsewhere. For that analysis, we must turn from Hicks to Constance Rourke.

An independent scholar and journalist, Rourke, due to her *American Humor: A Study of the National Character* (1931) is a foundational text for American cultural studies. Like Hicks, Rourke understood local cultures as simultaneously generating and challenging national identity. Whereas Hicks's localism could often seem generic, abstract and geoculturally transferable, however, Rourke focused on the specificity of cultures produced by distinctive communities within the United States, arguing for a specificity that has continued to characterize cultural studies, yet using the particularity of cultural formations as the basis, rather than simply a renunciation, of national identity. In so doing, she shows how national belonging can enhance the distinctive qualities—including the cultures produced by women, racial minorities, and laborers to challenge the hierarchies structuring governmental policies—that cultural studies scholars often celebrate today as intrinsically *opposed to* national belonging. Rourke's work prompts us to consider how our constructions of nationhood rely on *our* specific sociocultural and historical position as post–Cold War intellectuals, constructions that may be as untimely after the Cold War as they were before it began.

In order to examine Rourke's alternative nationalism and what it can teach us about critical methodology today, I will focus particularly on *The Roots of American Culture*, assembled after Rourke's death in 1942 by Van Wyck Brooks from pieces of a proposed three-volume study of the folk origins of American culture. In examining that work, I ask two questions. First, have we moved beyond the structure of exceptionalism in our critique of it today, or have we simply shifted exceptionalism to increasingly larger entities ("the hemisphere," "the transatlantic," "the globe") that carry many of the same supposedly superior characteristics formerly attributed to the United States? The possibility that postnationalism is the new exceptionalism leads to my second question: Has the problem with exceptionalism been inherent in the concept, or are some exceptionalisms (and some definitions of that term) better than others? To address these questions, I turn to Rourke's careful analysis of how transnational flows of culture interact with local conditions in which people live unaware of their context in a larger world. That analysis, I believe, offers a useful alternative to the rigid binary that opposes nationalism to a host of entities immune to the same rigorous investigations and therefore protects our own political investments, institutional positions, and methodological assumptions from undergoing anything like rigorous investigation.

Although Rourke is mostly forgotten by literary critics today, her critique and redefinition of American national culture had an enormous impact on her contemporaries, including F. O. Matthiessen, Newton Arvin, Richard Chase, Lewis Mumford, and Ralph Ellison, in addition to her posthumous editor, Van Wyck Brooks. We see her influence, for example, when Brooks invokes "a national culture," observing, "So far as our literature is concerned, the slightest acquaintance with other national points of view than our own is enough to show how many conceptions of it are not only possible but already exist as commonplaces in the mind of the world. Every people selects from the experience of every other people whatever contributes most vitally to its own development."[88] That America takes on different meanings when viewed from an international perspective, Brooks contends, is "a commonplace to anyone whose mind has wandered even the shortest way from home."[89] For Brooks, the imagination is a cosmopolitan affair, its ideals opening onto what Lewis Mumford called "a world civilization."[90] In proclaiming world citizenship, however, men like Brooks and Mumford maintained that among the accounts of America circulating globally, people within the United States might have one of their own. For Brooks and Mumford, being part of a geopolitical entity entailed certain forms of storytelling for self-comprehension, but those self-expressions were neither unmindful of nor superior to those created *outside* the United States (although in their accounts the attention of the world was still oriented toward the United States). Expressing these ideas, Brooks and Mumford reveal their debt to Rourke, who put forward an idea of transnationalism *and* of American exceptionalism that neither discounts national belonging nor locates its ideals only outside the United States, but rather opens nationalism's empty signifiers to the work of the poor, women, and people of color, the populations American exceptionalism is accused of excluding. Moving beyond facile oppositions of global/local, national/transnational, or critique/duplicity, Rourke offers us, as she did her contemporaries, an alternative to the impasses that have too often sapped the vitality from literary and cultural criticism today.

Rourke's thesis, in brief, is that while most cultural forms in early America came from Europe (her interest was particularly in British, French, Flemish, and German influences), in passing through specific material, spiritual, and affective needs and practices in the United States, those inheritances were transformed into something simultaneously national and transnational. While Rourke insists that there *are* defining experiences within the borders of the United States, she does not therefore claim a self-generated or superior culture, nor does she deny that the circumstances that she identifies in the United States might also have happened elsewhere. Exceptionalism means neither singularity nor superiority. It respects local practices within contexts, among peoples, and in response to historical necessities. For Rourke, affect, gesture, speech, and behavior developed in response to extranational inheritance and local needs, producing hybrid cultures that are nevertheless distinctly and identifiably American. The apparent paradox of Rourke's formulation—that local practices generated a national (and hence presumably transcontextual) culture—is what makes her analyses productive as a model for us today.

Part of what sets Rourke apart from other critics of the period, and helps account for her sensitivity to the transnational roots of American culture, is that she starts not with the geniuses of New England letters but with the folk arts of common people living along the mid-Atlantic seaboard, in the South, and in western Pennsylvania. Where other critics in her era turned away from regionalism in favor of a national "character," Rourke turned *toward* regions that retained their cultural specificity in defiance of the abstractions that allowed other critics to speak of "America." As they had been for Hicks, the people of the United States represented for Rourke an internal division that opened to deliberation over the meaning of "America," undertaken by citizens who, in addition to being laborers, are cultural producers. And although she celebrated national culture and claimed its origins in Europe, she was equally interested in the cultural productions within the United States of African Americans and Native Americans and was well aware that what gets called "European influence" often involves "migration, conquest and simple loot."[91] Combining critique and idealism, Rourke understood that living "as a citizen of a world that now seems to face many economic, social, and cultural crossroads," she, like the cultural innovators she studied, could "not in any conceivable sense . . . advocate a policy of artistic isolation,"[92] but she also knew that navigating cultural crossroads often generated and required national belonging, albeit one capacious and self-critical rather than exceptional in the post–Cold War sense.

In her understanding of national culture as a confluence of international and local influences, Rourke diverged from and opposed regional painters and critics of the time such as Thomas Hart Benton and Thomas Craven who positioned their isolationism against cosmopolitan modernism.[93] Even as she opposed the anticosmopolitanism of her contemporary regionalists, she also corrected those who ignored regional motivations in their accounts of transnational flows of culture. On that score Rourke most explicitly contradicted the historian John Fiske, who believed in what he called "the transit of civilization" in which "carriers" brought European cultures across the ocean.[94] To stop with that knowledge was, in Rourke's estimation, to engage in "one of the simplest, safest forms of scholarship," one that "proves nothing at all as to underlying creative forces."[95] While Fiske believed that "if we dipped deeply and often enough into the major European streams we might hope to witness their rise among us,[96] Rourke was less interested in dipping into European origins than in observing the forces that transmuted traditions in new cultural contexts. As Rourke summarizes: "Essential patterns of thought, emotion and imagination were freshly twisted, emboldened, pulled into new dimensional forms; and it is the resultant configuration that must concern us rather than the separated parts or their antecedent sources."[97] When European traditions came to North America, *something* happened, and Rourke was as interested in following cultural forms forward through their adaptation to specific experiences in North America as she was in tracing them back to their Continental origins. She saw the two activities as continuous, not, as they are often considered today, mutually exclusive.

To articulate her methodology, Rourke drew on the eighteenth-century philosopher and literary critic Johann Gottfried Herder and his contention that "history should portray the many layers of the cultures of peoples rather than the peaks of achievement. He believed that the basic folk cultures differed one from another," Rourke found, "and became concentrated in distinctive national patterns."[98] Following Herder, Rourke argued that what she meant by "American" culture is therefore extranational in its inception but modified by the "tastes, ideas and homely purposes developing over a long period," which "had created a special design."[99] Although "it cannot be sweepingly said that 'sky determines,' that is, that cultures are basically conditioned by environmental factors," Rourke writes, "nevertheless these factors were forces mingling with others in our early settlements. Strange horizons, a totally unknown continent, extremes in climate—these created a rigorous and electric medium within which all experience was shaped and colored. Yet there was a lush abundance of its promise everywhere."[100]

That lush abundance of promise was best realized, Rourke believed, in what she called "folkways," which she defined as "a common language of hand and eye—of familiar speech, which may be read as any speech is read to discover underlying patterns of thought, feeling or preoccupation."[101] Folkways, in Rourke's analysis, sprang out of what was greatly popular, and what was instinctively and sometimes perhaps waywardly preserved as a common possession. It is when these popular choices become deeply rooted and are free forms of expression and communication that they become folk arts. It is then that the social group that has accumulated such forms becomes a folk.[102]

Folk expressions, Rourke explains, may serve "to stir, instruct, reprove, applaud—and to establish social communication."[103] Their "contagions of feeling," arising in "comparative isolation," Rourke contends, reverberate "like loud voices in an empty room."[104] Taking the form of "idiom, intonation, gesture, dress, social choices," folkways express "underlying social ideas and emotions and motives in terms of typical form."[105] Folkways are not, Rourke acknowledges, always the cheerful and virtuous stuff of touristy kitsch; they "sometimes flow from the dark daemonic as well as from loftier or gentler emotions," giving rise to what she calls "folk-evil."[106] Whether working for good or evil, however, folkways refute a prevailing intellectual assumption that "the folk are simple, untutored, innocent and rooted in some secluded bit of countryside far from urban centers."[107] Focusing on "the whole dimensional pattern" of "minor figures" who became "symbols of a dominant creative effort," Rourke's analysis of folkways concludes, "Not merely the individual but the culture of a group, a town, a region may be significant of main tendencies."[108] When Rourke claims that "a continuous life of the folk" runs "through the history of the nation,"[109] then, she does not privilege the nation as the culmination of that folk history but offers a different model of nationhood. National culture, for Rourke, emerges from "the comingling of groups that often represented different races and different phases of culture and different communal aims," groups that do not simply "melt" into a homogeneous culture but retain their situational specificity *and* identities within the nation. "Nothing is static in such social groups," Rourke observes, and therefore nothing about American culture "was fixed or predetermined among the forces at work."[110]

Rourke's *Roots of American Culture* presents numerous examples of the ways regional, religious, and political communities shaped European-derived art forms into distinctive and idiosyncratic American cultures. Martha Beckwith sums up the range of Rourke's interests in this way:

> Woodcuts out of old almanacs, with their "sure lineal attack and a pungent humor;" Indian treaties "set down in amplitude as early as 1677" and constituting "essentially plays-chronicle plays-recording what was said in the parleys, including bits of action, the exchange of gifts, of wampum, the smoking of pipes, the many ceremonials with dances, cries, and choral songs;" the show-boat of the early nineteenth century, floating down the Ohio and Mississippi "like an ark or a flat boat, rigged up as a theater and home;" the first American opera, Tamany; the first American play with a native theme, Ponteach; the appearance on the stage of persistent native types: the backwoodsman, the Irishman, the Negro representing a "genuine native force" but corrupted under "the ecstacies" [sic] of the cult of the last ten years with its "glitter of newness . . . from which serious criticism is likely to turn with distaste," the figure of the Yankee, not Puritan, but "ground to its subtle edges within a society governed by Puritanism."[111]

Rourke discusses how the religious meetings of the Great Revival produced a new form of dance, carried out in "ecstatic, circling, swaying movements, in jumping, jerking, stamping and leaping when excitement rose to a height."[112] She offers the print dispute between Mary Dyer and her husband, both members of the Shaker community, as a prototype of a new psychosexual form of American novel. The Mennonites of central Pennsylvania, discarding standard musical notation, gave rise to an expressive song tradition adapted to their work rhythms. The cadences of verse circulated in newspapers and pamphlets throughout Philadelphia in the decades before the outbreak of revolution shaped a distinctive poetic style that found expression in works such as Francis Hopkinson's *Temple of Minerva* (1781), considered America's first opera.[113] That the Hopkinson who signed the Declaration of Independence wrote musical verse was no surprise to Rourke. As she writes, "The basses or volunteers or tenors might loudly drone or hum through various passages: they created other individual divergences and the struggle, which now seems crude and comical, undoubtedly produced an exhilarating sense of initiative and independence."[114] Translating English music hall ballads into American verse, writers like Hopkinson created "a spirited mode of popular communication or address, whether it set forth an argument or launched a satire or mourned the passing of a citizen."[115] Tracing the connections between political rhetoric urging the overthrow of tyrants and the abandonment of strict artistic conventions, Rourke explains the rise of William Billings, often considered the first professional musician in America. From "the embattled farmers," he decided that "rules distracted him" and instead developed "'the joys of conflict'" into the "early instinctive expression" of American music, in which the fife, "gay, triumphant" but also "comical," became, through improvised songs to honor George Washington, America's representative instrument.[116] In each of Rourke's many case studies, an artistic form begins in Europe and ends by being characterized as "American." The intervening process, in which the quirky situational relations between people gave rise to the different rhythms, movements, and beliefs that make up "folkways," describes a culture that was at once national and transnational, regional and cosmopolitan, transferable and exceptionalist.

It was, most importantly, a nationalism irreducible to the government of the United States or the specific class, racial, and especially gendered interests it served. For Rourke, one benefit of focusing on folkways rather than on the literature written by individual geniuses was that it allowed her to attend to cultural production by women. Rourke was determined to place women at the center of American culture, and in explicitly gendered terms. About the eighteenth-century authors Mercy Otis Warren and Susannah Rowson, for instance, Rourke wrote, "Shrewd, tolerant, hardy, they belonged to a provincial society but exceeded it: in a genuine sense, with their own particular bias, they were women of the great world," for "they had *esprit*, they had belonged to the Revolution."[117] Warren's plays "opened the way for the marked sequence of political and partisan plays to follow in later years,"[118] while Rowson, Rourke writes, "dispels the notion that gentility in this period was a negative quality. It was resilient, its fabric was strong, even tough."[119] Although Boston's "vigorous world seemed wholly masculine," the cultural forms produced by women like Rowson and Warren became the basis for what Rourke calls a "radical feminism" that "looked upon the male world with a skeptical eye."[120]

Rourke's interest in outsiders extended beyond women to include people of color. The great-granddaughter of a man who had as a child been taken captive by Creeks and who later, despite serving as Andrew Jackson's interpreter during his war against the Creek, "never felt comfortable with whites after he was returned to his people at his coming of age, and he often lived with the tribe for months at a time."[121] Rourke was astute in her treatments of treaty ceremonies as cultural performances and in her critique of representations of Native peoples in Anglo-American culture. Revealing "a troubled collective conscience, an effort to obliterate a wrong by handsome tributes," "Indian plays" in white mass culture contained nothing of "nature apprehended as the Indians had apprehended it" but instead drew nature "as the Indian characters were drawn, as fantasy, as belonging to the realm of untethered ideas."[122] Rourke also criticized white depictions of African-derived folkways as "primitive," "exotic," "strange," possessed of a "bold comic quality," and full "of nonsense."[123] She contrasted those depictions with slave songs, which gave a distinctive form to American humor: "Defeat was hinted in the occasional minor key and in the smothering sidelong satire. In American humor the sudden extreme of nonsense was new, and the tragic undertone was new."[124] Rourke advocated for "a full assembling of the Negro tradition" in order to create "a gauge . . . against false exploitation," and so that "the finer productions of the present day might take on unexaggerated values."[125]

Above all, giving concrete form to Hicks's often abstract references to "working people," throughout *The Roots of American Culture* Rourke argues for the value of cultures generated by laboring common people, who, for her, represented the independence, resilience, and creativity that I have described as characteristic features of hope. Rourke challenged Marxist critics who claimed that American culture had been ruined by "a persistent materialism," a thesis that "like many other generalizations about American life and the American character . . . does not bear the test of a close scrutiny."[126] The folkways Rourke celebrated, as Alan Trachtenberg observed, stood as "a model for newly formed communal relations imagined by socialist critics of the ferociously selfish and destructive capitalist order."[127] For Rourke, the material culture of the demos "developed out of popular movements and even with their limited numbers represented widespread popular concerns," manifesting the "impulse toward communal organization."[128] Rourke claimed populism in her choice of intellectual subjects, working against the "artificial division between the practical and the fine arts," with "the result that one tended to be lost or obscured and the other separated from vigorous and natural sources."[129] Wryly challenging the "mournful critiques" of scholars who worried over a lost or absent American folk culture, Rourke reminds readers, "Genius is never truly solitary though it is often proclaimed to be so."[130] Asserting that "our odd bias away from the popular" makes cultural criticism antidemocratic, Rourke concludes, "Critics might have accomplished more by a skilled and knowledgeable evaluation of the many more or less humble works at hand."[131]

Because she focused on popular folkways—including those created by women, African Americans, religious minorities, and workers—*without* opposing or disavowing national culture, Rourke offers a compelling model of how "America" might be approached as something more than exceptionalist, or perhaps as exceptionalist in a more productive way. Rourke, Trachtenberg points out, was not arguing for a reified, coherent, self-generated, or superior national character. Rather, presenting culture as fluid, ephemeral, contingent, and historically uneven, she depicted a national character that is continually changing.[132] There might seem to be a paradox in Trachtenberg's (or Rourke's) analysis: Why articulate a national character at the same time as one dismantles its exceptional status? But what seems like a paradox is, for Rourke, why nationalism makes sense. It is not only, as Rourke argues, that different geographic, economic, and religious developments taking place within the borders of the United States create particular forms of survival, labor, expression, and pleasure. It is that the rubric "national" became a way to see those particularities as participating in a larger project that mitigated the limitations or isolation imposed by folk specificity. Because they could imagine themselves as part of a national project, local communities gained a sense of connection to ideals that gave a transcommunal inspiration to local endeavors. Reviewing *The Roots of American Culture*, Alfred Kazin wrote: "She sought what so many modern Americans have lost, what so many Europeans have established as the first principle of a human existence—the sense of locality, the simple happiness of belonging to a particular culture."[133] Although they *were* spiritually, socially, and/or geographically local, however, members of these communities could imagine themselves as part of a national project. The particularity of these localities interacted with national signifiers—including "America"—in ways that gave a transcommunal inspiration to local endeavors while underscoring the malleability and historical contingency of these signifiers. And at the same time they gave a particularity to national self-definitions, generating what was specifically American about American culture.

Folkways thus become a way of "dislocating" the nation, to use Robert S. Levine's helpful concept. To dislocate is not, however, to abandon. If exceptionalism relies on abstractions of "nation" beyond the local practices celebrated by Rourke, the substitution of "transnationalism" or "hemispheric" or "oceanic" or any other abstraction in the absence of sustained attention to local practices that dislocate not just nationalism but also its alternatives leads to an exceptionalism different in name but not in function. The nation, Rourke teaches us, is *not* the same as its government (or, she might have said to Hicks, the economy). When we challenge national culture, we need to distinguish the policies undertaken in the name of the nation from the uses made by local cultures of the name of the same entity. The former often institutionalize and thereby place beyond redefinition national signifiers, while the latter may occupy those signifiers in ways that make them as variable and valuable as are local folkways. When we conflate the two, we not only make it impossible to say with Hicks that we like America but also do a disservice to those who, like Rourke, understand national belonging as an operation of resilience and pleasure for the disadvantaged, the unsettling possibilities that I call hope, or that Rourke imagined as the "possibility for criticism and scholarship of a most radical, refreshing kind."[134] Approaching national culture "in spite of criticism"—by which she means the "intellectualized, self-conscious attack [that] has become in a general way a national habit, even a rough technique" (here Rourke suggests that nothing could be more American than the critique of American exceptionalism)—Rourke believed that criticism "can be turned toward the definition and solution of our difficult cultural problems" not by disavowing but by acknowledging how, where, and why variant versions of "America" might be operating from different "exceptional" contexts and for different purposes, even those operating at cross-purposes.[135] For Rourke the most useful version of the nation belongs to the "imaginative folk-life of our short past [that] could gradually become a free possession,"[136] or, in a phrase from the title of her last chapter in *The Roots of American Culture,* "a possible future."

We are historically in a better position to see "where fulfillment has been impeded" by certain forms of national exceptionalism, and in arguing that we might reclaim "America," I am not talking about the Cold War state any more than Rourke was. I am suggesting that regression may be found not only in the deployment of and advocacy for "America" associated with the Cold War but also in the melancholic identifications with the Cold War state evident as well in critiques of America, that make suspicion seem like acuity and substitute negation for nuanced analysis. Being critical of a nation whose boundaries are represented as firm and whose character is claimed to be exemplary has been necessary, but perhaps too often at the expense of our purposive desires to make more of "our unstable and heterogeneous social life," including "underground movement" and "those ties with the natural world which are now being acutely missed in a machine civilization."[137] Rather than surrendering the category of the nation in a melancholy reproduction of the Cold War state, especially when we set out to critique that version of "America," we might better, in Rourke's words, "turn it to the purpose of the creative imagination and of self-understanding."[138]

I Like America was a best seller. Priced at fifty cents, the book quickly sold more than 50,000 copies,[139] reaching a broad audience that, during the Great Depression, was looking for a reason to believe in America. Hicks provided that reason with a thesis he summarized in his sequel, *Where We Came Out* (1954). "Sixteen years ago," he recounts, "I wrote a little book of Communist propaganda and called it, in all sincerity, *I Like America.*"

> I did like America, and it was natural that I should, for all through the thirties I was able to live the kind of life that I wanted to live. I couldn't help seeing, however, that I was a member of a privileged minority, and I found nothing un-American in desiring for other people, for all people, the privileges I enjoyed.
>
> I believed that there were great evils and injustices in American life, and of course I was right. I believed that these evils could and should be remedied, and I was right in that too.[140]

By the mid-1950s, however, Hicks had a different story to tell. "But I was dead wrong in believing that they could be remedied through the agency of the Communist party,"[141] he writes, going on to claim:

> I liked America in 1938, but I like it even better in 1954. For one thing, many of the evils I saw then have been corrected. Our nation is more prosperous than ever before in history, and prosperity is more widely distributed. Though inequalities still exist, the majority of working peo-ple labor in decent conditions, for reasonable hours, at high pay, while the aged, the sick, and the handicapped are better taken care of than in the past. How our high standard of living has been brought about and whether it can be maintained are questions to be looked into, but that high standard is a reality.
>
> There have been gains in other ways, too. In 1952, for the first time in our history, a year went by without a single lynching. Discrimination against Negros, though still powerful and evil, has diminished during the past ten years to an extent that the greatest optimist could not have believed possible. Other types of racial and religious prejudice persist, but we are on guard against them.[142]

The degree of complacency Hicks has acquired in the fifteen years between the two books becomes clear in his lament over what he names as a significant social problem of the 1950s: traffic. He claims:

> These successes and strains are most palpable when you have to travel from Astor Place, say, to 125th Street on New York City's Lexington Ave-nue subway at five-thirty in an August heat wave, or when, in a November ice storm, you drive from a factory in the southeast section of Detroit to a housing project on the northwest boundary. Who can reckon the price in irritation and frustration, to say nothing of the threat to life and limb, that is paid by each one of millions of commuters in an age in which home is here and work is there?[143]

That a focus on road congestion has pushed aside the fact that one would likely be traveling from Astor Place to Harlem by subway if one was domestic help or that people in industrial Detroit were still earn-ing so little as to require housing projects is a painful indication of the effects the Cold War had even on a committed Marxist like Hicks. Even when Hicks hesitated to attribute exceptional superiority to America, in the 1950s he attributed that caution not to doubts about government policies or to respect for other nations but to the American people he once trusted to found a different America. Hicks asserts that "as a people we are not fit for the responsibilities that are now ours" because Americans "need more wisdom and more humility than we have generally shown."[144] If "we are to overcome the suspicions of those who should be our allies," he advises, Americans must drop their tendency to "vacillate between smugness and a state bordering on hysteria."[145] He concludes, "I do not think that Americans are better than other people, or that the United States is always right and other nations always wrong," yet *despite* its people America is "the hope of the world."[146] Demonstrating the smugness he criticizes in other Americans, Hicks states that, albeit "not because of any particular virtue on our part, the modern revolution is farther advanced in this country than anywhere else and has shown clearer evidence of being a success." With tongue-in-cheek modesty he claims, "This at least suggests that we may have some qualifications for the tasks of leadership that have been laid upon us. If, to put it crudely, the world is going our way, it is not immodest of us to suppose that we may be able to give some good advice now and then."[147]

That Hicks could claim that America is "the hope of the world" is ironic given how uncomfortably the Cold War had interfered in his life. In 1953, Hicks was called before the House Un-American Activities Committee as a friendly witness, and he named eight men who had been communists when he was a lecturer at Harvard between 1938 and 1939.[148] Hicks later justified his cooperation, asserting that the worst consequence was likely to be that a few intellectuals were "bound to be embarrassed, even if nothing worse happened," a remarkably naive claim from someone who had been dismissed from an academic position because of his political beliefs.[149] Hicks had no objection to ousting communists, his challenge being only that McCarthy was going about it the wrong way, targeting academics when there were more serious threats weakening the fabric of American life.

Hicks, in short, was no hero, and my intention here has not been to present him as such (I would make a stronger case for Rourke, who, although she often ridiculed Marxist criticism, never surrendered her commitment to collective cultural resistance). But part of the problem with criticism today, as Latour and Sedgwick have pointed out, is a desire for politically "pure" positions, for our literary heroes and for ourselves. Such purity was no more available to Hicks than it is today. What I do want to argue, however, is that the failure to sustain ideals is not proof that one was wrong to believe in them in the first place. The lesson to be learned from the sad fate of so many midcentury critics—fired from jobs, driven to psychological and physical breakdowns, even suicide—is how powerfully determined the forces allied against idealism are, which is reason enough not to join them, however unwittingly, by disparaging idealism as naïveté, ignorance, or avoidance. When we wield those accusations against the men and women who defined American literature for a generation, no matter how radical the content of our critiques, we deny what is most socially transformative about them: their inspiration in ideals.

A dismissal of idealism—especially when, as in Hicks and Rourke, those ideals go by the name "America"—has become pervasive in literary and cultural criticism. Caught in our Cold War melancholy, we condemn previous generations of critics who ventured other definitions of and opinions about nationhood, blaming them, as Caren Irr claims, "for codifying the masculinist canon, solidifying the exclusivity of the great tradition, espousing nationalism, proselytizing humanism, and so on."[150] While there are legitimate reasons to criticize nationalism, Americanists today, Irr states, tend "to collapse all forms of nationalism into a homogenous other." What we have lost sight of is that nationhood, as Hicks and Rourke show, can be a powerful discourse for those pursuing social justice. However tempered, national belonging remained for Hicks and Rourke a potent site of both critique and idealism. Recognizing that, Hicks never quite surrendered his responsibility to defend America against its own government. American anti-communists, stirred up and sanctioned by government rhetoric, do not stop with avowed communists, Hicks notes in *Where We Came Out*; "they attack those whom they call 'Communist-minded.' They admit that so-and-so was never a Communist and never had anything to do with Communist fronts, but, they say, he has the kind of mind that makes him naturally sympathetic—'soft' is the word they generally use—toward Communism."[151] Such an accusation, Hicks argues, "aims not merely at getting rid of dangerous people but also at suppressing an idea,"[152] and the culprits, he charges, are more numerous than just McCarthy. Indicting a cynical government in terms that are just as germane today as they were in the 1950s, Hicks writes, "Many of the leaders of the anti-Communist crusade are fighting liberalism or progressive education or socialized medicine or the excess profits tax. Some are quite simply making political careers for themselves."[153] Although by 1954 he no longer believed "in dissent for dissent's sake," Hicks believed "even less in conformity for conformity's sake, or for the sake of money, or power, or prestige."[154]

Animating Hicks's critique of the U.S. government were ideals he made no bones about stating. "As I have tried to say before," Hicks wrote, "the health of society depends on the existence of free and vigorous criticism."[155] Although Hicks renounced communism, he refused to blame those who joined the party in the 1930s. Most of them, he wrote, "were convinced that they were following an ideal."[156] The ideals may have been wrong, but the idealism was not. American communists, for Hicks, were part of the "great tradition" of American populism, which included Emerson, Thoreau, and Whitman, all of whom "spoke for all the oppressed, and some of their words remain a call to arms."[157] Characterizing "the great tradition of American literature," which "has been a critical literature, critical of greed, cowardice, and meanness," Hicks makes explicit the connection between critique and idealism, writing, "It has been a hopeful literature, touched again and again with a passion for brotherhood, justice, and intellectual honesty."[158]

Does the basis of that "call to arms" still exist in literary criticism? I believe it does. The difference between the ideals articulated by Hicks and criticism today is not that we lack idealism but that critics like Hicks *acknowledged* those ideals, while we suppress ours, leaving them discernible only in their outcome as critique. Analyses of the failings of American nationalism, however, have their origin in concepts of the nation akin to Hicks's, although it is academic heresy to say so. But the claim is supported by one of the most forthright discussions in recent years of generational differences within American studies over nationalism and idealism. In 2005, Amy Kaplan published "A Call for a Truce" in response to an essay by Leo Marx, author of the "myth and symbol" study *The Machine in the Garden* (1964).[159] Acknowledging that "Marx eloquently attests to the political origins of the field [American studies] in multiple, complex, and radical roots that preceded what would later be characterized as a hegemonic Cold War consensus," Kaplan writes that "it was thrilling to imagine the political and intellectual turmoil, debates, and excitement of the era he describes so well" and to recognize in the criticism written by Marx's generation "the doubleness of critique and affirmation."[160] She regrets, however, that, looking at contemporary criticism, Marx "sees decline instead of recognizing that there are parallels between these generations or that the production of new and exciting scholarship that emerged from the social movements of the 1960s and '70s might have analogies to the work that grew out of the political ferment of his generation."[161] While Marx "attributes a sense of nobility and idealism to his generation," Kaplan observes, he "makes the political commitments of later generations seem merely angry and divisive, even when he agrees with their critiques."[162] Countering Marx's insistence on what he refers to as a generational "Great Divide," Kaplan asserts, "Like it or not (and I like it), we are very much the heirs of Marx and his generation, even in our rejections and critiques of the original project and the different, but equally passionate, personal beliefs and political commitments that inspire our scholarship."[163]

Despite their shared passion, however, Kaplan and Marx part ways, unsurprisingly, over national exceptionalism. Marx denies that the nationalist rhetorics in his era's criticism signaled support for the Cold War consensus, claiming that his contemporaries "were more committed— and, oddly enough, more *hopefully* committed—to the tradition of radical egalitarianism than Americans have been at any other time of my life."[164] Marx claims a different meaning of "nationalism" in their work, closer to what I have identified in Hicks's writings from that period. When the American nation was invoked, Marx claims, it was to mobilize opposition to "egregious forms of capitalist exploitation and injustice, or to unjust wars." Marx and his contemporaries expressed a "provisional belief in the idea of America" that was "a compelling means of exposing the discrepancy between a real and an ideal America,"[165] setting actual practices in sharp contrast to "the universal, egalitarian values of the Enlightenment represented by Thomas Jefferson, Thomas Paine, and Lincoln."[166] In so doing, Marx concludes, critics of his generation "combined harsh criticism with anxious affection for the world's first and largest experiment in multicultural democracy."[167] Turning this defini-

tion of nationalism on younger critics, Marx argues that their antagonism to American exceptionalism is itself quintessentially American.
Although later critics lost their faith in America because of the Vietnam War and Watergate, leading them to decry "as fraudulent the pre-
sumed commitment of the American republic to the principles—or (as
they said) the 'master narrative'—of the Enlightenment," nevertheless,
Marx insists, they "reaffirmed their own commitment to the egalitarian
principle at its core."[168] Instead of renouncing that vital principle, Marx
writes, "they relocated it."

> They disconnected it from the idea of America as a whole and reattached
> it to the aspirations of those subordinate groups of Americans—women,
> African Americans, the working class—ostensibly oppressed or victim-
> ized by an irremediably discriminatory social system. This redirected ap-
> plication of egalitarian political standards was a conspicuous—and highly
> revealing—exception to their all-but-total repudiation of the original
> American studies project.[169]

Yet whatever their intentions, Kaplan responds, the language of nationalism, once institutionalized, loses its progressive potential and becomes instead an oppressive force throughout the globe. Marx, Kaplan
claims, "believes that we need all the more to criticize the US 'as measured by the nation's own profession of values and purposes,'" while she
knows "that such professions have contributed to an exceptionalism that
justifies imperialism and injustice and that keeps the US insulated from
developing—in dialogue with others—ethical values that go beyond the
nation as a standard of measurement."[170]

This is the disagreement about nationalism that we would expect
today, when Kaplan's position is ubiquitous. We might profitably in-
troduce into that consensus some of the "turmoil" Kaplan admires
in Marx's generation, however, not for argument's sake (although in
this generation's distaste for awkwardness we shy away from internal
controversy far too often) but because it opens space for what Kaplan
calls a truce. Kaplan, more frank than many of her contemporaries,
acknowledges that critique—even that of nationalism—has its roots
elsewhere than in suspicion (the "doubleness" that thrills her in Marx's
position). Agreeing with Marx that "disillusionment presupposes the

loss of belief," Kaplan ponders "whether I do believe enough in the idea
of America to want to protect democracy, civil liberties, racial equality,
the Bill of Rights, checks and balances, and international obligations
from the dismantling of these institutions by the Bush administration"
and admits that she "may believe enough in the Enlightenment to think
that truth and knowledge, which this administration completely dismisses, should matter to politics."[171] Kaplan candidly acknowledges the
source of her critique in a set of ideals ("truth and knowledge") that
precede suspicion, although her concession to idealism moves quickly
to a condemnation of the Bush administration, as though she, like so
many Americanists today, is more confident in ideals when expressed
in the inverse form of critique. Nevertheless, this is a significant point
of convergence that indicates that criticism has remained a practice of
hope, even though its status as such has been by and large occluded.
The explicit articulation of ideals by both Kaplan and Marx invites not
only analyses of where those ideals have been distorted or betrayed but
about the meaning and potential manifestations of those ideals in more
hopeful forms. That is certainly the outcome of Marx's frank assertion
of his generation's ideals, which invites self-analysis and speculation on
Kaplan's part, leading to significant agreement where before there had
been only a "divide." The two points I draw from this exchange are that
idealism, despite Cold War melancholy's insistent critiquiness, has per-
sisted in American literary and cultural criticism, and that the entirety
of critique involves both Kaplan's skepticism *and* Marx's faith. When
the two come together, the result is a practice of hope. "America," as an
empty signifier, in this case becomes the site of that practice, as it was
for Hicks and Rourke. In the case of this particular exchange, however,
the convergence comes at a cost. The two critics communicate across
the generational divide by agreeing to a genealogy—leading from the
Popular Front to the New Americanists—that excludes an entire generation, present only as a trace invocation of the "Cold War consensus." In
leaping from the Spanish Civil War and World War II to Vietnam and
Watergate, Marx and Kaplan erase the intervening generation of critics
(even though Marx, who was sixteen in 1935, is more a member of the
Cold War generation than he is of the Popular Front critics of the 1930s
with whom he aligns himself, presumably to strengthen his defense of
pre-divide critical politics).

In the following chapters, however, I will argue that the idealism of Marx's generation continues in Kaplan's not because of a bridge across a chasm but due to a series of transformations of idealism and critique carried out by the generation the two critics excise. The critics discussed in those chapters—driven to suicide, confined to mental institutions, arrested for public drunkenness—had every reason to abandon hope. But they didn't. They translated it to fit changing times and different needs, "touched," like the authors they studied, "again and again with a passion for brotherhood, justice, and intellectual honesty."[172] Despite the disappointments they faced, critics who wrote during the Cold War continued to refuse, as Hicks wrote in *Where We Came Out*, "things as they are or things as they have been" and were "willing to examine freely proposals for change."[173] Richard Chase translated the socialism of Hicks's day into a liberalism adapted to a post-Freudian concept of human nature. What Hicks called a "critical liberalism" that would frustrate every "pattern of automatic response"[174] emerged in Chase's criticism, as the next chapter will show. Newton Arvin concurred with what he summarizes as Rourke's conclusion in *American Humor*: "As a people, we have hung together very imperfectly; and only out of rich and integrated sociality does thoughtful laughter, or tender laughter, or elevated laughter, arise."[175] He developed from that insight what, in the third chapter, I call his queer socialist humanism, which in turn became the formalist analysis of critics such as Marius Bewley and Richard Poirier, discussed in the final chapter. The usable past of translated hopefulness these critics offer finds its roots in the 1930s with Hicks and Rourke, for whom, in Irr's estimation, "there was a concept of national culture based not on an opposition between national and insurgent subjects but on an alliance between the two."[176]

Hicks wrote in *The Great Tradition* that the first reason "why books like this have to be written is to remind people of what America is really like. The second reason is to convince them that change is possible."[177] Unlike Hicks, we have become cautious, like former communists in the 1950s, of where, how, and to whom we express our hopes. To reclaim hopefulness for criticism will require more than another look at nationalism, however; it will involve what Hicks in a *Partisan Review* essay from 1947 called "a moral strength" that has "not only denounced the oppressions as immoral" but also "buoyed up the morale—significant word—of the oppressed by saying, 'The right is on your side.'"[178] A moral criticism begins "with self-analysis." As Hicks wrote at the start of the Cold War, "That is, the individual Leftist might state his ideas of the good society as explicitly as he can and then try to discover whence they derive. For the average intellectual today, this is like baring one's secret sins, but perhaps we are unnecessarily shamefaced about it."[179] Today when literary critics are trained to approach ideals—and especially those attached to "America"—with a totalizing suspicion and when the statement of our "ideas of the good society" again brings shame, when we shame *ourselves* by accepting uncritically the dogmas and dispositions of ritual critique, is there hope for a hopeful nation-based criticism? I would say, as Hicks did, "The marvelous thing is that it can be done."[180]

2

Liberalism

Richard Chase's Liberal Allegories

In a February 1950 letter to Newton Arvin, Richard Chase professed confusion over "just what we have been at loggerheads about" in the two critics' heated exchange in *Partisan Review* over Chase's interpretation of Herman Melville's *Billy Budd*.[1] In fact, as Gretchen Murphy notes, the stakes were high: the meaning of liberalism as a political philosophy and an interpretive methodology during the Cold War. Chase and Arvin continued their debate in an epistolary exchange over two years, and despite his rhetorical head-scratching over their disagreement, Chase went on in this letter to throw more fuel on the flames, asserting that *Moby-Dick*'s Captain Ahab is a progressive liberal who, unwilling to abandon his idée fixe about destiny and moral purity, destroys his ship and crew, as liberals like Arvin would, Chase claimed, ruin America. In response to Arvin's charge that Chase was using Melville to grind an ax, projecting contemporary political debates onto an author who could not possibly have engaged it in his own day, Chase wrote:

> I have assumed that by and large American culture has been for 150 years liberal-progressive culture. What else? Therefore I have assumed that the great types of this culture must have certain things in common with the general pattern. This has seemed a justification for speaking of Ahab, the Confidence Man, Hawthorne, Melville, et al., in their relation to liberalism and progressivism. Now you, having put a much more limited interpretation upon the word "liberalism" and having taken up a 19th-century rationalist view of history and politics, have naturally suspected me of loose thinking and being too friendly to reactionaries. You tend to see John Dewey and Henry Ford as utterly different, whereas what strikes me first is their amazing similarity.[2]

When Chase charged "progressive liberals"—United Front Marxists like Arvin who believed in the nobility of the working man and the teleological movement of history toward revolution—of taking a narrow view of liberalism, he was making the case for a "critically maintained liberalism" or what he called the New Liberalism.[3]

This argument often came down to semantic squabbling, muddled by Chase's habit of referring to both his philosophy and the one he opposed as "liberalism," though he also called the latter progressivism, socialism, or some combination of those terms. Underlying the contests over nomenclature, however, was a real dispute over the role of criticism at the start of the Cold War. Communist-identified critics in the earlier generation—men like Granville Hicks, Arvin, F. O. Matthiessen, and, in his early career, Lionel Trilling—believed in the elevation of the masses through an Enlightenment faith in rational, scientific examination and remedy of social ills. Good and evil were as easily distinguished as Dewey and Ford. Chase, however, wrote in the aftermath of the disillusionment resulting from Stalin's nonaggression pact with Hitler, his establishment of hierarchies of privilege and power, his purges of dissenting intellectuals, and his violent colonization of Eastern Europe. The development and deployment by the U.S. government of atomic weaponry, causing mass destruction and death, and the anticommunist purges like those conducted by the House Un-American Activities Committee further dampened the optimism of "progressive liberals." Scientific rationalism—and Enlightenment values broadly— could no longer liberate the masses, as science had enabled the nuclear arms race while rationalism had failed to account for the human ambition and greed that made inevitable the corruption of the Soviet experiment. These disappointments divided American liberals, generating a new intellectual class more politically centrist, psychologically oriented, and aesthetically highbrow than their predecessors. Unambiguous ideals became dangerous, and human action seemed rarely for the common good. The debate between Arvin and Chase indexes those changes. Part of a generation of leftist intellectuals characterized by anger, disillusionment, and fear, Chase diverged from the noble if often two-dimensional "common man" of the Marxists to embrace ideas of human nature as complex, self-destructive, plagued by depression, doubt, and anxiety. That shift produced an appreciation of literary characters possessed of deep interiority and uncertain motivations, over whom ideology could hold unconscious sway and who might therefore be subjected not to singular moral judgment but to ongoing suspicion. Chase's era of critics believed they were analyzing literary texts endowed with a "political unconscious" and populated by characters over and through which "symptomatic" critiques can legitimately operate.

The public squabbles between Old and New Liberals in which Chase became a lightning rod reflect the Cold War's growing influence on literary criticism. Cold War ideologies posited a dire opposition between ideological and mutually suspicious enemies whose absolute differences made overlap or resolution seem impossible. Chase and his opponents reproduced this structure, asserting unbridgeable doctrinal divisions between hostile enemies deeply mistrusting each other's motives and practices. Chase and Arvin's dustup over *Billy Budd* and *Moby-Dick* erupted at the start of the Cold War. But these disputes are something of a red herring. Though Chase and Arvin claimed antagonistic positions, their literary exegeses perform complex combinations of their seemingly irresolvable differences. Arvin was more skeptical about human nature than Chase allowed, seeing in Hawthorne, for instance, a troubled, almost pathological aversion to human society, while Chase was less averse to collectivity than Arvin seemed to believe, celebrating the social affection, strength, perseverance, and imagination of the crew aboard the *Pequod* in *Moby-Dick*. Above all, neither Arvin nor Chase saw negative affect as the opposite of social transformation but rather believed in something akin to what Michael Warner posits as an ethics of shame, a collective recognition of shared nonnormativity that is erotic in origin and leads to an ethical respect for divergence rather than a proscriptive imperative toward the social conformity both Arvin and Chase believed characterized postwar American life. For Chase, shame was hardwired into human personality, while for Arvin it arose from the conflict between noble ideals and social realities. Whatever their origins, shame, disappointment, and alienation led both critics to imagine other social possibilities beyond the consensus-oriented American culture of the early Cold War years.

Rather than seeing Chase's quarrel with Arvin as a break, then, we might better understand it as an adaptation, in which Chase kept alive ideals of collective sympathies, social critique, and hopeful idealism central to a previous generation's liberalism while adapting them to the changing conditions of early Cold War America. Understanding the differences between "progressive" and "new" liberals as an adaptation enables us to see that Chase—along with others in his generation of so-called myth and symbol critics—neither turned away from politics nor supported in any clear-cut way the Cold War consensus. Rather, they transformed a politics originally understood as a revolution in material conditions into a psychological struggle toward a social ideal that looked surprisingly progressive. If one consequence of this adaptation was to interiorize politics into something with potentially no social referent, another was the archiving of certain social ideals in the relative safety of academic literary studies at a time when articulated social dissatisfaction was tantamount to treason.

That transformation is most evident in Chase's discussions of allegory, which became in his handling a template for demonstrating the simultaneous intermixing of alienation and idealism, of human limitation and social aspiration. In this chapter I focus on the allegorical structure of Chase's *Herman Melville: A Critical Study* to show that Chase's interest in allegory was not a turning *away* from politics. On the contrary, from the first pages of *Herman Melville*, Chase makes clear the political motive for making allegories. At first Chase describes his motive in terms of the generational antagonism described above: he reports his desire to "contribute a book on Melville to a movement which may be described (once again) as the new liberalism—that newly invigorated secular thought at the dark center of the twentieth century, which, whatever our cultural wreckage and disappointment, now begins to ransom liberalism from the ruinous sellouts, failures, and defeats of the thirties."[4] Insisting on how much political philosophy owed to literary allegory, Chase asserts, "I have the conviction that if our liberalism is serious about its new vision of life, if it has the necessary will to survive, it must come to terms with Herman Melville."[5] As much as enactments of differences within liberal philosophy, however, Melville's allegories, in Chase's handling, combine a critique of a culture of conformity and a vision of how that society might be revitalized. Although he believed liberalism needed to acknowledge human foibles, he did not celebrate them, at least not in his interpretations of Melville. For Chase, the intellect "feeds and ruins and wastes" human potential, but he believed such potential must "be perpetually repaired, the wasted tissue restored," likening the dialectic of destruction and repair to "the rhythm of withdrawal and return," Chase's favorite of Melville's allegorical types.[6] Enacting the simultaneity of critique and idealism, Chase produced a literary disposition that, as he said of Ford and Dewey, was strikingly similar to that of progressive liberals like Arvin.

That simultaneity of critique and idealism is evident in Chase's particular fascination with the literary allegory he called withdrawal and return. Withdrawal involves removal—for the most part voluntary—from society into an isolation that allows meditation upon conventions and communion with the desires, affects, and beliefs those conventions foreclose. Melville sent his heroes on voyages away from civilization in order to find idylls where their emotional needs could be articulated, satisfied, and evaluated. In Chase's readings of Melville, physical withdrawal was also metaphysical, refusing proscribed "reality" in order to enter the "unreal" where new ideals sharpen the moral imagination. The cross-cultural and erotic bonding of Queequeg and Ishmael in *Moby-Dick* takes place at the threshold between social conventions and imaginative possibility, permitting the ideals of camaraderie found only in the allegorical space of Ahab's doomed voyage. Fantasy, emotion, desire, lyricism all become, through withdrawal, cartographies of dissatisfaction and reinvention legible only to "the mind which is *more* 'spiritual, wideseeing, conscientious and sympathetic' than other minds."[7] Withdrawal, in Chase's analysis, then, is more self-willed than abject alienation, being essential to the production of those forms of social imagination that he called visions, the diversity of which loosens the stranglehold of convention and allows the play of social invention. Taking Melville as an example, Chase explains that social visions must be "free of dogma and absolutism" but must remain socially relevant through their invitation to what he called "a kind of thought which is bounteous, in the sense that it is open-minded, skeptical, and humanist."[8]

Chase called the simultaneously physical and metaphysical withdrawal exemplified by Melville "beyondness." That term introduced a phenomenology of imminent vision in which the material world is saturated with the potential for its own not-realness, ontology released into the imaginative possibilities of interpretation. At the same time, imagination is given a materiality that renders it legible, capable of bringing material changes to the space of the seemingly unalterable "real." Giving textual form to a coming-to-being—what Chase called "return"— *beyondness* fills allegory's mundane content with imminent illumination and invites readers into an unsteady state both real and more than real, interpretable and ineffable. Melville's cosmos, Chase believed, gives sociality in particular a presence and, simultaneously, visionary excess. No truly progressive politics exists without beyondness, or what Chase also called a "visionary conversion,"[9] generating imaginative worlds at least partially free from the inevitable iteration of a dysfunctional past. When Melville sends his characters to sea, puts them on exotic islands, sends them to spiritual promised lands, or casts them backward in time, he is, Chase suggests, rejecting the facile utopianism of his age in favor of more inventive ideals that arise from and therefore find new ways to accommodate eroticism, creativity, desire, excessive emotion, bad faith, unconscious drives, cruelty, even failure—in short, the full range of human nature, available neither in material life nor in detached vision but in their simultaneity, their beyondness. In analyzing Melville's allegories, therefore, Chase combines the transformative collectivity of the preceding generation of progressive liberals with a more complex sense of individual psychology tempered by changing historical circumstances.

This chapter examines the debates over liberalism—and the divergent uses critics made of literature in those debates—in order to understand how literary scholarship participated in the changing politics of the early Cold War era. I argue that Chase's writings on Melville demonstrate how his New Liberalism, as a critical methodology, proved a practice of hope. In this chapter, I read Chase as he read Melville: with an eye for symbolic patterns that are affectively nuanced and socially engaged. The chapter ends by contending that similar dispositions to Chase's might structure literary criticism today, when critics confronting the end of the Cold War face comparable choices to those critics faced when entering it. Chase offers one model for responding to the limitations of middle-class Cold War culture in America and therefore suggests a way beyond the methodological melancholy that impedes criticism today.

Nineteenth-century American literature entered debates over liberalism in the pages of *Partisan Review* with the publication of Chase's essays

"Dissent on Billy Budd" (November 1948) and "The Progressive Hawthorne" (January 1949). In the latter, Chase contests what he calls the
"most common cliché about Hawthorne," namely, "that he thought solitude a crime and believed in the brotherhood of man and man's 'dependence on society.'"[10] Reviewing Randall Stewart's *Nathaniel Hawthorne*,
Chase faults the critic for misleading readers into believing that Hawthorne "thought that all men should be 'common men.'"[11] Countering
faith in man's inherent nobility, Chase argues, "This is good liberal doctrine. But, as it is usually presented, it is also such a vaporous idea that
you cannot imagine any serious writer of fiction worrying about it."[12]
Holding those vaporous abstractions as truth, Chase claims, critics "endowed Hawthorne's morality with a kind of liberalized Moscow-Trials
legalism."[13] Referring to a foundational Marxist critic of American literature, Chase claims that "half way between [Vernon] Parrington and
truth,"[14] progressive liberals needed to "come home to Nathaniel, who is
not an ideology, a religion, or a white whale, but only an old American
who was an artist and who knew a great deal about men, women, and
society."[15]

The real bone of contention turned out to be not the essay in which
Chase denounced progressive liberalism in the form of Nathaniel Hawthorne but the one in which he drew New Liberalism from the pages
of Herman Melville. His *Partisan Review* essay on *Billy Budd* was the
opening salvo in what became a full-scale war when Chase expanded
his essay into the monograph *Herman Melville: A Critical Study* (1949).
Shaping a Melville who looks very much like the one presented by scholars today, Chase asserts that the author presents "a vision of life capable,
by a continuous act of imaginative criticism," of countering "the facile ideas of progress and 'social realism,' the disinclination to examine
human motives, the indulgence of wish-fulfilling rhetoric, the belief that
historical reality is merely a question of economic or ethical values, the
idea that literature should participate directly in the economic liberation
of the masses, the equivocal relationship to communist totalitarianism
and power politics."[16] Melville, Chase claims, refused "the indulgence
of wish-fulfilling rhetoric"[17] and critiqued all "that was vague, utopia-
aspiring, and fuzzily ethical."[18] Instead of such imprecise ethics, Melville
shows a New Liberal awareness of the uneven and counterproductive
side of human nature, and the need for contemplative withdrawal from

society in order to evaluate and adjudicate the usefulness of one's ideals
for bringing about a better, if not utopian, society.

Chase's essays provoked a flood of dissent, both in print and in private correspondence. He received impassioned letters from Arvin,
Alfred Kazin, Philip Rahv, and Leslie Fiedler debating his reading of
Melville and Hawthorne. In the February 1949 *Partisan Review*, Arvin,
Robert Gorham Davis, and Daniel Aaron, a trio referred to in a subsequent essay as "the watchful eyes at Smith College,"[19] charge Chase with
avoiding "the exact and responsible semantic content of the words 'liberal' and 'progressive' when used, as they increasingly are, in a pejorative
context," making the terms "dangerously loose and emotive 'signs' for
intellectual inanity and political immaturity of any sort whatsoever."[20]
Chase, the Smith critics charge, creates straw men in place of responsible argument, and they express their "doubt whether anyone worth
arguing with has ever indulged in so crudely simple and sentimental
an interpretation."[21] Even when he characterized liberalism fairly, the
Smith critics claim, Chase failed to articulate his own political point of
view. "We do not suggest that only those who have attached themselves
to another dogma or orthodoxy have an intellectual right to criticize liberalism," they assert, but they insist that some critical position must exist
besides "pessimistic skepticism."[22] They complain, further, that when
a political position—Chase's New Liberalism—*does* emerge, it requires
"a gross oversimplification of Melville's intentions."[23] turning him into
a "self-righteous Liberal,"[24] upon whom Chase imposes values and beliefs Melville could not possibly have shared. Rendering facetious these
charges of anachronism, in "What Is the 'Liberal' Mind?," William Barrett, criticizing Chase's purported presentism, asks, "Did Iago vote for
Henry Wallace in the last election? Presumably, Mr. Chase must know,
or can find out the answer for us. We shall go on next to ask whether
Desdemona bought her clothes from Bergdorf Goodman."[25] In Chase's
work, Barrett charges, "all times, all places melt together in one contemporaneous, coterminous jelly of a present."[26]

These persistent charges of political presentism point to a productive paradox in Chase's criticism, in which he was both too far from and
too close to the literature he studied. The first charge—that Chase used
nineteenth-century literature unfairly as a screen for his political projections, distancing himself from the literature itself—was, to say the least,

hypocritical, since critics like Barrett and Arvin also used the past to support present politics, as when the former claimed that Hawthorne and Melville would have joined him in flying "our own reactionary banner with the slogan: Back to the Enlightenment!"[27] Perhaps because of their own deployments of what they denounced in Chase, these critics register a discomfort less with how far Chase's presentism distanced him from his objects of study than with how explicit he made a practice that, although ubiquitous, was, then as now, diligently obscured. The frank acknowledgments of his projections, rather than the projections themselves, were, I suspect, what disturbed critics, and such open expressions of critical *objectives*, disturbing the illusion of critical *objectivity*, continue to disturb critics to this day. Chase's explicit use of literature to express critical ideals challenged critical claims to "find" in literature the issues that conform conveniently to the critic's own political positions. Chase had little interest in critical hide-and-seek. In the preface of his *Herman Melville, for example, Chase* never pretends that his approach to Melville was anything but motivated by his New Liberal agenda. The world depicted in *Moby-Dick* was, for Chase, that of post–World War II America, peopled by "the good and loving mediocre citizen,"[28] whose "ineradicable emotional needs" were fulfilled by a "machinelike existence."[29] Decrying the sterility of the social environment of his day, Chase urges his readers to feel distress over "the decay of the spirit of freedom and humanitarianism; the whole enormous shell game of American commerce and American infantile uplift progressivism and cash-value philanthropy."[30]

For his critics, however, even more disturbing than Chase's explicit distance from the literature he studied was, I believe, his closeness to it, particularly to Romanticism's practices of hope. Unlike those who built methodologies from Enlightenment values, asserting "that the human reason, in its secular function, is capable of establishing the social conditions of freedom," Chase founded his critical practices on the distinctly antisecular qualities of Romanticism,[31] which showed "that something is to be gained by open and responsible controversy."[32] Chase's belief in critical Romanticism owed much to his teacher, Lionel Trilling, who believed that "literature is one of the cultural agents that forms the attitudes, even the categories, by which at least some part of life is apprehended,"[33] and therefore "a work of literature, or any art, has ultimately a moral and even a political relevance."[34] Trilling sets forth what he calls "*moral imagination*,"[35] which disabuses readers of the mistaken belief "that the life of man can be nicely settled by a current social organization."[36] Trilling instead encourages readers to use literature to arrive at their own ethical deliberations. Chasse found precisely those qualities of "moral imagination" and "ethical deliberation" in Romantic writers such as Melville, Hawthorne, and Whitman.

It is no coincidence that all the critics analyzed from this chapter on devoted their careers to the study of American Romantic literature.[37] Like Chase, they found there models for speculative thinking, for creating not-yet-real worlds that, not entirely divorced from the material conditions of the here and now, offered an imaginative space for ideals by which to measure their own society and to imagine new forms of sociality. It is not that Romantic literature self-evidently expressed such imaginings; rather, the critics *created* that literature, imagining it in ways that allowed it to reflect and inform, and especially to legitimize, their own critical practices of hope. In other words, they not only turned to Romantic literature but also read romantically. How and why they did so can teach us a good deal about the limitations of and alternatives to our Cold War melancholy and its dispositions.

In urging us to read romantically, as midcentury critics did, I am contradicting the argument put forth by Jerome McGann in his study *The Romantic Ideology* (1983). McGann identifies two dangers inherent in reading romantically. First, doing so erases the *otherness* of the past, turning it into a projection of the ideological concerns of the critic's own times. This refusal of the past's difference from the present prevents criticism from "achieving a critical distance, however provisional, from its own ideological investments."[38] Because the past "can know nothing of our current historical illusions," it provides a vantage point from which to judge contemporary critical illusions.[39]

McGann's second charge is that the Romantic Ideology makes criticism, to put it colloquially, too upbeat. Objecting to "these happy and upright days when so much emphasis is placed upon Romanticism as a 'creative,' 'enthusiastic,' and 'celebratory' ideology,"[40] McGann takes to task critics like M. H. Abrams, in whose treatment of Romanticism

"Despair" is an emotional state to be shunned if not deplored, and it is associated explicitly with "the unbounded and hence impossible hopes" of political and social transformation. "Hope," on the other hand, is a good thing, and it is associated with an "infinite Sehnsucht" which is possible to achieve: that is, with a psychological victory, a religious and spiritual success which can replace the failed hope of social melioration.[41]

In the end, McGann insists, such a happy depiction "falls victim to the deeper critique announced by the subject matter itself,"[42] which offers what McGann calls "data" showing that "numerous works widely acknowledged to be Romantic are nihilistic, desperate, and melancholy."[43] Because criticism seeks to mislead readers into a belief in subversive celebration characteristic of the "loose critical thinking" that "is more characteristic of our period than one likes to remember,"[44] the reader "must therefore be on his guard to demystify"[45] the critic's "crippling illusion,"[46] despite the fact that this task is rendered nearly impossible, since "the chief disciplines of cultural analysis are themselves vehicles for the production of ideology," containing criticism "within the larger system."[47]

McGann objects to criticism that "sidesteps the concrete, human particulars of the originary works, either to reproduce them within currently acceptable ideological terms or to translate them into currently unacceptable forms of thought,"[48] but he, like the critics he critiques, displaces the ideological investment of *his* day—a suspicion of ideology—onto what he problematically calls Romanticism "itself." McGann thus critiques—while reproducing—the problem of a critical ideology that does not recognize itself as such. While the denial of pastness is, as McGann claims, damaging to critical perspective, he is wrong to assume that such a vantage necessarily leads to a critique of celebration, an assertion that relies on McGann's claim, made with the force of critical objectivity, that "nihilism" is a production of the past "itself" and not a projection of his own ideological expectations. McGann is right to assert that a purely celebratory representation of Romanticism denies poetry the complexity of its self-representations, but he substitutes for this reductive reading his own claims for a literature distinguished by a single outlook, in his case one of despondent nihilism. Similarly, McGann's representation of other critics is remarkably flat, denying them perspectival nuance in order to assert an absolute division in which he transcends the "Romantic Ideology" while they deceptively involve literature in their own simplistic ideologies. Finally, while McGann is no doubt correct that making ideology explicit is important to criticism, he can assert the secretive nature of critical Romanticism only by representing it as hidden in the first place, creating the impression that any claim to find celebration in the past is in fact an obfuscation of the critic's real motive, which is to dupe readers into "loose thinking." Whereas the critique of idealism apparently has no hidden motives (so far removed is the critic from imposing his own ideologies, in fact, that the "deeper critique" is offered by "the subject matter itself"), the expression of ideals, albeit projected into the past, always does. Despite McGann's assertion, "Needless to say, I am not suggesting here that the ideological polemic of criticism should be sacrificed to a (spurious) critical objectivity, or vice versa,"[49] the disclaimer suggests that on some level he realizes that if critics *were* to own their ideals rather than displacing them onto the past, making criticism a self-conscious "polemic," he would be no happier with "celebration" than he is when it is said to characterize Romanticism. If critics claimed those ideals explicitly, they might purposefully deploy, rather than unwittingly enact, mystification, turning the mystical into a vantage point, like the past in McGann's account, from which to evaluate and imagine alternatives to the social, economic, and political present. Claiming, "It is the aim of this study to bring critique to the Ideology of Romanticism,"[50] McGann makes clear his belief that critique and idealism are mutually exclusive, never two sides of the same coin. He not only brings critique to the study of Romantic literature, in other words, he brings critiquiness.

My intention here is not to offer a "gotcha" moment in relation to McGann's critique. Rather, I want to show how McGann's argument is embedded in its own historical moment, one I have identified as the beginning of a Cold War melancholy. Only by establishing the epistemological structure he uses to analyze Romantic Ideology, centered on the opposition of extreme values, can McGann establish himself as the uniquely ("exceptionally") astute critic transcendent in his capacity to distinguish "fact" from "ideology." Because the methods of distinguishing the two are never explicitly stated, McGann imagines a vigilant and suspicious reader whose aim is to "demystify" submerged ideologies, despite the fact that the location of criticism within a mystifying system of cultural institutions makes such vigilance impotent and, therefore, perpetual. This is also the reader Chase's critics imagined, not coincidentally, at the start of the Cold War. My intention, however, is not to belabor the point that the mid-1980s produced a melancholy relation to Cold War state epistemologies. Rather, I want to suggest how and why Chase and the other critics discussed in subsequent chapters chose to read romantically precisely *because* doing so involved the critical strategies McGann presents as flaws and weaknesses. It was to counter that characterization—used socially against dissidents and social critics in 1949 in similar ways to how it is used in criticism of the 1980s—that led midcentury critics to romantic literature as subject and as methodological model.

Part of Chase's particular version of Romanticism, evident in his treatment of Melville's allegories, was a combination of critique and idealism that contradicts McGann's assumption that one necessarily cancels the other. Chase's New Liberalism was, like McGann's critique, a repudiation of what he saw as criticism's bland optimism. Yet Chase did not turn, like McGann, to Enlightenment reason (the same faith in objectivity Chase found objectionable in Barrett and that allows McGann to see the past as a mine of discernible data). Rather, Chase understood that idealism is the motive for the most stringent critique, that ideals, to survive, must accommodate the foibles of human nature and the consequent unpredictability of history. Chase also valued the idealism that keeps criticism from lapsing into cynicism. Despite his clear-eyed view of progressive liberalism and of early Cold War America, Chase did not abandon the rich sense of wonder that turns quotidian literary symbols extraordinary. Wonder brings both dejection and joy, and Chase registers both by making embodied sensation and emotion, abject as well as exultant, the center of his New Liberal interpretations of Hawthorne and Melville. By shaping a Romantic writer capable of critique and idealism, critique *as* idealism, Chase made Melville—and himself—effective practitioners of hope.

Chase's resistance to the clean separation of idealism and critique arguably stemmed from his observation of an emerging Cold War discourse that asserted an absolute difference between the United States and the Soviet Union, both of which claimed an innocence that quickly became despotic when turned against an equally extreme evil. Writing in that context, Chase was skeptical of claims to innocence—like those made by progressive liberals in their heroic struggle alongside the equally faultless "common man"—because they deny the darker aspects of what Chase called "personality," comprising unpredictable mixtures of shame, desire, sincerity, depression, and wonder.[51] Earlier liberals had failed to achieve their goals, Chase believed, because they refused to acknowledge the combinations of virtues and flaws in human nature, turning them, in Chase's opinion, into hypocrites like F. O. Matthiessen, who "loves Melville and Hawthorne, has a tragic view of life, believes, even, in original sin, and *nevertheless* commits himself to the most childish, shallow, and unexamined political liberalism."[52] Resisting what he saw as a liberal hypocrisy, Chase believed that historical change, like human nature, is uncertain, halting, death-driven but also full of hopeful possibility. Seeing Cold War America as similarly complex, implicated in the evils it denied in itself but also comprising divergent socialities that are strongholds of admirable values, Chase turned Melville into a social critic who could also be a shameless idealist, finding both roles most clearly in Melville's allegories.

As the previous examples suggest, while Chase located allegory's critique and idealism in Melville, they were explicitly and implicitly responsive to Chase's own day. The progression of Chase's readings of Melvillean allegories becomes a sustained critique of early Cold War America, as well as a subtle prescription for social redemption. Most explicitly, Chase consistently used Melville's allegories to criticize the multiple fantasies and self-delusions that marked America's transition from World War II to the Cold War. In that moment an affable innocence transformed into tyranny, or, rather, both existed simultaneously, the former being the lure and cover for the latter. In *Moby-Dick*, for example, Ahab is both deplorable and compelling, a despot because he is so likable (Chase acknowledged to Arvin, "I like Ahab, and fear him").[53] Chase's mixed feelings about Ahab stem from the latter's resemblance to the ambitious, progressive hero of the Cold War consensus, who, despite his affability, represents for Chase the acid corroding American society. Ahab, in Chase's reading, both attracts and destroys, demonstrating how false idealization negates what it nominally seeks to preserve. Projecting all negativity onto the White Whale, Ahab becomes "a terrifying picture of a man rejecting all connection with his family, his culture, his own sexuality even . . . for a vision of spotless purity and rectitude attainable only in death, drifting into the terrible future, a catastrophe which annihilates a whole world."[54] In that "terrible future" awaiting those charmed by a tyrannical manipulation masquerading as innocence, Ahab, the representative American, is "a dummy already dead and wonderful in his righteousness—in the midst of historical catastrophe."[55]

That "historical catastrophe" was, in Chase's day, America's antagonism to the Soviet Union (and vice versa), which the U.S. government rationalized as the necessary defense of a democracy that rhymes with capitalism. The latter, for Chase, comprised mindless pursuit, bottomless greed, and reckless inhumanity. In Chase's analysis, "The American cultural fate which Melville feared may be deduced from the dénouement of *Pierre*," in which "the only probable emotions and intellectual endeavor . . . become those which protect wealth and position with force."[56] Capitalism, in Chase's analysis, creates "commercial classes," the members of which are "willing to be the most abject kind of dupe if only they were given in return the comfortable sense of having mastered and destroyed every high or fierce emotion."[57] Ahab, whom Chase believed fits this description exactly, is motivated by a relentless pursuit of profit, making him "the epic transmutation of the American free enterpriser" and Moby-Dick "the transmutation of the implicit spiritual meaning of free enterprise."[58] A "free enterpriser" is most dangerous, for Chase, when he seems most likable, passing as "a builder, a large scale operator, a searcher, a killer of monsters"; only when he is unmasked do we find ourselves "so easily bemused by a silly and impossible ideal."[59] This was, for Chase, what made Ahab most despicable: posing as a caring father to his crew, charming them into acquiescence, he is all the while already a spiritually dead man determined to take everyone down with him.

Beguiling father figures, in order to assume the role of benevolent protectors, require gullible and complacent children, and the latter, as Chase argued in his interpretation of Melville's *Pierre*, are as dangerous as the former. America, Chase believed, invented adolescence, possessing neither childhood's innocence nor adulthood's wisdom. Although the postwar United States was said to be "coming of age" as a world power, national maturity in fact became perpetual adolescence, plagued by narcissistic self-satisfaction and hackneyed ideals. In such a state, American critics, "many of them writing from the point of view of the older liberalism of the 1920's and 1930's, have not taken *Pierre* seriously enough, either as art or as a cultural document." Critics, Chase argued, should embrace Melville's late romance for "pointing out to us, as it does, the enormous difficulties to be encountered in coming of age."[60] Melville's critique of America's perpetual adolescence was, Chase believed, as relevant as ever a century later, when Americans, figurative adolescents, accepted a world in which genuine innocence and responsible maturity, especially when embodied by social outcasts like Pierre, could not thrive, but becomes distorted and shrill. "Until we have constructed a culture in which our Pierres can survive and be fruitful," Chase writes, "we must as liberals with hopes for the future come to terms with Melville's novel. Pierre's madness is our own as no other is."[61]

America's adolescence, as I have suggested, relied on a stubborn faith in its own deceptive innocence, conceivable only in opposition to the equally extreme evil of the Soviet empire. The disastrous consequences of this phantasmagoric opposition become clear, Chase claims, in the adversarial relationship between Billy Budd, whom Chase describes as "nothing but a beatified child,"[62] and his apparently unmotivated antagonist, Claggart. Leveling unfounded charges that result in Billy's death, Claggart represents the evil supplement to Billy's innocence, both characters appearing "evil" or "good" only in opposition to the other. For Chase, though, the real villain in *Billy Budd* is Captain Vere, who represents an America so invested in its own faultlessness that it perpetuates the oppositional structure in which Billy and Claggart contend. Vere finds his fantasy of an impossibly innocent Billy threateningly elusive, yet that very threat—arising from within Vere but projected outward onto Claggart and Billy—justifies his power, which derives from the imposition of "order, authority, and legality."[63] But an innocent law requires an equally guilty lawlessness, so Billy precariously flips from the idealized child to culpable criminal. Vere knows both positions are fantastic, but a fantasy on which legal fictions rely. His consequent compulsion to reconstitute a continually faltering innocence allegorizes America's always incomplete self-construction as faultless, which compelled it to feast on the rest of the supposedly innocent and vulnerable world imperiled by an evil antagonist that draws attention away from the imperial aggressions of the United States and turns murderous the democracy it supposedly defends.

More dangerous even than extreme distinctions between good and evil, however, is the incapacity to draw from painful and unavoidable experience any moral judgments at all. Determined "to destroy moral distinctions, to keep our fallible minds from making choices," the Confidence-Man, in Chase's reading, creates "a universe where everything cancels out, where moral distinctions disappear," and "where consciousness, vitality, and action are purged of all natural grossness and efficacy."[64] Like his progressive counterparts, the Confidence-Man "preserves himself from self-knowledge by refusing to admit that moral choices have far-reaching consequences and that thought, no matter how ordinary or work-a-day, has its complex resonances of moral, allegorical, religious, and cultural meaning."[65] In a statement that raised the hackles of his critics, Chase concludes that the Confidence-Man, disallowing moral choices even for himself, "was what is now called 'just a confused liberal.'"[66] Rendering an amoral refusal of distinction as a virtue, liberals like the Confidence-Man had allowed Americans "to present ourselves to the world as neutrals,"[67] distracted from noticing that behind the guise of neutrality lurks "the sullen and defensive sell-out to a center of power or authority" into which one enters "passively, and without heroism."[68] The result of that passive acquiescence was, for Chase, the Confidence-Man's stock-in-trade, cynicism. Ready-made hope and cost-free progress, *The Confidence-Man* shows, create "a universe where everything cancels out, where moral distinctions disappear."[69]

Unlike the Confidence-Man's naive victims, however, Chase did not succumb to cynicism, any more than he took refuge in easy optimism. Rather, he created an image of Melville as a secular prophet, able to "deal with what I have called 'the alienated passions,' that range of emotion which extends to the comprehension of social-historical tragedy and spiritual failure, realms of experience which remain opaque to less imaginative views of life."[70] Although Melville's work was filled with crafty liberals and guileless dupes, evidence of their creator as a master of critique who could "denounce and exhort with all the dark gloom of an Old Testament prophet,"[71] there are also characters who, because of their awareness of suffering, express the author's idealism through their imaginative countersocialities. Often pushed to the margins of Melville's texts, these "true heroes" nevertheless offer a model of psychological negotiation and ethical judgment. Understanding that "civilization, precious on any terms, is the fruit of human suffering and anguish, as well as of human joy,"[72] they are characters like *Pierre's* Charles Millthorpe, who represents "rebelliousness, idealism, and the kindness of the heart."[73] The true hero, Chase says, must be "the young Promethean revolutionary who battles against the old reactionary gods in order to liberate man and give him his creative intelligence," but he "must also be Oedipus—the man who has accepted the full moral responsibility of his fallible humanity" and "has suffered and grown wise in the leadership of his fellows."[74] Such a hero, for Chase, gains "the full knowledge of his human guilt and his human nobility" and thereby "makes himself the symbol of a culture formed in the rich magnitude of wisdom and love."[75] *Moby-Dick*, for Chase, shows the social possibilities of one such collectively held vision of human frailty. The crew members aboard the *Pequod*, not entirely taken in by Ahab's progressive promises, are, Chase writes, "companions, storytellers, defenders of freedom, revolutionaries; their brotherhood with other men is open, frank, and based on the deepest ties of common humanity."[76] Knowing as they do that "life must be understood and lived in lower worlds of ecstasy,"[77] these men form "a heroic democracy" where a people "free, frank, and proud" stand "opposed to the modern Diana of ill fame, 'unanimous mediocrity.'"[78] Although these explicit statements of Chase's social vision are striking in their unqualified idealism, more often, in his work, hope is easy to miss, mixed as it is and must be with human fallibility and venality. These contradictory notions—the idyll of camaraderie and the dystopia of life in capitalist America—turn paradox into productive hopefulness, the friction that occurs when visions attempt to materialize in a disenchanted world. That friction is, for Chase, at the heart of Melville's allegories, which, even as they level their stern critiques, are motivated by visions too fragile to exist but too powerful to relinquish.

My discussion of allegory has thus far concentrated on content. For Chase, however, aesthetic form also expresses social commentary. Although Chase's allegorical content was typically critical, his idealism, this section will argue, more frequently emerged in his choice of aesthetic form. In this, Chase followed Melville, for whom, he argues, "ideas have profound aesthetic value," and therefore his "'position' is an aesthetic device or context which he uses in his art, besides being a set of explicit intellectual attitudes."[79] Melville, Chase claims, achieved the distance necessary for a realistic evaluation of social relations through "the infinitely moving lyricism of certain passages in *Moby-Dick* and *Benito Cereno.*" In those passages, Melville gives ideals aesthetic form in "a kind of closely knit textual style reproducing the complexity of subdued psychic experience,"[80] and thereby reflects "qualities of pathos and lyricism and pity, of rage and acceptance and courage."[81]

What Chase admired in Melville's style was precisely what his critics found most troubling in Chase's. To be sure, they railed against the New Liberal content of Chase's allegorical readings, as the opening section showed. But his critics became especially nasty when they dismissed Chase on the basis of style, tone, symbolism, and, above all, allegory. Although his *Partisan Review* had published Chase's essays, Philip Rahv labeled *Herman Melville* "a Talmudic elaboration of mythology pretentious to the point of stupefaction" and dismissed Chase as practicing "the new pedantry of myth" in his "addiction to the more aberrant tendencies of the contemporary literary mind."[82] Calling the book "static and even provincial," "astonishingly immature," "full of the most reckless guesses and assumptions," "raging rather incoherently," and, despite its rage, lacking "emotional authenticity,"[83] Alfred Kazin attributed Chase's sacrifice of "the truth of his own experience" to his "symbol-extracting machinery" that revealed the "great weakness of the myth approach in criticism," namely, "that it freezes man to the universal," making him a mere "figure of speech."[84] Kazin went so far as to blame Chase's use of symbolism for those who "had the atomic bomb tested on eighty thousand human beings at Hiroshima."[85] Less hyperbolic, Harrison Hayford complained of Chase's "casualness about facts: his allegorizing both literature and life."[86] Most directly challenging Chase's use of allegory, Kazin mockingly characterized *Herman Melville* as "a morality play, in which The True Prometheus, The False Prometheus, The Confidence Man, The Ordealist Critic and the New Liberal vie with each other in this period of intense political introspection, for the Soul of America the Alienated at the Mid-Century."[87]

In his eagerness to dismiss Chase as an allegorist, however, Kazin underestimates the work that genre performed for Chase. Kazin's version of allegory presents the genre in its simplest form: a story in which objects, events, or people suggest abstract, pedantic, or moral meanings. But

Chase had a more complex understanding of the genre, one more related to his depiction of Melville as the creator of a "beyondness" that suffused the everyday events of his characters with a deeper, more ideal, and even spiritual significance. And, precisely because that significance is both experienced and illusive, opening predetermined correspondences to unpredictable associations, Melville passed allegorical wonder on to his readers. The content of Melville's allegories, in Chase's handling, could be as transparent (a "symbol-extracting machinery") as his critics claim. But the form itself was anything but predictable, becoming the aesthetic form of idealism that is different from, yet always conjoined to, critique. Allegory as form becomes the animating spirit in excess of, but never divorceable from, its content. To understand how allegory operates for Chase, we must step away from his criticism momentarily to consider the phenomenology of allegory more broadly.

Allegory might be defined as an assemblage of symbolic presences that suggest, in their totality, an absence that becomes presence ("meaning") only in retrospect, once the reader has finished reading. But allegorical reading is never finished, being a process of constantly and actively revising one's sense of each episode's or character's meaning retrospectively, repeatedly unsettling and reshaping meaning, and thus rendering the meaning of experience more flexible, adaptable, and resilient. As Walter Benjamin writes, "The intention which underlies allegory is so opposed to that which is concerned with the discovery of truth that it reveals more clearly than anything else the identity of the pure curiosity which is aimed at mere knowledge with the proud isolation of man."[88] The impossibility of finding a single, ultimate truth in allegory provokes, in Benjamin's words, "speechless wonder."[89] That sense may be what gives allegory its unending potential for transformation, for conceiving a world made otherwise—one translation of "allegory" from the Greek is "other-speaking"—or what John Cassian calls revelation, "mysteries prefigured in history."[90] Allegory thus functions in the early Christian sense of signs pointing not to codified morals but to a divine quintessence suffusing the world, sensed yet never seen.[91] Allegory gives spirit an imminence, infusing what is familiar with an excess of significance, irreducible to any conclusive interpretation. As another way of putting this, Benjamin cites the "profounder truth" of Carl Horst's pronouncement, "The proximity of the gods is indeed one of the most important prerequisites for the vigorous development of allegory."⁹² The idea of multiple gods inspires a supple belief prescribed less by an epistemological mastery—the assurance of one inalterable, passively received "meaning"—than by a willingness to create (and recreate) meaning in the image of one's imaginative ideals. Chase took a decidedly secular approach to allegory, but his use of the form retains this sense of imminent revelation in what he called *beyondness*. He was drawn, for instance, to Romanticism's investment in what the Roman philosopher Macrobius called *fibula*, "a 'fabulous narrative'" that takes on the texture of a dream.⁹³ Allegory thus conjoins the spiritual and the secular in a social realm where what is commonly taken as real or true gives way to a vision of the world organized otherwise, a *not-yet-realness* that Ernst Bloch called anticipatory illuminations. When Chase refers to Melville as a visionary, he means more than the author's incisive critiques expressed in the plots of his romances. This symbolic beyondness, the wonder Chase identifies in Melville's aesthetics, conjoined with the content's critique to make allegory a practice of hope.

The lyrical beyondness enabled by allegory is not the same as blind optimism, however. Chase understood that the painful experiences that tie us to an unjust world generate both a critique of that injustice and the imaginative idealism of hope. Both are implied in allegory's restriction to material forms, which are nevertheless suffused with a wonder that inspires the possibilities of a not-yetness that makes reality into an anticipatory illumination necessary for resilience. Plato's *Republic* offers the paradigmatic allegory, in which prisoners watch images projected on a blank wall they are doomed to face forever. The Allegory of the Cave is, famously, a lesson in the impossibility of direct perceptions of reality, which is knowable only in images and shadows. In this regard, Plato offers an allegory about allegory, where hints and figures seem to picture forth an obscured or displaced reality—a "meaning" or "moral"—that can never be determined definitively because its existence is simultaneous with its diffusion through those hints. As Benjamin suggests, however, it is the incommensurability of shadows and reality that undoes the chains and turns frustration into wonder. In an allegory, mundane objects are endowed with a surplus of significance that turns them into symbols with always-contestable meanings. It is not that these objects are *like* a more ineffable entity, but that discernible form and ineffable significance exist simultaneously in the same figure, leaving the reader to decide what elements of a story are "allegorical," thus making all elements potentially allegorical and suffusing the "real" world with a supplemental significance that denies the empirical finality of self-evidence. The conviction that objects and people have a mystical *something* that gives them more than predictable (absence of) significance, that the shadow and what throws the shadow are one and the same, gives allegory the sense of wonder referred to by Benjamin. Experience is not given but derives from collaboration between self and nonself, sense and speculation, discernment and belief that makes allegorical "experience" an imaginative practice of hope.

The description of allegory I have just offered anticipates ways the critics I discuss in my final chapter understood symbolism. I argue there that the condition of gays in Cold War America led to that understanding of symbolism, and Chase's investment in allegory, I believe, had a similar inspiration. When Chase found idealism in Melville's plots, he did so in same-sex socialities made by men who, pushed to the margins of their world, generate the best hopes of that world. Chase's ideal is, in his words, the "blissful, idyllic, erotic attachment to life and to one's comrades, which is the only promise of happiness,"[94] a sentiment that, if it does not assert same-sex desire (Chase's or Melville's), points to the way erotic communities represented an ideal ("promise of happiness") not found anywhere else ("only"). It is not a stretch to imagine that Chase, living in New York at a time when the city was becoming home to a new erotic subculture simultaneously visible and inscrutable, might have found in same-sex sociality a model for the allegorical hopefulness he located in Melville and—tellingly—Whitman. His stringent critique of the oppressive normativity policed by the Cold War state might well have occasioned an identification with the group of people—homosexuals—who, along with communists and other social dissidents, came to represent un-Americanness at that period. Some gay literary critics at the time—Newton Arvin, Marius Bewley, and, later, Richard Poirier—turned queer sexual sociality into literary form, as subsequent chapters will show at greater length. But even for an apparently heterosexual man like Chase, the existence of same-sex countersocialities might have exemplified the anti–Cold War ideals he located in Melville.

And the aesthetic form of the "only promise of happiness" became, for Chase, allegory.

For allegory is the genre of desire. Joel Fineman ascribes to allegory a perpetual lack (of meaning) that he calls "the insatiable desire."[95] Allegory, Fineman writes, "will set out on an increasingly futile search for a signifier with which to recuperate the fracture of and as its source, and with each successive signifier the fracture and the search begin again: a structure of continual yearning."[96] When Fineman writes that "allegory seems regularly to surface in critical or polemical atmospheres, when for political or metaphysical reasons there is something that cannot be said," he underscores two features—the capacity to "surface" and the function of speaking the unspeakable—central to both allegory and the queer subculture consolidating in postwar American cities, including Chase's New York.[97] Like allegory, queer life in the Cold War involved continual masking and "surfacing," a dynamic arising from as well as perpetuating the desire (sexual and world-making) in the regulated conformities of Cold War America. The claim to be able to recognize homosexuals based on an authorized set of signifying characteristics started with the military in the 1940s and expanded through other governmental institutions in the 1950s.[98] But allegory refuses the certainty of such epistemologies, rendering relationships of signifier to signified dynamic, reliant on the desires of those who look. As numerous historians have documented, urban gay networks that arose after World War II were variable and contingent assemblages of signs, sites, and embodiments. Because of the prosecutorial environments in which they formed, these networks shared a visibility apparent to those who desired to see them. The queer subcultures of Cold War America existed not in postliberation urban "ghettos" but in the midst of apparently and normatively knowable objects, locales, and figures, which were rendered queer by their adaption to counternormative purposes. Queer networks in Cold War America, that is, required those in them to read allegorically, speculatively connecting seemingly mundane or random signs into meanings that emerged retrospectively and suffused the ordinary with a desirous excess of significance. Seeing allegorically became a form of queer world making (form *as* world making), inscrutable to authority yet filled with relational possibilities.

And here we can return to Plato's allegory. It would be understandable if an allegory about people chained to a fate that, forbidding them to examine each other or themselves, socially estranged and self-alienated, appealed to those who, in the 1950s, felt similarly caught between their culture's normativity on the one hand and, on the other, the need to forestall further alienation by suppressing self-knowledge or abstaining from seeking others in a similar condition. Thus Plato's cave might seem an apt allegory for homosexuality in the early Cold War, visible, like the projections on the cave walls, only in shadows and projections. As an allegory *about* allegory, however, Plato's holds for modern readers a different, less predictably depressing lesson about the uses of a literary form premised on the desire to undo the chains of suspicious certainty characteristic of governmental scrutiny and to release those schooled in shadows to make a world in the beyond-ness possible in allegory (in Plato's allegory the one prisoner who escapes the cave finds reality too harsh and decides to return to where he feels more comfortable, among those who know how to live among shadows). Being unchained, however, is not the same as being freed from the cave. Living allegorically can confine as well as protect, and even that protection is often vulnerable. Resilience, not utopianism, is the nature of hope. Chase knew that, as is clear from the catalog of sad fates—deception, despair, civic death, and suicide—that befell the characters he most admired in Melville's allegories (fates that also ended the lives of many queers, including critics like Matthiessen and Arvin, in the early Cold War decades). For Chase, however, pain, disappointment, self-destruction, or cynicism cannot be, indeed *should* not be, avoided, being part of human experience, and therefore necessary to any literary model for a social response to the legal and physical violence aimed at queer Americans at midcentury.

The complex nature of allegorical living—resilient yet confined, filled with possibility including that of violence and shame—becomes clear in the last allegory I want to consider here, one taken from an episode from Chase's biography. Six weeks after Chase married Frances Walker in 1940, he turned up in a strange local item in a Kennebunkport, Maine, newspaper. The details are sketchy: Chase went to see a circus, wandered into the woods, got drunk, and either fell or rolled into the river from which he was rescued by the police, who kept him in jail overnight. The police would neither confirm nor deny rumors of foul play, and Chase claimed to remember nothing about the episode.[99] It seems unlikely that Chase would have considered this incident an allegory, although its elements—circus, woods, river, and jail—lend themselves to reading more in this story than meets the eye. Newly married and assuming the responsibilities of career and family, Chase perhaps felt drawn to the giddy permissiveness of the circus, an intoxication he then literalized. It is possible that the woods offered a further sense of freedom, providing cover for a drinking spree. Maybe he did not drink or go to the woods alone. Chase certainly would not have been the first man to have drunken sex with a stranger, particularly another man, in a secluded place and conveniently remember nothing about it afterward. What was behind the rumors of "foul play" that the police would not confirm or deny? Perhaps as he wrote *Herman Melville*, the river incident took on allegorical meaning for Chase, who turned to figures like Ishmael— another near-drowned adventurer escaping civilized responsibilities with an exotic (and erotic) comrade—to forge tales of withdrawal and return, of estrangement and transformation, imaginative possibility and tempered ideals.

All of this is conjecture, permitted by the uncertain meaning of allegory, an indeterminable truth that always risks wandering from the verifiable. Among the critical sins Harrison Hayford charged Chase with was "his way of ignoring or misinterpreting the primary surface of works, [and] his unconcern with Melville's actual biography."[100] But I think the risks of misreading are endemic to allegory, opening the "meanings" we find "in" literature to an understanding of interpretation as *fabula*, perpetually yearning for, rather than suspiciously hunting beneath, the inventiveness a text enables. If I am guilty of misinterpretations, I can only own my desire to *make* rather than *find* meaning in Chase's criticism, creating a usable past that brings together literary language, queer life, and the difficulties of saying the unsayable in academia and beyond. That, I hope, is what Chase did with Melville as well.

Perhaps because Chase found resilient idealism in representations of same-sex countersociality (the "blissful, idyllic, erotic attachment to . . . one's comrades"), six years after the publication of *Herman Melville*, the critic turned his attention to Walt Whitman. His *Walt Whitman*

Reconsidered (1955) directly critiques Eisenhower's America, which Chase presents as a land of complacent conformity, unchecked greed, and seemingly benevolent violence. *Leaves of Grass* was not, for Chase, a celebration of American democracy but a reflection of an America in which annihilation became a primary political goal.[101] According to Chase, "the period of deformed sensibility we have been living through" created a corollary to social conformity in the popular taste for literary works "that display conservative values."[102] Scholars in the early 1950s charged that Whitman's "moral view is indiscriminate, infantile, ignorant of the tragic dilemmas of life."[103] Unlike 1950s America, where society had become so normative that it could not see Whitman's social vision, Chase argued, "The culture of his time admired (much more so than our culture does today) the prophet, the orator, the sententious democratic reformer" and "would condone oddity of behavior (more so than now) so long as the main requirements were met."[104] Reflecting a freer America, *Leaves of Grass*, in Chase's reading, retains the imaginative idealism of the allegory, depicting "the dream activity of the mind as the way in which universal equality and unity are achieved, the way in which joy and vitality are released."[105]

At the same time, however, by 1955 Chase's belief in "allegoricalnesss," to borrow Melville's neologism, had become more fraught with ambivalence, less confident in its moral judgments. Ambivalence and the loss of moral distinctions had, in his earlier book, been the objects of his critique, but by 1955 allegory seemed to involve a violence and resignation absent from his earlier scholarship, more limited in aspirations and aggressive in tone. Rather than a triumphant return with renewed ideals, Whitman "entirely destroys society."[106] And rather than transforming "reality" into a regenerated world hospitable to his vision, Whitman's poetic persona absorbs that world "into the native sensations, desires, and aspirations of the non-social man."[107] Still "a great releasing and regenerative force,"[108] allegory had become as abrasive and imperative as the world its hero had escaped, designed "symbolically to assault and overwhelm."[109] Chase's allegorical idealism was undone, ironically, by the concept of personality for which he had advocated earlier in his career. Whitman, in Chase's handling, turned the regeneration enabled by withdrawal and return into a psychologically individuating rather than a socially collectivizing phenomenon. No longer a social dialectic between two (or more) experiential accounts of reality, allegory now expressed conflicts within a single subject, "a cat-and-mouse game going on . . . between the conscious and the unconscious, when unexpected dreamlike images emerge apparently unheralded and have to be dealt with by an imaginative intelligence which is not often capable of large-executive organization of meaning but which is triumphantly capable of local forms of order produced by a comic or elegiac sensibility."[110] Far from world making, the return of Whitman's hero, according to Chase, is unwilled and ineffective except in a proscribed ("local") terrain, full of insecurity and self-doubt; the poet, far from the exuberant self-celebrator Whitman might seem, was helpless before the "yeasty eruptions from the unconscious depths, turning uncertainly from self-assertion to self-recrimination and despair, brooding with the same sense of mystery on the most sublime and the most vulgar and sordid aspects of life."[111] In light of that diminishment, the poet yearns not for transformation but for annihilation, leaving Whitman's triumph in his depictions not of democracy or sex but of death. "A walk along the shore at ebb tide," Chase writes, "has led the poet to muse on the transiency of life, the fragility of the resistance to annihilation which the individual can put up, the instability of organic existence, the evanescence of ideas and 'identities.'"[112]

Not surprisingly, given that the writer under discussion is Whitman, the battle between the conscious and unconscious mind, creating a psychological distress that proves socially alienating, took the form, in Chase's readings of Whitman, of sexuality. What *is* surprising is the deep ambivalence that marks Chase's readings, as the collective representations of same-sex idylls become the vexed psychology of individual homosexuals. As eroticism became sexuality, Chase grew increasingly ambivalent, his faith shaken by the same emergent cultural identity that had, just years earlier, enabled his understanding of allegory. To a large extent, the crisis in Chase's celebration of male camaraderie was symptomatic of the anxiety generated by suspicious injunctions against homosexuality that broke up the postwar gender-segregated intimacies in order to make the privatized family into the separated units of a newly policed conformity known as the American Way of Life. The differences between Chase's treatments of same-sex eroticism in Melville and Whitman index the speed with which state homophobia took hold in American culture. The difference shows as well the effect of that homophobia, especially among liberals, in making sexuality a psychological rather than a cultural phenomenon. Same-sex eroticism was creating neuroses as well as worlds by 1955, and the widening gap between the two becomes evident in Chase's personal and critical ambivalence.

To be frank, Chase already was ambivalent about sexuality and its place in society at the start of the Cold War, not in his literary criticism but in his correspondence with his wife, Frances. Those letters show erosion—perhaps the sign of growing sexual liberation as much as of intensified homophobia—of the divisions Chase attempted to maintain between literature and "real life," camaraderie and the psychology of sex, tradition and radicalism. The id as an abstract force or a literary trope had the power to revolutionize, but as a lived experience it got dangerously close to home. Writing to his wife during the summer of 1949, Chase recounts a discussion with F. O. Matthiessen and Allen Tate about Leslie Fiedler's "Come Back to the Raft Ag'in, Huck Honey," which controversially claimed that allegorical homoerotic relationships between men of different races lay at the heart of classic American fiction. When Chase, in a queer version of exceptionalism, claimed that "homosexualism [sic] as Fiedler discusses it was still in a special sense American," Matthiessen responded with resentment at "the tone and what he calls the know-it-all attitude of Fiedler." Chase reported to his wife, "Aha, says I to myself, a defense mechanism."[113] Flippant as he was about Matthiessen's defensiveness, Chase perhaps shared his anxieties. Just four days after relating the conversation about Fiedler, Chase, in another letter to Frances, extolled the normative virtues of "the family culture as both the repository and source of our humanity: our sentiments, attitudes, affection, values, and manners," adding, "So you see, I should think we are heroes of some sort. You've seen the psychological wreckage amongst our contemporaries. We've been on the margins of that wreckage ourselves and, anything we do to overcome it is jolly well admirable."[114] Yet the family is no bulwark against desire, Chase knew, and that is to the good. Chase wrote to his wife ten days later, "It's this very Id—the ambiguously wonderful murderous and loving unconscious mind— which deserves the tenderest and most perpetual care. It's the source of EVERYTHING," inquiring of Frances (whose response, unfortunately, does not survive), "Am I wrong, then, to think that the rituals of the family home, the family bed, the family routine, etc. ought primarily to support, restore, and celebrate the Id?"[115] These letters are nothing if not ambivalent. On the whole, however, Chase seems more emphatic about the possibility that the libidinal unconscious—murderous, loving, and, most tellingly, wonderful—might hold sway over the mundane world of marriage and family (and everything else). For Chase, the id would, without being seen, suffuse everyday life, rendering it less static and predictable.

But that vision of the disseminated libido did not reassure—much less inspire—Chase when he turned to Whitman's poetry. In writing about Whitman's sexuality, Chase's ambivalence is palpable. On the one hand, Whitman's treatment of sex is "neurotic," since "when he objects to 'sentimentality' in literature . . . he is always speaking of erotic, heterosexual emotions."[116] On the other hand, Whitman's critique of heterosexual sentimentality occasions one of Chase's most witty condemnations of Cold War America. "Whitman may have gone off the deep end in pursuit of sympathy and comradeship," Chase writes, "but at least he does not come bounding up to us with that doglike guilelessness our contemporary culture admires."[117] Chase claims that Whitman had "the tragic but purgative and liberating experience of recognizing and accepting the fact that he was homosexual," but he also asserts that the poet was "of dubious sex,"[118] and his sexuality was "so diffuse and sublimated that it could never have generated in him any definitive disposition or crucial recognition and acceptance of such a disposition."[119] Chase proclaims, "There can be no doubt that 'Song of Myself' made sex a possible subject for American literature, and in this respect Whitman wrought a great revolution,"[120] and yet his treatment of "sex as a subject" is "remarkably ironic, covert, elusive, and given to skipping back and forth between the personal and the generic."[121] For Chase, Whitman wrought a great revolution, but the poet "was conservative and nostalgic."[122] In any consideration of Whitman's work, Chase asserts, his "bisexuality must figure prominently,"[123] yet his treatments of sex with women "are fatally lacking in emotion,"[124] "remote and theoretical, however much he may have been in favor of it."[125] Whitman's homoerotic world of comrades "is a utopian vision of the future democracy,"[126] yet he possessed only "a vague, diffuse, and psychically infantile feeling of 'comradeship.'"[127] Chase's descriptions of Whitman as a sexual being are riven with ambivalence, making the poet "quirky, ironic, 'indirect,' guileful,"[128] "indeterminate, neurotic, power conscious, furtive, given alternately to dreams of order and of annihilation,"[129] both "confused" and "heroic."[130] But these terms are just as appropriate to describe the lives of many gays in Chase's day, who, furtive and quirky, neurotic and ironic, found ways to live in the culture of conformity Chase, like Melville and Whitman, condemned. In using those terms pejoratively, Chase deploys a psychojuridical homophobia even as, in the same passages, he attempts to preserve faith in the same-sex intimacy prone to legal and medical characterization and condemnation. In *Herman Melville*, Chase's adoption of an ideal of male camaraderie seemed to have been an imaginative effort to preserve the social collectivity prized by an earlier generation of progressive liberals in an age that suspiciously policed bonds between men for signs of sexual deviancy. By 1955, however, Chase was at some pains to distinguish it from the vilified image of homosexual love. His efforts to do so were haunted by ambivalence.

Chase could resolve his ambivalence only through an appeal to futurity, imagining an age when readers could again appreciate Whitman's poetic vision, presumably because attitudes toward his sexuality had changed. In such a future, readers "may not think it an extreme case if someone should remark to him that Whitman's utopian rejection of society is under modern conditions the necessary first step toward the preservation of what is vital in society and the revitalization of what is not."[131] Such readers were not to be found, however, at midcentury, "an age of moral gloom."[132] Unlike his future of perceptive readers, in 1955, Chase reports, the "radical politics that inspired an admiration for Whitman in the thirties has largely disappeared, and Whitman's reputation suffered from the general dissolution."[133] Confronting that gloom, Chase surprisingly reverses his dismissive attitude toward an earlier generation of progressive liberals, acknowledging for the first time that he sought to preserve and defend, not defeat, the radical implications of their philosophy.

The accepting future Chase imagined was less assured than he seemed to believe, however, in large part because his (imagined) reconciliation with his liberal opponents came too late. Both groups were, by 1955, ignoring the rise of a new "moral gloom" posing an even worse threat to Whitman's democratic camaraderie, which Daniel Aaron identified in the same year Chase published *Walt Whitman Reconsidered*. Looking back at the critical debates with which this chapter began, Aaron saw that both sides of the controversy, fighting each other, missed the rise of forces that threatened the cultural authority of liberals of any stripe.[134] While progressives and New Liberals squabbled, Aaron argues, New Conservatism arrived, no longer dedicated to "the moral imagination" but to "fetishes and stereotypes."[135] New Liberalism, in Aaron's account, did the dirty work for a new breed of knee-jerk conservatives, who followed in the wake of the dismantling of Enlightenment values. The New Conservatives, in Aaron's view, were the extreme extension of New Liberal philosophy, sharing with the latter "a profound mistrust not only for the theory and practice of socialism but also for the progressive mind itself."[136] Both groups, Aaron alleges, share a "revulsion from the excesses of liberal rationalism, the crimes of collectivism,"[137] in favor of prejudice, emotionalism, and self-interest.

More striking than his alignment of New Liberalism and New Conservatism, Aaron, in a vertiginous remapping of the political terrain, associates liberals of his generation with those he calls the Old Conservatives, both groups having a rational concern for the fate of the common interests of principled members of a democratic culture. Though sometimes "wrong-headed and ridiculous," Old Conservatives "understood (with all of their suspicions of celestial railways to paradise) why visionaries dreamed of more harmonious societies."[138] Like Aaron and the other "watchful eyes at Smith," Old Conservatives "felt a compassion for and an identification with the 'damned human race' and were not blind to man's capacity for nobility," which allowed them a "sympathetic regard for much of what they opposed, their conviction that truth was a blending of contrarieties."[139] Continuing in the tradition of making nineteenth-century authors speak for mid-twentieth-century political philosophies, Aaron enlists Hawthorne and Melville, who, like the traditionalists on both the right and the left, had "a standard of moral realism by which the ideals and achievements of a democratic society can be tested."[140] Their philosophy, Aaron claims, did not "sever them from the human community whose imbecilities and crimes they report."[141] No longer liberals, those writers "show what conservatism can do," namely, "point out the excesses and fallacies to which a democratic society like ours has always been susceptible: the sanctifying of majority will; an uncritical faith in manifest destiny; a delight in the new-fangled; an over-simplified conception of human nature; a predilection for short-cuts and panaceas of all kinds; an intense absorption with the mechanics of life."[142] Unlike those nineteenth-century Old Conservatives, their off-spring occupied a political position that Aaron saw as a series of "failures or betrayals," such as the identification of conservatism with single institutions or interests or short-term policies; the overemphasis on human depravity; blind resistance to change; the ignoring of the community; excessive distrust of the majority together with an unwillingness to recognize the danger of a tyrannical elite; ignorance of the social process; refusal to understand fundamental conservative values in other parties and programs; negativism that leads to the stifling of dissent rather than an attempt to understand its causes; and failure to consider the psychological as well as the economic needs of a society.[143]

Are we the heirs of the "moral gloom" generated by the conflict between Arvin and Chase? Or are our critical tales of disenchantment just its newest iteration? Aaron's essay is sobering, especially when he places the blame for political conservatism at the door to the academy. Claiming that "it is in the universities that their [New Conservative] doctrines are most attentively regarded," Aaron holds accountable conservative academics who "dominate the literary quarterlies" and who "have been characteristically doctrinaire in their politics as they have in their aesthetics, contemptuous of the mass-mind, and brilliantly articulate in their criticisms of the literature of liberalism."[144] In Aaron's account, the movement of literary criticism into the academy in the early years of the Cold War sacrificed liberalism's faith in human nature, its advocacy for collectivism, its loyalty to local resistance, its insistence that "politics" are not only a matter of incisive reading. After its move to the academy, Aaron claims, literary criticism became characterized by cynicism, distrust of common people, suspicion of humanism, increased abstraction, the uncompromising critique of a unified (and abstract) opponent, and belief that reading literature replaces or even transcends political activism carried out in local collectives. Those, for Aaron, were the signs of a new conservatism in literary criticism.

I leave it to the reader to assess to what extent Aaron's characterization can be applied to literary criticism today. But we might pause over his characterization as *conservative* the academic opposition to localism, Enlightenment values, liberalism, humanism, and sympathy with one's opponents as people with interests and practices and not simply as abstractions. Insofar as scholarly discourse today requires these repudiations, we continue the trend in literary criticism Aaron called New Conservatism, reproducing, even as we believe we oppose, a Cold War containment of cultures of dissent. A certain academic radicalism—Aaron points out that academic conservatives very often position themselves as revolutionaries—may be yet another form of Cold War melancholy. Although Aaron does not make this case, a fundamental danger of the New Conservatism (then or now) is how its belittling of the beliefs that bring people together in social collectives (local or national belonging, social identities, liberal politics, belief in progressive humanism) undermines the possibility of what Leslie Fiedler, in a 1949 letter to Chase, calls faith.[145] Fiedler wrote Chase to convince him that Melville's Confidence-Man is not, as Chase claimed, a cynic but a trickster who leads his interlocutors (and by extension the reader) from despair to faith, the former inspiring, rather than extinguishing, the latter. "The Confidence-Man *betrays* people into *faith*," Fiedler writes. Among a people convinced that any faith is the hallmark of naïveté, Fiedler claims, the Confidence-Man "is charlatan enough to stir faith." For Fiedler, faith is not blind but "extraordinarily bitter-hopeful," motivating resilience in the face of painful experience. Only faith, Fiedler suggests, can motivate a hero to give the unbelieving world a shake.

But Chase already knew this, at least at the start of his career. As the Cold War began, he saw how conformity, destruction, false rationality, repressive ideas of mental health, and unrestrained capitalism made critique necessary. He also saw, however, that without idealism and imagination, without hope (which I believe is what Fiedler meant by "faith"), critique is a charlatan's game no one can possibly win. Entering the Cold War, Americans were, "like Ahab, the votaries of the white icon," Chase claimed, adding, "We shall continue our murderous lopping and cutting and severing of the great body of Leviathan, until all of life is hacked out."[146] Have we hacked the life out of faith? In so doing, have we turned the "great body" of allegorical literature into a carcass gutted of its valuable justifications for hope? At the end of his diatribe against his fellow Cold War citizens, Chase, like a critical Jeremiah, holds out hope, quiet and constrained: "But if we are Ishmael, we may live to love Leviathan, who is the mythical body of the world, of our cultures, and of our-selves."[147] At the start of the Cold War, Chase used literary allegories to turn criticism into a practice of hope that balanced cogent analysis and unembarrassed idealism, pain and resilience. Leaving the Cold War (at least in our melancholic methodologies), we can join him in putting the wonder back in allegory and, in the process, make criticism the "mythic body" of our day.

3

Humanism

The Cant of Pessimism and Newton Arvin's Queer Humanism

We are in the habit of assuming that the most serious and
profound apprehension of reality is the Sense of Tragedy;
but it may be that, in assuming this, we ourselves are mistaken. It may be that there are points of view from which
the Tragic sense must be seen as serious and profound indeed, but limited and imperfectly philosophical. It may even
be that there can exist a kind of complacency of pessimism
as there is certainly a complacency of optimism; and that
many of us in this age are guilty of it.[1]

What Newton Arvin wrote of his colleagues in the field of literary studies in 1959 is true of many of its practitioners more than half a century
later. The language of tragedy, trauma, and cynical disbelief—what
Arvin called "the cant of pessimism"[2]—saturates literary and cultural
criticism, turning it into an ongoing disenchantment tale. To disavow
pessimism as "cant," however, is not to call for "positive" criticism, nor is
it to disparage the value of critique. Arvin acknowledges that "there are
points of view from which the Tragic sense must be seen as serious and
profound."[3] An avowed communist when he began his academic career,
Arvin well understood the important confluences of literary critical
methodology and a sustained and generative social and political engagement. Even after disavowing his allegiance to the Soviet Union, Arvin
maintained well into the 1950s his critique of Cold War geopolitics, of
nationalist myths of noble individualism and heteronormative privacy,
and of military and scientific heroism.

At the same time, however, Arvin was right to acknowledge that
some forms of criticism, especially when taken up as the axiomatic
capital of academic advancement, have proved "limited and imper-

fectly philosophical." Privileging ever more abstract concepts of power, criticism often implicitly dismisses as undertheorized, provincial, and narrow attention to local operations of injustice; focusing on the repressive and xenophobic operations of state and extra-state power, it often overlooks—and renders ineffective—resistance and alternative social identifications; by offering overextended and totalizing explanatory accounts, it leaves little room for the imaginative and collaborative interventions that make criticism less didactic, more inspirationally engaging; and, finally, by making cynical disbelief—the "cant of pessimism"—the affective sign of muscular acuity, it forestalls the hopes that generate social resiliencies. In the airless abstraction of much criticism, then as now, it is hard for hope—and its constitutive features, imagination and idealism—to breathe. But Arvin understood that the problem lay just as much in efforts to respond to performative pessimism with an equally dangerous "complacency of optimism," which contributes to the widespread and erroneous belief that hope and critique are necessarily opposed. Wrongly associating hope with blind optimism or political quietism, or cynicism with a lack of idealism, criticism too often occludes the constitutive *simultaneity* of hope and critique. The problem, in short, is that criticism is often formulaic, especially when it most claims its avant-garde status: equating rigor with absolute positions within a binary logic (even while critiquing binary logics).

In a very different vein, Arvin found balance in an evolving project of queer humanism, a combination of the progressive socialism of the 1930s and the experiential innovation of an ethics of enhancement. Rather than positing a liberatory trajectory, Arvin, acknowledging the near ubiquity of alienation in modern society, among the middle class as well as among the abject and the working classes, imagined enhancement as a project with mobile starting places and negotiable trajectories, leaving open the creative and collective work of local consultation, collective negotiation, conflict resolution, and collaborative imagination to *generate* (rather than "discover") the truth of core values important to those involved in the processes of imaginative negotiation. The goal of such processes is similar—the enhancement of creative imagination, social idealism, and human solidarity, a combination of literary and political skills—although the "problems" (including epistemological or ontological ones) will differ from community to community and across social strata.

The hope necessary to fuel such basic operations of what Arvin called a "radical democracy" underpins what the Frankfurt School named socialist humanism. Revising materialisms that dismiss as bourgeois indulgences all human experiences unrelated directly to production—including those that most interested Arvin in sexuality, namely, fantasy, pleasure, sensuality, emotion, and leisured sociality—socialist humanists such as Erich Fromm, Herbert Marcuse, and Ernst Bloch insisted that "Marx's ideal was a man productively related to other men and to nature, who would respond to the world in an alive manner, and who would be rich not because he *had* much but because he *was* much."[4] Unlike those invested in the cants of pessimism or optimism who, as Arvin writes, inculcate "a hard complacency, a shallow self-righteousness" so over-blown as to generate a "feeling of unreality,"[5] socialist humanists take up the brave and hopeful aspects of human nature, and the forms of social alliance they occasion: "tenderness, affectionate sympathy, benevolence, good-natured companionableness, and diffuse and fruitful social feeling."[6] Just as important, the Frankfurt School provided an alternative account of production, especially the production of humanism, as analytical truth making, the creative and collaborative production of the "human" as historical agent, capable of generating and revising new meanings for supposedly self-evident values, a willed mode of collective becoming.

Arvin used literature to develop such a model to comprehend the conditions in which humans approach and work through suffering to reach, collaboratively and imaginatively, an ethics of resilient enhancement. His humanism was neither unmindful nor curative of pain. It arose from pain, was impossible without it. Arvin's queer humanism acknowledged the deep relationship between pain and joy, the latter arising as an exhilarated resilience available from the stuff of everyday experience. On April 23, 1953, Arvin wrote to his friend and Smith College colleague Daniel Aaron:

> The staple of life is certainly suffering, though surely not its real meaning, and we differ mainly in our capacity to endure it—or be diverted from it. I myself never found it consoling to have this denied or minimized: it seems to me to give one *some* strength just to know that pain is normal, and disappointment the rule, and disquiet the standard—and that the

things that have the other quality (work, friendship, the arts) are the wonderful incredible exception & mitigation. And I can tell you, from a fund of experience, that one can be taken down from the rack, closer to death than to life—and then still have the most exquisite joys ahead of one.[7]

On one level, the passage is a straightforward attempt on Arvin's part to see a silver lining in the anguished depression he struggled with throughout his life. But Arvin's claim is more philosophical than personal. His assertion that suffering is not the "real meaning" of life is not a facile denial but an articulation of his Neoplatonic belief, arrived at through Emerson who in turn inherited it from Augustine, that evil has no *positive* meaning but is the lack of good, which is the only true presence.[8] When Arvin, paraphrasing Emerson, claims that "suffering is a kind of illusion, that it has no absolute or ultimate reality," he stresses that Emerson did not mean that unhappiness does not exist or that suffering is self-delusion, but rather that, in Emerson's words, "'all melancholy, as all passions, belongs to the exterior life,'" being circumstantial rather than internally generated.[9] Freed from pain-inducing conditions, one finds that "'progress, amelioration, and upward movement of things is a law of nature, like gravitation or natural selection.'"[10]

As I discussed in the previous chapter, later liberals like Richard Chase and Lionel Trilling found objectionable in Arvin's generation precisely this Neoplatonic belief in a drive toward happiness that pushes humans to overcome circumstantial hardships, evil coming from the outside rather than from within. What Arvin's critics failed to note, however, is that even while ignoring the Freudian death drive that became so central to Trilling's revisions of liberalism, Arvin nonetheless interiorized socialist politics in ways that both enabled the psychological analyses of culture undertaken by Trilling *and* preserved progressive ideals *as* human nature in a historical moment when such ideals were viewed as seditious. Arvin's concept of human nature, insofar as it interiorized pain as experience, avoided the facile optimism of which progressives were often accused. Yet it retained faith in resilience, the equivalent of the ongoing collective struggle advocated by Popular Front socialists, as the prevalent quality in human nature. In claiming with Emerson that suffering is "'for the most part fantastical,'"[11] Arvin brought critical recognition to the resilience, the critical hope, he believed was necessary to turn suffering into what he called a "philosophy of intelligible change."[12] Arvin believed that the critical endeavor—in everyday life as in literary criticism—is not to look through the apparent good in order to find the bad beneath but, conversely, to work through the conditions of badness so as to arrive at (to generate, to hone the perspective capable of discerning) the good it obscures and stifles. Pain is the obfuscation of good, and not the other way around, as is often claimed today. The hopeful articulation of and movement toward good, rather than the uncovering of bad, in short, is, Arvin believed, the most effective critical response to pain.

Because the notion of an *essential* humanity might seem to doom individuals to unchangeable predispositions (to optimism, say, or to pessimism), however, the idea of a fixed human character was anathema to Arvin's belief that experience and concentrated effort can change dispositions. Arvin, like Emerson, believed that one can move from suffering to joy, can be "taken down from the rack," through the accumulation of and sustained attention to a necessarily varied and contingent "experience." Neither suffering not joy is given an ontological status; both function as affective coordinates in a transformational process arising from the materiality of "experience" and generating a fictive space of possibility—the invisible hand that takes one from the rack—that, in turn, translates back into "experience" as affective and imaginative resilience. Suffering, then, is for Arvin an experience that can be transformed, not transcended. Arvin captures that transformation in the word "endure," which suggests an ongoing practice without a predetermined object or even the possibility of final satisfaction. Without surrendering the possibility of progress, then, Arvin revised socialism to make it more responsive to the restrictive social conditions and policed dispositional politics of early Cold War America.

Arvin suggests what that practice comprises when he makes a counterintuitive turn in values in the letter quoted earlier. Arvin takes comfort, he tells Aaron, in knowing that suffering is "normal," "standard," "the rule." This language seems to show Arvin conflating the universal "human" with the disciplinary production of docile bodies. But Arvin elsewhere expressed contempt for "the new science of statistics," which believes "that human behavior can be reduced to mathematical terms and predicted as confidently as the procession of the equinoxes."[13] Arvin did not associate such statistical knowledge, as Foucault did, with the maintenance of life but rather with death, thereby turning discipline, as Foucault frames it, back into punishment, as in his reference to "the rack."[14] To a homosexual man living at the height of the HUAC persecution of those viewed as the embodied agents of domestic anti-Americanism, someone who dealt repeatedly with the psychiatric profession, and who had his career ruined by juridical prosecution, Arvin would have been keenly aware of the mortifying and historically specific effects of statistical standardization. What is significant here is that Arvin associates the "normal" not with institutional power-knowledge but with the informal sharing of experiences of pain, from which, paradoxically, he draws *strength*. Arvin reclaims normalcy for the diseased, criminal, and pathological, making suffering the basis of a countersociality of the abnormal, or what he calls the "wonderful incredible exception."

Arvin does not leave his countersociality subject to the rule of the real, moreover, but quickly attaches it to the enchantment of the "wonderful," which was, for him, the distinguishing trait of Romanticism. That is itself paradoxical—distinguishable traits of the exceptional and ineffable—but in a world where gay men circulated in a continually shifting and barely marked network, the paradox takes on material plausibility. Or, to put it another way, subculture, for Arvin (and for many of his critical contemporaries), is the lived experience of Romanticism. While on one level Arvin's humanism may appear essentializing, then, through Romanticism he recasts essence as wonder, the affective response to the unexpected, the immaterial, the *joyous*.[15] By making Romanticism the basis for countersociality, moreover, Arvin *queers* humanism, making it not legible and predictable but informal, contingent, inscrutable to all but those who have experienced suffering within institutional logics. Making Romanticism the ground for a sociality of the pained and marginal, Arvin, in short, creates a queer humanism. When queered, humanism is not an identity or a political position but a *practiced* response to suffering.

That is a lot of philosophical work to load onto one relatively brief epistolary passage. Yet the steps shorthanded in that passage are central to Arvin's development across his scholarly career of a practice of hope that was at one and the same time a humanist philosophy and a critical methodology. Six years after his letter to Aaron, Arvin gave that practice its fullest expression in the *Hudson Review* essay "The House of Pain: Emerson and the Tragic Sense" (1959).[16] Arvin begins the essay by characterizing critical accounts that dismiss Emerson for legitimizing competitive and self-interested individualism and for providing a bourgeois rationale for the rich and powerful. There is, Arvin concedes, a grain of truth in such depictions. Elsewhere Arvin reminds readers that Emerson was a close friend of John Murray Forbes, whose son, later president of Bell Telephone, married Emerson's daughter Edith, making Emerson grandfather to a governor of the Philippines. Arvin acknowledges "the line of class privilege is virtually unbroken."[17] Emerson's, Arvin admits, was at least partially "a philosophy of power, a metaphysics of success, a religion of enterprise and self-help"[18] that pushed "the foggy idealism of the Transcendentalist epigone."[19] It would not be "far-fetched," Arvin writes, to blame Emerson for "such tangible realities of our political life as resistance to the 'demoralizing' dole," concluding that "without the essays and addresses, without the Emersonian clichés, how much less spiritual authority the ruling class would have had."[20]

Critics in his day, however, had turned these strains in Emerson's writing—strains that are, Arvin claims, guilty projections of critics' own complicity in bourgeois individualism and competitive capital— into the totality of his philosophy. What such accounts disregard, Arvin contends, is Emerson's critique—*not* his endorsement—of middle-class values. Arvin went so far as to claim that Emerson had predicted that class's downfall. "From the beginning," Arvin writes, "there has been a deep disequilibrium in middle-class culture, as there have been deep contradictions in its economy."[21] The source of that disequilibrium is the paradoxical middle-class commitment to "change, to a dynamic and essentially revolutionary program" necessary to the continued generation of consumer desire around supposedly new and improved commodities, and, simultaneously, a reliance on the fiction of stability required by hierarchical economic, sexual, and social reproduction.[22] Especially in relation to the latter, Emerson's radicalism emerges, for Arvin, in his claim, "Everything . . . looks permanent until its secret is known," leading Arvin to continue, "literally everything, including the elective system at Harvard, the strenuous life of the Roosevelts, rugged individualism, and the middle-class culture which made this generalization possible."[23] Missing Emerson's critique in their rush to condemn the "great 'glad' glow of Emersonianism," critics turned transcendentalism into "a vulgar optimistic superstition, a cant of self-seeking concealed beneath a butter of altruism, a gospel for the aggressive, the unscrupulous, the interested."[24] Such misunderstandings were predictable, Arvin claims, because in an age "when we all seem agreed that anguish, inquietude, the experience of guilt, and the knowledge of the Abyss are the essential substance of which admissible literature is made," it is impossible for most to read Emerson "with respect," preferring to add to "the stench sent up by a rotten individualism."[25]

Two decades earlier, Arvin similarly accused literary scholars of endorsing the very bourgeois individualism they purported to condemn in another nineteenth-century writer. In his *New Republic* review "Whitman's Individualism" (1932), Arvin contests portrayals of Whitman as "merely the jolly and complacent spokesman of American middle-class democracy, undiscriminating, uncritically affirmative, and committed to the dogmas of self-help and self-expression in their simplest and even crudest forms."[26] To show that on the contrary Whitman was keenly critical of middle-class individualism, Arvin quotes from a column in the *Eagle* in which Whitman writes, "'Has any one of our laboring fellow citizens such thin perceptions—does he imagine in his most abstracted dreams—that all this hubbub made by the pale-fingered richly housed Whig manufacturers, and their organs, is for *him*, the laborer?'"[27] The more complex Whitman remains invisible, Arvin claimed, to critics who are "naturally inclined to read undiluted liberalism and individualism into whatever writers they find praiseworthy."[28] The date of these essays is telling. The Whitman review's privileging of the collectivism of the working class over liberal individualism is understandable in 1932, when Arvin was still actively involved in Popular Front communism. More surprising is that twenty years later, after the disappointments that purportedly drove critics to a more conservative celebration of the values they had critiqued in the 1930s, Arvin was still defending Emerson against charges of bourgeois individualism. Arvin's defense of Whitman and Emerson suggests that the beliefs he held while a communist did not simply vanish but transformed into something closer to a literary methodology, one that built not only on the negative critique of capital but also on what he called "moral courage," discernible in—rather than despite—the "exhilarating fluidity" that Arvin believed sustained "a conviction that development is the secret of life, and movement the hallmark of reality." Subjecting the static "real" to the fluidity of change, Romantics like Emerson and Whitman turned literary imagination into "irreverence toward the *status quo*."[29]

That irreverence was not, it bears repeating, a denial of pain or suffering; indeed, resisting the status quo almost certainly increases one's suffering. Emerson was far from a naive optimist, Arvin argues, quoting the writer's letter to his aunt, Mary Moody Emerson, "'He has seen but half the universe who has never been shown the house of Pain. Pleasure and Peace are but indifferent teachers of what it is life to know.'"[30] Keenly aware of "the problem of moral evil," Emerson, Arvin contends, "was really deeply stirred by the spectacle of systematic cruelty and injustice."[31] What critics often see as Emerson's risible optimism was, for Arvin, "a conviction he had arrived at after youthful years during which he had as good reasons as most men—poverty, ill health, bereavement, anxiety—for questioning the absolute rightness of things" and had therefore developed in his writings "the strain of sadness, apprehension, and doubtfulness of the good of existence."[32] Emerson's work, Arvin saw, combined "a celebration of the powers of the human will" with "an insistence on its limitations—on the forces in nature that are not friendly but hostile and even destructive to human wishes, and on the discrepancy between what a man aspires to do and what nature and circumstance allow him to do."[33] Emerson knew, even if his middle-class readers did not, "that the laws of the world do not always befriend, but often hurt and crush us."[34]

What Arvin focused on in Emerson, however, was the side that concerned "the human will" as a force of resilience and moral courage rather than as "the product of good fortune or of a natively happy temper."[35] Building on experiences of and sympathy with suffering, Emerson believed that hopeful resilience "was an achievement both of intellectual and emotional discipline."[36] Out of such discipline, Emerson trusted, would come the capacity to change what he called fate, which, without promising inevitable success, becomes a practice of hope. In the end, Emerson's disposition was, for Arvin, "not a fatalistic acceptance, but an exhilarated and courageous activism," for "the true lesson to be learned from the facts of determinism is that we can afford to be brave."[37] Emerson's "activism" was, for Arvin, a willed process of self-transformation from resignation to resilience, and ultimately to what he called joy, the recognition of developed strategies of survival, both individual and collective. Emerson, Arvin reports, did not "simply *find* himself" beyond a state of fated powerlessness but rather "he had *moved* beyond it."[38] In contrast to most readers, then, Arvin foregrounds what he calls "the strenuous strain in Emerson's optimism," which is not a naive expectation that all will work out well—Emerson knew that "we must learn what not to expect"—but rather a moral commitment to resilient hope.[39]

It is tempting to speculate that, in formulating this hope-generating askesis, Arvin had in mind William James's *Varieties of Religious Experience* (1902), a text that also looked to Emerson for an account of active hope. In Lectures IV through VII, James distinguishes between "healthy-mindedness" and the "sick soul." Turning to the Transcendentalists, James at first sounds like one of those critics of Emerson and Whitman Arvin disparages. James asserts that in the Transcendentalists one finds evidence "of a temperament organically weighted on the side of cheer and fatally forbidden to linger . . . over the darker aspects of the universe."[40] Whitman, according to James, "owes his importance in literature to the systematic exclusion from his writing of all contractile elements. The only sentiments he allowed himself were of the expansive order."[41] As a consequence of his willed obliviousness, Whitman, for James, "ends by persuading the reader that men and women, life and death, and all things are divinely good."[42] As Arvin suspected of other critiques of Emerson and Whitman, however, James's was at least in part projection, as James urged readers to reject "the pining, puling, mumping mood" of pessimism, which "perpetuates the trouble which occasioned it, and increases the total evil of the situation." Pessimism, James claims, sounding very much like his caricature of Whitman, is "a pathological melancholy" or a "pathological depression" to be cured or banished.[43]

At other moments, however, James imagined "the compound world," composed of evil and good, optimism and pessimism, health and illness. Pathology, then, arises not only from a determined pessimism but also from a refusal to see that optimism and pessimism are *never* separable, do not ever exist as *absolute* states. "Withdraw or pervert either factor of this complex resultant," James warns, "and the kind of experience we call pathological ensues."[44] To be entirely optimistic or pessimistic, for

James, epitomizes "forgetfulness and superficiality," a "blindness and insensibility to opposing facts."[45]

Since neither optimism nor pessimism is an absolute state achievable without pathological delusion, what James is calling for is an awareness that what he calls "experience" necessarily involves both, that hope is impossible except in the acknowledged experience of suffering *and* joy. One can face experience, however, with a variety of dispositions that are not determinative but can be altered *through* experience. What James called "the twice-born" state comprises a change in disposition, a choice that does not come naturally but rather involves what Arvin calls moral courage. That courage enables movement across what James describes as a psychological "threshold," or "the point at which one state of mind passes into another."[46] What appears evil "can so often be converted into a bracing and tonic good," James asserts, "by a simple change of the sufferer's inner attitude from one of fear to one of fight."[47] Religious experience—and here James quotes Kierkegaard's claim, "'It requires moral courage to grieve; it requires religious courage to rejoice'"—is for James a *practice*, a building of hope from the stuff of despair, generating the resilience characteristic of what he calls the twice-born state.[48]

That process is hardly as simple as James claims, however, since the painstaking labor to bring "the entire frame of reality under a systematic conception optimistic enough to be congenial with its needs" requires that one face the "pity, pain, and fear" caused by and reinforcing "the sentiment of human helplessness" in order to reach an earned and *critical* hope. James insists that "the securest way to the rapturous sorts of happiness of which the twice-born make report has as an historic matter of fact been through a more radical pessimism than anything we have yet considered."[49] In the end, then, James, like Arvin's Emerson, "was a philosopher of intelligible change."[50]

In turning to Emerson (or James) as a model of activism, Arvin sacrificed some of the realpolitik engagement of the 1930s (Hawthorne wryly characterized Emerson as "the mystic, stretching his hand out of cloudland, in vain search for something real'"),[51] making it more psychological, philosophical, and interiorized. Perhaps Emerson was appealing to Arvin precisely because, except "when he was really deeply stirred by the spectacle of systematic cruelty and injustice," he "took but a cool interest in the radicalisms of his day."[52] Yet Arvin was doing something more:

not only was he adapting and preserving the values of his early politics during increasingly unsafe times for the expression of such values, he was collating social politics with the psychological needs of those at the front lines of Cold War persecution, finding ways to address those emotional and spiritual needs that must be met if social activism is to have a future. Showing how attention to human interiority may have realer political consequences than does abstract dogma, Arvin turned in 1937 to William Dean Howells, who, Arvin writes, might seem "useless" because he "made relatively little, in fiction, of the terrible sacrifice of personal wholeness among the industrial workers."[53] But not all interior states are tragic or triumphant, Arvin knew, and he found his literary equivalent in Howells, defending him as he had Emerson and Whitman. Arvin asks, "Who can fail to discern, in so many of his middle-class characters, restless or ill occupied or discontented or self-seeking men and women that they are, his implicit criticism of an egocentric culture?"[54] Amid what Arvin called "the ugly disharmonies of monopolism and empire,"[55] Howells showed us not armed revolt or crushed despair or even metaphoric triumph over abstract systems of power but restlessness, boredom, discontentedness, ambition—the dispositions, in short, that animate characters to develop—or not—"imaginative understanding,"[56] a "fatal courage,"[57] in a world "dominated not by purpose and control, but by accident, hazard, and whim."[58] And the combination of his interest in dispositional askesis and his concept of enhancement made clear that the first step in achieving social change is to take the psychic distress caused by contemporary life and transform it into a twice-born state of resilient critique and commitment to life.

That is to say, Arvin understood—as he believed Emerson had—that before politics there must be what he called "apprehension of reality" or "points of view," or, in short, critical disposition. Given similar backgrounds and similar experiences of injustice, what makes one person fight and another flee or fold? It is not correct to say that the choice depends on character but rather that it is the result of what Arvin calls "a fund of experience" the negotiation of which develops, alters, and hones dispositions. One becomes "political" not only by adopting or refusing an ideological structure, in other words, but beforehand, in the dispositional askesis I am calling a practice of hope. That practice is the glue of social assemblages; it teaches what not to expect and yet is necessary to what Arvin calls Emerson's radicalism, "accessible as always to those who wish not merely to 'interpret the world variously' (in Marx's phrase) but to change it."[59] Through Howells, we learn not how to negotiate power and production but what makes—or unmakes—the dispositions that compel us, in contingent way, toward the choices we make. In a perfect dispositional state, however, one *does not* choose but rather combines resilience *and* resignation, maintaining what Arvin saw in Henry Adams, "balanced between the poles of hopefulness and despair, affirmation and denial, belief and skepticism."[60] Arvin understood the political need for an outlook, an orientation begun in suffering but trained into something more capable of wonder at the unprecedented, more *hopeful* possibilities of life. For Arvin those practices of hope are the *positive* good that constitutes humanism, generating both personal and social dissatisfaction (generating critique) and endurance (ensuring the perpetual life of ideals). The accumulation of endured experiences over time abrades what Arvin called "the status quo," becoming a collective and socially engaged practice, a *socialist* as well as a humanist queerness.

But even more than a socialist, humanist, or queer project, the practice of hope is for Arvin a *literary* skill, for it involved, in addition to depictions of social realism, the imaginative idealism that motivates us in all our everyday activities, although it is often an unseen and unacknowledged force in a society that discredits both idealism and imagination. Literature gives us the distance to see what we already, on some level, know, exaggerating as it does the imminent materials of hope. The remainder of this chapter explores three of Arvin's monographs to show how he developed a lifelong commitment to queer humanism. Just as important, however, those readings will suggest how Arvin turned a pedagogy of dispositions into a literary methodology, generating a queer practice of hope still available to us as readers today.

Although Arvin was in the first half of the twentieth century one of the best-known critics of nineteenth-century American literature, his critical reputation, to say the least, has dimmed since his death in 1963. If Arvin is recalled at all today, it is more often in relation to his biography than to his criticism. In September 1960, Massachusetts state police arrested Arvin for "lewd and lascivious behavior" for receiving and sharing with other gay men physique magazines featuring nearly nude male models. Arvin, who had taught for thirty-eight years at Smith College, named to the police younger colleagues with whom he had shared these magazines, was convicted, forced into retirement by Smith, and died three years later after repeated hospitalizations for depression.[61] While Arvin's work has been all but forgotten since his death, some critics—especially Robert K. Martin—have worked "to restore Arvin to the position he deserves in the history of American literary criticism."[62] To continue this project, we must, as Andrew Delbanco encourages, stop turning "everything that Arvin wrote into a repository of clues to his ultimate self-destruction" and turn again to Arvin's critical studies.[63]

If we do so, we gain a good deal of insight—less evident in his life—into his understanding of the relationship between humanism and imaginative resilience. What is remarkable about Arvin's career is not that he found socialist humanism—he was active in Marxist reading groups in the 1920s and remained interested throughout his life—but *where* he found it: not in the history books or the newspapers or even the hard-boiled realist fiction of his youth but in the broody Romanticism of the 1850s. As Martin astutely observes, through that literature Arvin worked out the relationships between sexuality, sociability, and imagination, turning them into what I consider a hopeful ethics of enhancement.[64]

Beyond the insight offered by any one of Arvin's books, however, three studies together form a tale of dispositional changes necessary to a queer humanism. His first book, *Hawthorne*, published in 1929, describes the debilitating limitations placed on the imagination by shame and secrecy, and argues that Hawthorne's fiction—to say nothing of his emotional life—would have been greatly enhanced had he been able to escape his self-imposed exile in a fantasy world of his own creating. In *Whitman* (1938), Arvin marvels that, faced with many of the same forces that kept Hawthorne in self-doubt, the author of *Leaves of Grass* willed himself into a public poetics of homoerotic pleasure. Finally, in *Melville* (1950), winner of the first National Book Award for nonfiction and today the only of his studies in print, Arvin recognizes that queer humanism, without a community of fellow travelers, is an empty achievement. Melville, Arvin observes, conceived an erotic fraternalism that combined Whitman's daring and Hawthorne's imaginative fantasy to create the first glimpses in American literature of the dispositions necessary to a queer humanism.

While Arvin's three critical biographies are notable enough for placing sexuality at the heart of a new canon of antebellum letters, they are
even more remarkable for understanding a socially transformative humanism as essentially literary as well as political in origin. Arvin was
no reformer, any more than were the authors he admired. Organizing
laborers, cleaning out brothels, educating the poor: these are important
reforms but not necessarily the only valuable ones available to critics,
whose skill is to enhance the power of imagination—to visualize a social organization that breaks the seemingly imperative precedents of the
"real"—and to yoke that imagination to the dispositional idealism fundamental to queer humanism. Imagination and idealism arise, as Arvin
well understood, from the hard materials of human history, but they are
animated when the conventions of prescribed life give way to the fantastic, extraordinary, and unprecedented. In such moments—the moments
that Arvin recognized as central to the romance—new assemblages are
worked out in the service of human possibility. The same conditions
that threatened to drive Melville and Hawthorne to despair—"the worries and humiliations of poverty, the daily pressure to make money and
get ahead, the settled warfare between intellect and feeling, the ever-
renewed clash between impulse and conscience"[65]—also pushed them
to use the imaginative form of the romance to "reach through tragedy"
in order to find a preferable, if (because) unprecedented social arrangement, rooted in human feeling, pleasure, and aspiration. This combination of fantasy and social enhancement, of hope and will, is what
Arvin called "vital materialism," a socialist humanism both sensuous
and social.[66] When that combination is achieved, as it was in the finest
moments of *Moby-Dick* or *The Scarlet Letter*, humanism—and of a particularly *queer* stripe—thrives.

Arvin pauses with evident admiration on a passage from *Redburn*
in which Melville uses precisely such an imaginative evocation of the
fantastic to picture an erotic attachment between the eponymous hero
and another sailor. "But Harry! You are mixed with a thousand strange
forms," Melville writes, "the centaurs of fancy; half real and human, half
wild and grotesque. Divine imaginings, like gods, come down to the
groves of our Thessalies, and there, in the embrace of wild, dryad reminiscences, beget the beings that astonish the world."[67] The combination
of fantasy and experience ("wild, dryad reminiscences") has the power

to "astonish" us out of our security in the tried, the conventional, and the "real." Inviting us to invent without surrendering the root of fantasy in material experience, this queer humanism—Melville's excited sense of possibility palpitates from his rhetorical excess—is importantly, for Arvin, a *literary* moment, as imagination functions both as a mode of social enhancement and as a disposition toward sensing the pleasurable beyond the plausible. In highlighting such passages, Arvin combined imagination, sexuality, and humanism, placing the hybrid—the dispositional ethics of hope—at the center of the American literary canon and of critical practices oriented toward it in his time and, potentially, in ours.

While Arvin's analyses of how their sexuality influenced the work of Whitman and Melville may no longer seem as provocative as they once did, Arvin was perhaps the first—and still one of the few—critics to suggest that same-sex desire animates Hawthorne's romances, a line of analysis he published, daringly, in 1929. Secluding himself from society for twelve years following his 1825 graduation from Bowdoin College, Hawthorne, in Arvin's account, became a prisoner of a paradoxical mixture of shame and pride. That combination, in Arvin's telling, becomes characteristic of the closet. Hawthorne's inability to participate in mainstream social activities produced "his ignorance of so deep a human experience as the love between the sexes," causing in turn "the incurable emptiness of his life."[68] Hawthorne, whose avid if not always appreciative consumption of sentimental novels allowed him to court Sophia Peabody from a distance, found physical intimacy excruciatingly awkward. Yet an emerging middle-class ideology made private intimacy a training ground and—in large measure—a substitute for public participation. Hawthorne, believing himself "failed" at heteronormative intimacy, therefore accepted his alienation from civic life as well. Lost to the possibility of private fulfillment or public companionship, Hawthorne withdrew into "a cold or selfish or marginal way of life" antithetical to "a healthy perception of human reality."[69]

Exhibiting a good degree of identification with his subject, Arvin vacillates between blaming Hawthorne for his self-seclusion and, with increased vehemence, condemning Hawthorne's era for its uncritical investment in public and private conformity that offered a free-thinking and imaginative individual no choice but to withdraw, as Hawthorne did, from public life. In Arvin's interpretations of *The Scarlet Letter*, Hester, like her creator, is a haughty figure, separated from her community as much by her pride as by Puritan edict. For Arvin, however, the principal sin in the romance is not Hester's but the townspeople's, who sin against human nature by insisting on a regulated normalcy that necessitates a split—not just in adulterers but in every citizen—between the wayward force of individual imagination and the outward show of regulated conventions. As Arvin knew, a mortifying view of democracy, relying on the conformity of diverse opinion into a unified voice of an abstract "people," requires homophobia, as Christopher Newfield has argued, in order to vilify nonconforming invention as danger, disease, and sin.[70] Imagination is isolation only in the presence of stern conventionality, Arvin believed; allowed to thrive, it creates communities of compassion and appreciation. The "essential sin lies in whatever shuts up the spirit in a dungeon where it is alone," Arvin writes, "beyond the reach of common sympathies and the general sunlight. All that isolates, damns; all that associates, saves."[71]

At the same time as he condemned the isolation imposed by social convention, however, Arvin did not advocate for a triumphant pride. Enforced isolation that results in shame is blameworthy, but what the isolated make of that shame is paradoxically liberating. If "the sense of guilt . . . is the product of solitude,"[72] shame may also radically reconfigure social ethics, as Michael Warner has contended.[73] Already alienated from the regimes upholding "normal" society, the shameful are liberated from imperatives to reproduce that normalcy and are free, instead, to imagine ways of life, sources of pleasure, inventive fantasies that may in turn generate new social alliances. Shame, as has often been the case in startlingly imaginative literature, thus becomes the catalyst that transforms an "abnormal inaction"[74] into a radically active hopefulness. While "the shadows in the midst of which he lived seemed to deprive him of all credence in the reality of human life, all confidence in the truth of the visible world,"[75] Hawthorne's alienation from "reality" generated a capacity to restructure "human life," imaginatively, into a less competitive, less driven, and more sociable realm. A "good deal given to daydreaming,"[76] Hawthorne willfully transformed shame into creative social ethics, a process his contemporary Donald Grant Mitchell in his defense of "bachelor reveries" called "realm-making," and which, a half century later, Lauren Berlant and Michael Warner celebrated as urban queer "world-making."[77] Out of Hawthorne's isolation, Arvin recognized, grew "a resourceful fancy" that provided him with a "fictitious world in which to take refuge from the here and now."[78] Hawthorne's closet became, paradoxically, his freedom, releasing him from "'seeing the thing as in itself it really is'"[79] and allowing him instead to populate his phantom public with others who, like the sinners who flock to Hester's cottage under cover of darkness, provide a countersociality that is no less hopeful for being fantastic.[80] Like his infamous heroine, "Hawthorne found himself, during those eventless years that would have seemed to all other men alive so tame, so poor, so frosty," Arvin writes, "entertaining angels—fallen angels, if you will—whose presence was intolerant of boredom."[81] When contact with the "'Present, the Immediate, the Actual'" threatens to take away, as Hawthorne reports it did for him, the "'desire for imaginative composition,'" then "'scatter[ing] a thousand peaceful fantasies upon the hurricane that is sweeping us along with it, possibly, into a Limbo where our nation and its polity may be as literally the fragments of a shattered dream as my unwritten Romance'"[82] may be the safest way to become, in Arvin's words, "a wanderer in time and place, a native of a hundred far countries more congenial than Massachusetts."[83]

The power of imagination Hawthorne wielded over actuality was, however, neither absolute nor fully sanguine. The imagination, Arvin knew, must compromise with reality, drawing on its materials in order to push them to their limits: "He wrote," Arvin notes of Hawthorne, "not as he would, but as he found he could."[84] It is not true, Arvin acknowledges, "that the will is all-powerful, that the universe is consciously beneficent to mankind, and that conflict infallibly issues in victory for the hero. These assumptions were the basis of conduct in Hawthorne's day, if no later, and had inspired, as they were to continue to inspire, most of American literature."[85] Part of Hawthorne's imaginative power, paradoxically, was its capacity to see through that myth of inevitable triumph, to show the truth behind deceptive promises of individual transcendence. It is not only that shame gives rise in Hawthorne's romances to a renovated ethics; it is also that failure becomes the paradoxical strength to deny the absurdities of facile optimism. This is what Arvin meant when he spoke of a fraudulent cant of optimism, as dangerous as its pessimistic counterpart. The imaginative power he admired in Hawthorne, who in Arvin's estimation "was the first of American writers to go in his own person to the very center of human experience, and demonstrate this facile optimism as myth,"[86] was his capacity to balance hopefulness and skepticism in ways that allowed him to deploy his creative powers to enhance very specific conditions of suffering injustice.

While Arvin saw the benefits of shame and failure in generating Hawthorne's creative powers, however, as long as Hawthorne's imagination operated in solitude it ultimately proved unsatisfying to Arvin, who remained dedicated to the possibilities of collaborative public sociality among more than mere imaginary friends. Arvin worried that romantic isolation threatens to release fantasy from its connection to human suffering and, "uncorrected by any appeal to the full normal life of humanity," surrenders the give-and-take that provides the opportunity for revising opinions, fantasies, and, ultimately, public opinion about what constitutes "normal" life.[87] While Arvin, in other passages, was more skeptical of collective public wisdom, his fear was that, in an age of accelerated individualism fueled by market innovation and competition, the concept of the "social" might be entirely subsumed by the assertive eccentricities of the "human." Arvin, showing how shame creates abstract counterethics superior to normative social conventions, made Hawthorne into something like a queer theorist today. But with that resemblance comes queer theory's limitations as well. Queer theory often privileges the anomalous, the eccentric, and the outlawed, neglecting— even ridiculing—efforts at community-building necessary for safety and pleasure.[88] Even at the risk of normativity, Arvin refused to romanticize moves "away from the center toward some waste and dismal region." In "an age given over to the centrifugal,"[89] citizens find themselves united only "in their refusal to work together on any but a false basis. United, finally, in paying the penalty for disunion," Arvin continued with unaccustomed heat, citizens become "partial and lopsided personalities, men and women of one dimension, august or vulgar cranks."[90] "Dispersion, not convergence," Arvin laments, "has become the American process."[91] In such a world, Hawthorne's "very estrangement from his fellows was but emblematic of their own estrangement from one another or their collective estrangement from the main body of human experience."[92] Only a very careful disciplining of disposition can resist "the free expansion of temperament"[93] and restore "ethical and cultural centralization."[94]

The "center," in Arvin's vision, is elastic, however, organized by ethics built not on the power to stigmatize but on the experience of shame. Nor is "centralization," for Arvin, synonymous with consensus, for the work of collaborative deliberation might—indeed should—occasion conflict and disagreement, the skillful negotiation of which is necessary to a functional democracy. Arvin dismisses Hawthorne's tales, which, he asserts, trade "conflict" for undemocratic dispositions of "resignation, inertness, passivity."[95] Conflict is not one of "those social and psychological forces that lead to disunion, fragmentation, dispersion, incoherence";[96] rather, the false harmony of superficial conformity, according to Arvin, "is irreconcilable with a truly human solidarity." Conflict is a sign of a viable democracy, for when citizens "lend themselves to a general and articulated purpose,"[97] those purposes will at times clash. Prevented from reaching the point of violence by patient and imaginative deliberation, conflict is a productive corrective to "the illusion most Americans have suffered from, that they could achieve social integrity by learning to 'cooperate' and attain harmony by striving for standardization."[98]

Arvin clearly wanted what seemed, in Hawthorne's case, irreconcilable goods: individual imagination *and* social collaboration. "Certainly it was not easy to manage two horses at once," he wryly comments of Hawthorne, "when one of them was a hackney and the other Pegasus."[99] Yet without a combination "of the marvelous, of the picturesque, of the exceptional" and "our sense of the generally true, of the commonplace, of the racily normal,"[100] individuals like Hawthorne must suffer from "a deadly creeping paralysis."[101] The ideal balance, for Arvin, came through humanist socialism, which Arvin turned into a theory of literary production. Standing in opposition to New Critics, those "little writers of syllogisms" who "had no more notion of what literature is about than a mole has of astronomy," Arvin declared himself "quite willing and even eager to be 'impressionistic,' 'intuitional,' 'appreciative,' 'unsystematic,' and all the other sins in the tight little Eliotine decalogue."[102] The difference between New Criticism and Arvin's humanism, in short, was the dispositions that revel in messy, intuitive, emotional, in short, *human* experiences shared by readers with commitments to imaginative idealism. Arvin sought a critical methodology to correspond to that experience. In the first place, Arvin wrote, the critic must discern how an author "shared fully and directly some central spiritual experience of his people and his time, must have been moved by desires not merely personal or fugitive, and have won some typical triumph or gone down in some typical defeat."[103] A literary work is not simply a transparent register of its historical moment, however, any more than a single person embodies the spirit of an age. Rather, the imagination transforms history in the process of its inscription, making "typical" experiences "embodied, artistically, in the idiom of personality" and translating "from its native formlessness, abstractness, subjectivity, into concrete and dramatic terms."[104] Combining "the facts of human character" with "catholicity,"[105] Arvin saw criticism as a solution to the dispositional impasse that paralyzed Hawthorne. In so doing, he moved, in his own form of Jamesian threshold, through "'the hard-boiled or the 'objective' or the tough-minded school of my own generation'" to create "'an open . . . literary universe.'"[106] This literary methodology would find its corresponding subject a decade later in Walt Whitman.

"'Of course I find I'm a good deal more of a Socialist than I thought I was,'" Whitman told Horace Traubel, "'maybe not technically, politically, but intrinsically, in my meanings.'"[107] This quotation opens Arvin's second critical biography. *Whitman* focuses on the question of the poet's socialist meanings, which, by 1938, had become a matter of controversy. H. S. Canby, who claimed that the ideological "specialization" of modern poetry contributed to its divergence from established patterns of thought and feeling and hence to poetry's apparent irrelevance for contemporary readers, argued that "the idea of a world proletariat based on economic grounds would have been repugnant" to Whitman.[108] The socialist poet and journalist Floyd Dell, managing editor of Max Eastman's magazine *The Masses*, called Whitman "'the most complete and thorough-going anti-Socialist in all literature,'" while the Marxist critic V. F. Calverton called the poet "'just as much a petty bourgeois individualist in social philosophy, just as much a believer in private property, as were most of his contemporaries.'"[109] The poet-critic Mark Van Doren claimed that Whitman's poetry "has no serious meaning—certainly no serious political meaning—for healthy men and women" due to its author's "abnormal sexuality." Arvin summarizes Van Doren's argument: "His 'democratic dogmas,' since they base themselves on this eccentric and unwholesome emotion—this 'wateriest of foundations for democracy'—are wholly without meaning, wholly invalid for the men of to-day and of the future. 'No society can be made out of him,' said Mr. Van Doren of Whitman. 'We could not be like him if we would. He has revealed himself to us, and that is all.'"[110]

Arvin appears to agree with both Whitman and his critics. On the one hand, he too found in Whitman the voice of the modern bourgeoisie, "the highly affirmative poet of American middle-class culture."[111] With "a great fund of conservatism" and "unexpected practical conformities" in his temperament, along with "an instinctive love of the show of power,"[112] Whitman, in Arvin's judgment, suffered from a "happy economic fatalism" in which "the real is in fact the rational, and that somehow good fortune and high deserts are one and the same."[113] "Reflection might tell him," Arvin interposes, "that all this building and bartering, though certainly the necessary basis, was *only* the basis for a civilized life; and he might come to see that its questions were anything but democratic in their effects."[114] At the same time, however, Arvin saw in Whitman a social critic aware that "'there are hundreds and thousands of men who go on from year to year with their pitiful schemes of business and profit, and wrapped up and narrowed down in those schemes, they never think of pleasant and beautiful capacities that God has given them.'"[115] While Whitman might "cling to his petty bourgeois ideal of a world of small owners," moreover, his poetry forbids all "doubt that the drift of his work as a writer was violently against a crass possessiveness."[116] Whitman, who once reported in a notebook his awareness of a dispositional shift—"'*a new feeling* a profound & tender enthusiasm for the people, & especially for the poorer & less favored & educated masses'"—wanted his poetry to reinforce "'the great pride of man in himself.'"[117] When all was said and done, however, the poet who once planned to write a work entitled "Songs of Insurrection" was well aware that "the actual tendencies of American economy were threatening the political and social program of democracy"[118] and that "the process of getting ahead in the world" was "an appalling waste of priceless hours and beautiful faculties."[119] "He was a heretic," Arvin asserts, "in that bourgeois carnival, say what he might."[120]

Whitman's apparent contradictions in relation to capitalism were, for Arvin, also America's: just as Whitman sought "to reconcile democracy and economic individualism,"[121] so those around him strove to balance "both the middle-class contentedness of the century's end and the surviving strains of petty bourgeois radicalism which rumbled beneath it."[122] Given that Whitman's conflicts were ultimately historical, Arvin could no more reconcile them than could Whitman, nor could he settle the question of the poet's socialism, at least insofar as men like Dell and Van Doren understood the term. Instead, Arvin worked to redefine socialism in relation to Whitman's innovative aesthetics. For Arvin, this entailed a three-part process, each of which is part conventional materialism and part the imaginative idealism expressed through Whitman's sexual poetics. First, socialism's goal is not comfortable consensus but a productive conflict that requires citizens to take rational positions and to develop the negotiating skills required to debate and, if possible, resolve conflict when positions clash. Second, those skills are imaginative: resolution will not come by attacking another's beliefs but by imagining third options that combine aspects of each position without replicating its shortcomings (for Whitman, this was the work of "free verse," which could "contain multitudes" and their contradictions). Finally, resolution comes not through enforced consensus but through enlarged fellow feeling, a bond made *through* difference, that is always, for Whitman, erotic. Arvin tells us that for Whitman it is only through conflict, imagination, and community that we can achieve "radical democracy,"[123] not "rational or programmatic" but "personal, naïve, concrete, and intimate."[124] Such a vision, as Whitman expresses in *Democratic Vistas*, "is mainly ethical and cultural; and almost its leading thought is the relative insignificance of political mechanisms in the building up of a full democratic life."[125] What Arvin calls Whitman's "ethics of socialism, with its rejection of the fixed, the final, and the static, and its assertion of the reality of time, the value of struggle, and the dignity of conscious development,"[126] was Arvin's ideal of a queer and socialist humanism.

Among the struggles Arvin saw in Whitman's poetry was a conflict between centuries, in which the eighteenth-century Enlightenment battled a vulgar nineteenth-century American Romanticism for expression in Whitman's aesthetics. This conflict represents a tension within

Arvin's own outlook between the scientific rationalism characteristic of progressive liberals of his generation (as discussed in the previous chapter) and his attraction to the illogical and fantastical aesthetics he admired in the nineteenth-century authors he studied. While liberals took the Enlightenment as the apex of human civilization, its scientific rationalism authorized the legal, psychiatric, and educational authorities that repeatedly threatened the well-being of Arvin and other Cold War dissidents. In response to those authorities, Arvin turned to the otherworldliness of Romanticism, but he knew that it fuels the excesses of American capitalism and the politics it generates. While Arvin never articulated this tension—much less its resolution—in terms of his own time, he addressed it directly in Whitman's and found in the poet a synthesis of the two that allows for a humanized rationality and a restrained Romanticism, a combination essential for a democratic aesthetic.

Whitman's concept of productive conflict was, for Arvin, his inheritance from the eighteenth century and its Enlightenment trust in rational public debate. Only that rationalism could check Americans' "undernourished sensibilities and over-disciplined emotions" in full "revolt against the humanistic rationalism of the previous century."[127] Without that restraint, Americans gave vent to "bias and desire and 'purpose,'" to "all possible sources of subjective error,"[128] all of which threatened the viability of what Jürgen Habermas calls rational-critical debate and all that "make[s] dynamic" the material conditions of public life. Only through rational debate, Whitman believed, could a right understanding of human society come about, and his poetry, which presents no ideological position without also airing its counterposition, "bringing many contradictory or apparently contradictory thoughts, feelings, and perceptions somehow into creative focus," turned rational conflict from a disharmonious threat to an enlivening poetics comprising "the most elastic dialectical fullness."[129]

Whitman knew, however, that public debate did not always tend toward elasticity but could take the form of dogmatic entrenchment and a panicked rush to consensus. Nineteenth-century America, Whitman saw, was losing the capacity "to maintain the intellectual and philosophic gains of its great century, the eighteenth," not only because it was too Romantic but because public debate had failed "to enrich, to humanize, to make dynamic, that bold if too mechanistic materialism it had attained during the Enlightenment."[130] Compromise was becoming increasingly impossible between "faith and knowledge."[131] Public life tended only toward comfort, complacency, and harmony, typically taken as signs of public health, but Whitman understood these as profoundly antidemocratic. Arvin notes, "However much others might hold up peace," it was Whitman's "intention to hold up agitation and conflict. 'As for me,' he once wrote, 'I love scheming, wrestling, boiling-hot days.'"[132] "To young Walt Whitman," Arvin observes, "the turbulence of democracy in action—the vulgar turbulence, as fine gentlemen called it—was a sublime spectacle, and he threw himself into the fray with a whole heart."[133]

Although Enlightenment values are superior to the Romantic irrationality characteristic of Whitman's day, therefore, *some* version of Romanticism is necessary to keep public life humanistic, in the fullest and most disruptive sense of what human life comprises. If adherents to Romanticism were "crying down logic and analysis and 'exact demonstration' more and more truculently," theirs were also "the voices that rose more and more bravely in behalf of feeling and imagination."[134] At the same time that he maintained the eighteenth century's faith in rational debate, then, Whitman was ultimately in "the camp of the romantic idealists,"[135] his "natural allegiance to an idealistic ethic and the free, beneficent, disinterested career of the creative artist."[136] From Romanticism Whitman drew his most characteristic features: "Freshness of feeling, certainly, unguardedness in expression, boldness and bigness in work-making, enthusiasm for daring and heroic action, contempt for mere prudence and calculation,"[137] all of which culminate in "that weird, wild, perverse style of his."[138] For Whitman, this Romantic strain, generating "something more radical, more personal, more livable,"[139] was also necessary to democracy, arising from "thousands of ordinary Americans with whom his fellow-feeling was more instinctive,"[140] and this camaraderie—not official representations of "the people" and their issues—led him to reject even those bold public pronouncements with which he agreed if tainted by a "supercilious disdain for average, ordinary people."[141] Just as Enlightenment reason turns Americans from their excessive emotionalism, the potential sterility of public debate is enlivened by "the marvelous, the picturesque, the half-incredible."[142] Arvin contends, "Wonder and reverence and a mystical faith that based itself upon them, this—and not respect for demonstrable fact—was what" Whitman revered.[143]

It was not simply that his materialism and his Romanticism remain compartmentalized in Whitman's poetry. Rather, the "marvelous" and "half-incredible" produced social possibilities—new forms of alliance, of pleasure, and of justice—that take citizens from their overadherence to the already-seen, motivating them to build something new from the ideas generated in public debate. Although the "muffling and soothing idealism which became the literary habit of his time" often closed Whitman's ears "to much of the appeal that socialism might have made to him,"[144] the poet also combined rationality and Romanticism to form "a vital materialism"[145] that suffused socialism not only with the lived productions of labor but also with fantasy, desire, emotion, and wonder—the very things Van Doren and his circle invoked to disqualify Whitman's socialism—in ways that made Whitman's "imaginative sympathy"[146] more humanist and very queer. For Arvin, the salient fact of Whitman's imaginative collectivism was its origins in "Whitman's own urgent, passionate need—despite his love of independence—for sympathy and friendship, for the physical presence of crowds, for intimate and affectionate association with his fellows, for the vital sense of participation in a common life."[147] For Arvin, that drive toward social intimacy is not, like much Romantic sentiment, "flickering, fanciful, metaphorical, and transient, any more than it is something base and sin-ridden"; rather, "it is a thing immitigably real and good and lasting, adequate in itself to all the physical and spiritual needs of man."[148]

Arvin emphasized that the "passionate need" that gave rise to this communal vision was, for Whitman, primarily sexual. "'Children of Adam' chants," Arvin recognized, "for the express purpose of revindicating, in the teeth of all corrupt asceticism, the dignity—he himself said rather the 'sacredness'—of the human body, and the high worth—he himself said even the 'divinity'—of all its functions and acts."[149] Contradicting Van Doren's claim that a poetics derived from homosexuality has nothing to teach to the "normal" man or woman, Arvin asserts that, throughout *Leaves of Grass*, the "line that can be drawn between the normal and the abnormal, through a real one, is at best an uncertain and somewhat arbitrary line, drawn rather for practical convenience than for the sake of absolute distinctions, and it is one of the profoundest lessons of modern mental science that the extreme abnormalities are only exaggerations, distortions, unhealthy over-growths of the most normal traits and tendencies."[150] Anticipating Alfred Kinsey's findings, Arvin identifies "the warm fraternal emotions that are not only latent but active and efficient among average men"[151] and asserts, "There is, so to say, a harmless, wholesome, sane 'homosexuality' that pervades normal humanity as the mostly powerless bacilli of tuberculosis appears in the healthiest of lungs."[152] Unlike Hawthorne, who cowered in secret embarrassment, Whitman proved that attraction is not destiny but that we are free to follow the poet who "delighted without shame"[153] and turn whatever is apparently "eccentric or anti-social"[154] into a shameless proclivity for imaginative public delight. Such proclivities—akin to what I am calling dispositions—are essential to "common living in a society from which arbitrary distinctions and the privileges of caste and fortune have been banished."[155] As Whitman demonstrated in the Calamus poems, "essentially, no other bond than this bond of sentiment and emotion would effectually unify the society of the future,"[156] generating "a humanistic emotion."[157] From his experience "of friendship, of neighborliness, of union, of companionship,"[158] Whitman forged an ethos "of tenderness, of affectionate sympathy, of benevolence, of good-natured companionableness," a poetics "of participation, . . . of common work, of common play, of common struggles, of common aspirations."[159] Whitman expressed to Traubel his fondness for "'solidarity, intercalation . . . all together, all nations—the globe: intercalation, fusion, no one left out.'"[160] "What really interests us in Whitman," Arvin concludes,

> is not that he was a homosexual, but that unlike the vast majority of inverts, even of those creatively gifted, he chose to translate and sublimate his strange, anomalous emotional experience into a political, a constructive, a democratic program. In doing so, he made himself the voice of something far larger and more comprehensive than his own private sensibility, and this in a manner that is not at all necessarily invalidated by the facts of that sensibility.[161]

Responding to Van Doren on Whitman's behalf, Arvin snaps, "'We could not be like him if we would,' says Mr. Van Doren: so much the worse for us if we cannot be like Whitman the citizen, the neighbor, the friend."[162]

Despite his obvious admiration for Whitman, however, Arvin ultimately faults the poet for not subjecting his idealism to a dispositional discipline. He believed that Whitman's idealism could turn facile, the poet too often believing "that with social and with ethical and metaphysical questions it was unnecessary to subject oneself to any difficult discipline of study and analysis; that here, too, one could safely rely upon feeling and intuition."[163] Optimism cannot exist without critical thinking, and Arvin found in Whitman a too "breezy illogicality"[164] and "the germs of a lethal obscurantism."[165] The "backward drift of his idealism,"[166] unchecked by critical analysis, too often led him "away from the realistic, the demonstrable, the purely natural, and toward the wishful, the unarguable, the dimly and cloudily mystical."[167] Above all, while Whitman goes far beyond Hawthorne's closet, he perpetuates an apparent choice between a sexual companionship restricted to the couple or a broad fellow feeling cleansed of its sexual impulse. While Whitman usefully demonstrates "how all the strong instinctive powers, all the fine natural responsiveness of bodily life can be endowed with plastic and imaginative value by the secular poet,"[168] his translation of bodily instinct into imaginative value seems to make their coexistence impossible. For this tempering of breezy Romanticism with open-eyed criticism, Arvin turned to Melville, the exemplar, in Arvin's trilogy, of queer humanism.

Against Hawthorne, with his often antisocial cynicism, and Whitman, with his too-breezy optimism, Melville was Arvin's ideal of "a romantic idealist with a passion for actuality," a writer possessed of a "critical imagination" who still maintained "a strong intuition of human solidarity as a priceless good."[169] More than any other writer of the nineteenth century, Melville possessed what Arvin calls "double vision," the position of those who, sympathizing with the abject and their insights into the operations of unjust power, nevertheless live in a world structured for and by the instruments of that power.[170] For Melville, however, such doubleness became the ideal position from which to formulate a critical hopefulness, at once confident in the transformative powers of human collectivity and keenly aware of the obstacles of bullying individualism and artificial cultural difference that must be worked through, meticulously and often painfully, before idealism can do its work in the world.

Melville, Arvin believed, was as much an idealist as Whitman, suffusing his Romantic allegories with "a democratic and humanistic reference"[171] while "struggling to avoid 'a brutality of indiscriminate skepticism.'"[172] Melville's early religious schooling, Arvin contends, taught him that "beyond all the apparent formlessness, wildness, and anarchy of experience, there was an ultimate Rationality, an absolute order and purpose, in the knowledge of which one could reassuringly abide," and that "beyond all the moral and physical evil in human affairs, beyond wickedness and suffering, there was an absolute Goodness or Justice on which one could unquestionably rely."[173] At the same time, Arvin recognizes in Melville a "tiger-pit of emotionality,"[174] a "restless, excitable, mercurial, and experimental"[175] temperament arising from "skepticism, humorous contempt, and the anger of an outraged sense of right."[176] Plagued by "doubt and anxiety,"[177] keenly aware "of the full and anguished consciousness of modern man,"[178] Melville, unlike Whitman, realized the uselessness of "avoiding the clash between consciousness and the unconscious, between mind and emotion, between anxious doubt and confident belief, but in confronting these antinomies head-on and, hopefully, transcending them—in that direction, as Melville intuitively saw, lay his right future as an adult person."[179] Melville remained, for Arvin, a dedicated humanist and a true socialist, aware of the realities of human brutality and kindness, knowledge he acquired by "rubbing shoulders with the brutalized, exploited, and mostly illiterate seamen of the merchant vessel."[180]

The "actualities of the human struggle"[181] were not all Melville learned from such rubbings, however. For Arvin, Melville's socialism is most admirable for having its ultimate source in the author's "strong, deflected sexuality."[182] Unlike Whitman's confident awareness of his same-sex attractions, Melville, Arvin observes, maintained an "unperceiving perception" of his homosexuality,[183] combining in his consciousness the knowing ignorance constitutive of the open secret. Nevertheless, from Melville's early works, obsessed with "a Greeklike cult of physical love" and "a frank and astonishingly free celebration of the power of a Polynesian Eros, an unashamed and sometimes orgiastic sexuality,"[184] to the later romances depicting an "unappeased, perhaps unappeasable, but never quite abandoned reaching out for the perfect mutuality of an ideal friendship,"[185] Melville remained preoccupied with "that easy, youthful, irresponsible, bachelor association with his own sex that was clearly necessary to him."[186] In "After the Pleasure Party," Melville states, "One's sex asserts itself," and this is certainly true of his romances, which, for Arvin, are continually "confessing the ambiguity of his feelings toward his own sex and the opposite sex,"[187] turning "the theme of repressed sexuality and the vengeance it takes on life and spirit"[188] into "the central fact behind his work."[189]

Few critics in 1950 were as well positioned to discern that theme in Melville's work as Arvin, who, as a professor at a women's college in a relatively remote and conservative Massachusetts town, struggled for years to maintain an active sex life, including a long relationship with the novelist Truman Capote. What drew Arvin to Melville, arguably, was not simply Melville's use of sexual themes, however, but the persistence with which he advanced from the "vengeance" of repression to the hopeful solidarity of what Arvin called "radical democracy." *Moby-Dick*, for Arvin, is an allegory of the heroic resilience of a "sensitive imagination, enriched by the humanities of romantic idealism," struggling "against the ruinous individualism of the age."[190] The latter is, for Arvin, represented by the quintessential "modern man," Ahab, "forcible will and unbending purpose all compact, inflexible, unpitying, and fell, but enlarged by both his vices and his strength to dimensions of legendary grandeur."[191] Ahab, in Arvin's reading, "has refused to accept the interdependence that is the condition of genuinely human existence,"[192] and therefore wins not independence but "isolation; and, since he is after all human, it is unendurable."[193] Ahab's inhumane individualism is countered, for Arvin, by Ishmael's embodiment of "a singular intensity of sentiment and tenderness,"[194] a disposition that inspires his belief in "an all-embracing love"[195] that proves to be his salvation. Love, as Arvin understood, was neither free of risk nor conducive to romantic freedom, but its importance comes from the limitations it visibly places on free will. Making Ishmael keenly aware of his dependence, for good or ill, "on the mistakes and the misfortunes of other men," love proves the surest instrument of material humanism, of critical hopefulness, generating in Melville's great romance "the creative dependency of fraternal emotion that prevails."[196]

Although Melville claimed that he "was neither an optimist nor a pessimist,"[197] Arvin's careful redefinition of hopefulness through a mixture of Emersonian askesis and 1930s socialism brings forth a writer whose faith in "a democratic humanism" was acutely critical, incessantly imaginative, and thrillingly hopeful. Melville's was not a conventional socialism but combined an "indictment of arbitrary political power and an inhumane or rigidified inequality" with a repudiation of "a cluster of delusions and inessentials that, as he felt, had got themselves entangled into the idea of democracy in American minds: the delusion that political and social freedom is an ultimate good, however empty of content; that equality should be a literal fact as well as a spiritual ideal; that physical and moral evil are rapidly receding before the footsteps of Progress."[198] Above all, Melville understood that hopefulness is hard work; as Arvin observes, Melville's later novels represent the most admirable efforts of "toilsome recuperation."[199] Arvin writes of Melville's last hero, Billy Budd, that his is "not mere blank innocence; it is an active and disarming *good nature*."[200] Active good nature is another way of describing a dispositional practice of hope, which must be daringly imaginative as well as critical, for "after the doubts of adolescence and the disbelief that follows them, one comes to rest at last in 'manhood's pondering repose of If.'"[201] Only through the hard work of that If, what Arvin describes as Melville's exhausted but unexpired "Yea-saying of the most reserved and melancholy sort,"[202] can we arrive at the combination of unprecedented invention and already-existing human possibility that, Arvin believed, was Melville's lifelong goal: an "unwarlike, undistinguished, unhistoried, tranquil human living."[203]

At the start of *Whitman*, Arvin engages in a moment of speculation, asserting, "The clearer it becomes that the next inevitable step in human history is the establishment and construction of a socialist order, the more interested every thoughtful man is in scanning the work of writers and artists of the recent past for whatever resources there may be in it on which a socialist culture may draw."[204] For Arvin, that "recent past" was American Romanticism, which he felt was returning to American literature in his own day with positive results. Arvin wrote to Daniel Aaron in 1946 of his "preference for the 'new movement in writing' which was revealing itself . . . as (in some as yet undefined new sense) a romantic and even Gothic one, and . . . I am infinitely more at home in the midst of it than ever I was in the midst of the hard-boiled or the 'objective' or the tough-minded school of my own generation."[205] We "should be selling our birthright for a mess of feeble skepticism,"[206] Arvin believed, if we overlook that heritage of "everything enlightened, positive, hopeful, and human in our recent heritage. We should feel this," he insists, "if only because the ugly menace of decivilization presses upon us,"[207] threatening the queer humanism of Whitman, Hawthorne, and Melville.

Discernible through Arvin's readings of Hawthorne, Whitman, and Melville, as the preceding sections show, is a critical disposition that became a practice of hope. Yet that practice had its flaws. Chief among those is Arvin's tendency to conflate "socialism" and "humanism." While the Frankfurt theorists brought the terms together to make each, as a distinct philosophy, modify the other, Arvin often used them interchangeably.[208] As a result, an important shift that occurs between *Whitman* and *Herman Melville* is almost imperceptible. Arvin's emphasis in the former is on socialism, his argument being that Whitman's robust sexuality enabled him to imagine collectivities devoted to economic and social equality, or what Arvin calls "radical democracy." In his study of Melville, however, the balance between sexuality and solidarity reversed: the collectives Melville imagined served the goal of healthy sexuality (primarily the author's), and not the other way around. The equality established by groups like the *Pequod* crew remained important to Arvin, to be sure, but as a sign of "human solidarity" as a "priceless good" for its own sake, not as a means toward larger social change. A subtle effect of this shift is discernible in Arvin's depiction of politics. In *Whitman* an erotics of social engagement generated unpredictable, messy, lopsided positions that made clear-cut distinctions between complicity and opposition hard to maintain. In Arvin's treatment of Melville, however, politics are contained within (what the critic presents as) the logic of the text (man versus abstract "structures" or "systems"), making attention to the complexities of human motives and practices unnecessary. This shift in perspective is not altogether surprising, given the two books' dates. In the 1930s, when Arvin wrote *Whitman*, he was still active in movement politics, whereas by 1950 the fears generated by HUAC and other agencies of

Cold War state homophobia (such as the state troopers who arrested him for lewdness ten years later) had made the protective maintenance of psychological well-being a primary and often exclusive goal, particularly for homosexuals.[209] Even for critics not so directly threatened by Cold War normalcy, such as Lionel Trilling and Richard Chase, Freud became more essential than Marx with the result that human nature trumped social relations as a critical preoccupation. One sign of Cold War melancholy is the persistence of Arvin's (and many of his contemporaries') later conception of politics, in which easily distinguishable and abstracted forces contend in skirmishes subject to the controlling power of both author and critic; as a result, the critic's satisfaction in discerning recognizable yet previously obscured patterns that confirm what the critic already believes becomes the objective. Critics today reach for ever-expanding, purportedly descriptive, and clearly differentiated abstractions, losing in the process the complex imbrications of resistance and complicity, and ignoring—or disparaging—local forms of struggle that show how muddy and slippery the political terrains can be. It is not that literature, then or now, has an imperative responsibility to transparently represent "real life" or that representation does not perform a social engagement of its own. The point is that Arvin, like many after him, came to conceive politics as too simple, clean, and modest in terms of social (or representational) goals.

Criticism today goes even further than Arvin did, sacrificing not only socialism (at least as Arvin imagined it in *Whitman*—embodied, local, and without clear heroes and villains) but also humanism (as Arvin pictured it in *Herman Melville*, as a "priceless good"). Universal constructs like "human nature" are anathema, usually (but perhaps not always) rightly so. And when we focus on affect, we tend to move to cruelty, depression, shame, and grief, all of which are important emotions deserving careful critical attention, but hardly the full range of human affects. About others—compassion, generosity, happiness, or, central to this book, hopefulness, the ones on which Arvin continued to focus—we have less to say, even though, as Arvin's treatment of the three authors shows, these have a good deal to do with understanding both social life and textual politics. I think the loss of humanism is unfortunate, not because I want criticism to be more upbeat or to focus on humans at the expense of the nonhuman world, but because we have much to learn from humanism about supporting struggle when outcomes are uncertain and strengthening the imagination needed to picture the possible worlds envisioned in human ideals. Humanism, as Arvin knew, is not only critically productive but also essential, as he put it, "in our own guilt-ridden and anxious time,"[210] when cynicism has rendered risible any attachment to socialism *or* humanism. Arvin, however, never lost sight of the important psychological, spiritual, and social work done by humanism, especially in the face of devastation, disappointment, and dishonor. Rather, he turned it into a critical philosophy that made explicit how reading and teaching become practices of hope.

That philosophy is most evident in an unpublished manifesto, "The Grounds of Literary Judgment," based on lectures delivered in 1952 to Smith College undergraduates. In those lectures Arvin sets forth evaluative criteria based on social and critical generosity, assuming that literature "should not be thought of as wholly independent of moral and intellectual implications."[211] Literary judgment, in Arvin's account, involves three components: subject matter, "consistency," and emotional tone, which together form what Arvin calls literature's "dimensionality."[212] Reading in the way Arvin instructs his undergraduates changes dispositions, becoming the "threshold" between "the cant of pessimism" and a "twice-born" hopefulness built upon human compassion, love, and humane identification.

In his discussion of content Arvin moves from didactic moral subject matter to stimulations of readers' sensations that create forms of consciousness disposed to generosity and compassion. On the simplest level, Arvin claims that good writers conceive people to be "'better rather than worse.'"[213] He turns away, however, from comedy or epic, with their triumphant resolutions, in favor of "the *complexity of the moral issues*" typical of tragedy. That genre is not "so much a matter of showing a simple conflict between perfect good and absolute evil," Arvin contends, "as it is a matter of exhibiting conflicts between (or within) imperfect embodiments of good and evil."[214] Unlike Cold War oppositions between absolute virtue and villainy, Arvin offers tragedy as "the spectacle of human beings suffering in ways that cannot be said to be wholly deserved, and sometimes they are hardly deserved at all."[215]

The moral complexities of literary and social judgments not only warn against occupying positions of unimplicated discernment but also initiate what Arvin calls "a process of *identification*."[216] Such identifications are not only with suffering but also with the transformation of pain through wonder. The previous chapter suggests that allegory suffuses the everyday world with *beyondness*, an ineffable significance that gives material existence an aura of immanent revelation. For Arvin, a similar phenomenon takes on moral implications when tragic identification activates the universal in the particular, and vice versa. "What you get in literature when it rises above a certain level," Arvin writes, "is not simply the particular on the one hand or the general on the other, but the general *in* the particular, the permanent *in* the temporal, the intangible *in* the tangible."[217] The imbrications of the known and the infinite become social, as Arvin explains, when they achieve "a very special balance or fusion of the new and the strange with the old and the recognizable."[218] Without sacrificing the "old and recognizable" that can serve as points of entry for the reader, a literary experience introduces the "strange" into the familiar, suggesting that what is considered customary already contains the uncanny possibility for its own beyondness, an experience of wonder that elides the Cold War era's Manichaean logics of good and bad, insider and enemy.

Arvin's account of his second criterion, consistency, is an argument for respecting difference. Arvin distinguishes the predictable trajectories of conventional fictions from "*imaginative logic*," which he defines as "consistency of development, fidelity to the governing spirit of the work and to the demands of imaginative probability."[219] Consistency is an unfamiliar faithfulness, a fidelity discernible not in the inevitabilities of conventional narrative but in the "author's attitude toward his materials, and the philosophical outlook which directs his handling of them."[220] Describing the imaginative logic of Thomas Hardy's fiction, for example, Arvin writes that "not everything that happens is inevitable, nor are all the ills from which the characters suffer irremediable." Rather, the "courage and the dignity with which Hardy's characters meet their afflictions, their resistance to defeat, deepens the significance of their author's portrayal of them."[221] In this understanding of literature, the juridical and medical fates that render persecutory outcomes unavoidable are interrupted and resilience enabled.

For Arvin, the most significant aspect of literature's "dimensional-ity" is the emotional identification awakened in the reader. Great litera-ture, Arvin states, stirs "a heightened, free, and intense experience"[222] through appeals to "a large body of significant experiences, ranging from bliss to loss, from hopelessness to utter love."[223] The progression of emotions Arvin names reproduces the course of Arvin's queer human-ism, in which the ecstasy of physical contact is matched by the equally overwhelming loss caused by imperative conventions, and the resultant hopelessness is in turn transformed into the "utter love" enabled by social solidarity. This dynamic animates what Arvin describes as the center of great literature, the "love relation," which goes beyond "the primitive sexual drive" (although that is part of the experience) to an experience of "love, tenderness, and devotion"[224] that is the heart of the camaraderie Arvin admired in Melville's work. Immediately following love, however, Arvin moves to fear in "its countless shades of intensity" and from there to pity and compassion, which he describes as "seri-ous or profound" emotions.[225] This progression from love to fear to pity increases readers' sensitivity to "afflictions," inspiring the same state of wonder that arises from the intermixing of the particular and universal. In the case of emotion, "great works give their readers an impression of *inexhaustibleness*."[226] This is the condition of beyondness that arouses not the objectivity necessary to judgment or even to forgiveness but to the condition of continual possibility necessary to hope without the promise of utopian satisfaction.

Arvin performed the theory of literary judgment he developed in his Smith lectures in his last critical study of nineteenth-century literature, *Longfellow: His Life and Work* (1963). In that monograph, Arvin defends Longfellow's reputation and demonstrates his compassionate identifica-tion with the psychologically troubled poet. The critic knew well, by the end of his life (*Longfellow* was published the year of Arvin's death), what depression and the loss of reputation feel like; as a result, he knew the urgent need for the values he claimed literary judgment could foster. It is possible to read *Longfellow* as a defense of his own depression and a repudiation of the authorities that ruined his career. Readers of a 1963 newspaper article connecting Newton Arvin with references to "certain so-called 'psychosomatic' difficulties" including an "obsessive preoccupation with suicide," to "neuroses" arising from a "crisis" in sexuality, and to misinterpretations of "evidence" making for a weak "defense" exacerbated by "confessional" and "self-exhorting qualities" in the defendant, all leading to a "tarnished reputation," might have imagined the subject under discussion was Arvin himself.[227] Despite its use of the legal and psychomedical discourses that seem to characterize Arvin's end, however, the *New York Times* article in question, "A Tarnished Reputation Reappraised," by Lawrence Thompson, was a review of *Longfellow*. The review indicates that the implications of Arvin's critical practice of hope extend beyond his biography to counter the Cold War ideologies that allowed those sad events to unfold. Even if Thompson was unfamiliar with Arvin's story, his terminology typified literary criticism in the early 1960s, which had absorbed the state-sanctioned logics of "healthy" sexual and social conformity, making the humanism Arvin advocated in *Longfellow*, as he had in his previous monographs, as suspect as Arvin's life.

On a more fundamental level, Thompson's review, which faults Arvin for not making more of Longfellow's hardships, represents its era's expectation that texts "reveal" psychological "depth," especially when that textual "unconscious" reflects what Arvin called "the cant of pessimism." Arvin's analysis of Longfellow is flawed, according to Thompson, because it overlooks references in the poetry to Longfellow's mental distress and fails to realize "Longfellow's repeated tendency to use his art as a conscious and deliberate form of psychotherapy for himself."[228] It is unlikely that Arvin, who wrote several books of psychobiographical literary criticism in no small part to release himself from severe depression, would have "missed" these aspects of Longfellow's work. Rather, I believe Arvin grew uneasy with offering distress, despair, and pessimism as proof of a writer's worth. Arvin does not ignore Longfellow's pain, but he does not privilege it as the "meaning" of the poems. And far from overlooking the poet's willed dispositional movement from depression to hope, Arvin not only describes that transformation but *enacts* it in an exercise in critical judgment consistent with his Smith lectures.

The hopefulness underlying Arvin's study is clear in the poem he offers as proof of Longfellow's capacity for literary greatness. In "The Light of Stars," the narrator addresses Mars in the night sky:

> The star of the unconquered will,
> He arises in my breast,
> Serene, and resolute, and still,
> And calm, and self-possessed.

The poem concludes:

> And thou, too, whosoe'er thou art,
> That readest this brief psalm,
> As one by one thy hopes depart,
> Be resolute and calm.

> Oh, fear not in a world like this,
> And thou shall know erelong,
> Know how sublime a thing it is
> To suffer and be strong.

Longfellow offers a lesson in resilience, "To suffer and be strong" even "in a world like this." The critic similarly contends that reading and writing literature are determined responses to pain and depression; he presents Longfellow as "a representative American liberal of his generation, hopeful, humane, generous, and idealistic."[229]

Like Arvin's earlier monographs, *Longfellow* offers a tutorial on critical disposition that demonstrates the relative value and implications of dismissive or hopeful reading. Arvin was moved to write the book to counter Longfellow's "ostracism"[230] from the canon by critics who dismissed him as a minor poet. That judgment came from a range of critical methodologies, from the Marxism of Calverton and Hicks, writing in "a period in which one could [not] expect that even-handed justice would be done to a poet so largely nonpolitical as Longfellow,"[231] to the New Critics, whose professed interest in "close reading and textual analysis" became a rationale for sneering at Longfellow's "confessional directness."[232] Longfellow was least likely to thrive in his own age, Arvin charges, due to its Cold War insistence on suspicious exclusion. "Our own age," he says, is "dominated by" minds with "a strong bias toward elimination," noting that some great critical reputations have been based *partly* on the success with which the critics in question have shown reasons for holding on to as few writers in the past as possible. The passion for proscription, in literature as in other realms, is one of the prevailing passions of our time, and better writers, as well as worse writers, than Longfellow have found themselves on the lists of the proscribed.[233]

In response to the era's imperative to police, Arvin warns, "There is a danger in the habit of leaving out, just as in the habit of taking in,"[234] and he adds, "There is such a thing as a wholesome fear of losing something precious as well as of being deceived by something second-rate."[235] Expressing a hope that "we may well be moving into a period when . . . the case for inclusion may be heard more frequently than it has been for a long time,"[236] Arvin insists, "An eclectic taste is not inevitably promiscuous, and there is now a certain urgency in the necessity for restoring some damaged reputations" at a time when "the canon of acceptable writers has grown alarmingly small."[237]

To hasten that inclusiveness, Arvin offers a criticism based on clarity, directness, and generosity, the traits he most admired in Longfellow and that took on greater worth at a time when concealment and circumvention were imposed on gay men like Arvin. The critic knew all too well that critical tendencies toward accusing, judging, and expulsion had dangerous real-world correlatives. Instead, he imagined a criticism based on humanistic ideals, which he found in Longfellow's determination "to be sympathetic and descriptive rather than judicial or censorious, and to linger on excellences rather than defects."[238] Such a criticism would appreciate "the poetic virtues of directness, of simplicity in statement, of the incomplex [sic], of 'easiness' on a certain level."[239] In his way, Arvin, countering Cold War culture, anticipates the current turn away from suspicious reading practices that, as Stephen Best and Sharon Marcus contend, are based on "the assumption that domination can only do its work when veiled."[240] Sounding very much like Arvin in his defense of Longfellow, critics dissatisfied with critical suspicion have turned to description and textual surfaces in the belief that literary texts "can themselves indicate important and overlooked truths"[241] Humanism tempered Arvin's turn toward surfaces, however, in ways that distinguish him from theorists today who counter suspicion by overinvesting in critical objectivity, bolstered by strong identification with the social sciences. Neither suspicious nor surface reading imagines criticism as an act of identification; Arvin, however, considered his empathy with

Longfellow as central to his humanistic criticism, in which the "truths" reflected by textual surfaces are not "factual" in the sense of being detached from the needs, ideals, and principles held by readers as well as writers but are imaginative utterances of forthrightly held values of generosity, compassion, and sympathy.

Conceived this way, criticism was not, for Arvin, suspicious, judgmental, or objective but "exuberantly 'appreciative'; unapologetically imaginative or fanciful; sometimes dramatic, sometimes pictorial; sometimes charmingly allusive or metaphorical."[242] The criticism Arvin advocates for is not blindly optimistic but rests on the willed conversion of pain into wonder, a transformation enabled by the sensations inspired in readers by literary dimensionality. Longfellow, in Arvin's account, was just such a figure. He experienced "bereavement, frustration, loneliness, or just 'causeless' dejection,"[243] being "by no means free from the painful and problematic complexities that are the familiar penalty of fine gifts."[244] But by reading and writing literature Longfellow moved beyond "a bearable despondency";[245] poised "between the confession of suffering and the voice of the resisting will,"[246] the poet refused to "make a coherent world-view out of his sufferings." Rather, Longfellow opposed hopelessness with "a doctrine of earnest struggle, of courageous resolution, of cheerful and productive action,"[247] and his accomplishments were not temperamental characteristics but *willed* actions. His "resolute hopefulness" arose from the "conscious effort and self-discipline"[248] that gave rise to William James's twice-born soul. That his hopefulness was strengthened by intense male friendships, feeding and protecting a nature "tenderer, more vulnerable, more exposed to injury than most men's,"[249] made Longfellow the combination of Hawthorne's refusal of solitary suffering, Whitman's exuberant self-affirmation, and Melville's redemptive camaraderie, and thus the exemplar of Arvin's queer humanism. And Longfellow's failures—those moments when he was unable to produce the hopefulness that, for Arvin, was his strength, are evidence of an inhospitable social environment that privileged conformity over eccentricity, unfeeling competition over compassion, and easily attainable success over imaginative striving. If Longfellow "sometimes essayed to do a larger kind of thing than his gifts warranted," it is his aspirations, not their execution, that should be judged.[250]

We might say the same for Arvin and his aspirations. The power of Arvin's imaginative idealism, grounded in the qualities he considered essential to social resilience and compassion, exerted on some readers the kind of sensational transformation he attributed to Longfellow's poetry and, in his Smith lectures, to humanist interpretation. One of the pioneering scholars of gay literary study, Robert K. Martin, testified to the impact of Arvin's scholarship on his life and work. In reading Arvin, Martin learned the simultaneity of shame and strength, defeat and determination, central to critical practices of hope. Sounding very much like Arvin defending Longfellow against critical dismissal, Martin, in an act of compassionate identification, frames his account of Arvin's influence on him this way:

> I write this story in order to render justice to Arvin's career, to pay tribute to all of those who suffered because of the raids in Northampton, to try to help prevent it happening again. But I will also write this because of the shock of recognition I felt in the fall of 1960, when I knew that in some sense this was my life. I will write it because I promised myself then that it would not happen to me, at least not in that way, because I would not ever give them the pleasure of discovering a secret that was available for anyone to see. Newton Arvin's career came to an end, and its end helped me come out. I have hoped since then that my practice as a critic might be worthy of following in the tradition he established, and that my life might be one that he was never able to know.[251]

Martin, who like Arvin turned to Melville to tell the story of the hopefulness of male intimacy, made from his predecessor a usable past in which Arvin, stating ideals—even those he could not quite live up to—allowed Martin to articulate his in the hypothetical ("might be") of his final, moving aspiration.[252]

When I was a graduate student at Columbia in the mid-1980s, trying to figure out how to do criticism as a gay man, particularly one studying in a deeply homophobic academic environment in a city devastated by AIDS, I invited Martin to campus to give a lecture. After he delivered part of what became *Hero, Captain, and Stranger*, his study of homoeroticism in Melville, the faculty in the audience fired one hostile and dismissive question after another, while Martin, calm and dignified, answered as if the questions were asked with earnest curiosity. Afterward he took me out for a hamburger and said, "I think that went OK." It had. Because when my professors tried to subject Martin to the treatment Arvin had received, he refused to "give them the pleasure of discovering a secret that was available for anyone to see." Years later, at a conference on nineteenth-century American literature held in Northampton, where I was sitting with Martin at an outdoor café, he pointed out across the street the door to the public lavatory where Arvin used to cruise. It was a bittersweet moment, for Martin and I had both delivered papers at the conference on queer Romanticism on the Smith campus where Arvin had given his lectures on literary judgment and from which he had been expelled. But Arvin had inspired Martin, who in turn inspired me, and that chain of critical identifications had realized an unashamed criticism, a public male intimacy within sight of the police station, and a retrospective compassion that Arvin, even at his idealistic best, never imagined. That is what is possible when criticism is a practice of hope.

4

Symbolism

The Queerness of Symbols

Look back and you will see, drifting in and out of the books of history, appearing and vanishing in the memoirs of more aggressive and more acceptable minds, all manner of queer geniuses, wraith-like personalities that have left behind them sometimes a fragment or so that has meaning for us now, more often a mere eccentric name.
—Van Wyck Brooks, "On Creating a Usable Past"[1]

In James Merrill's epic poem, *The Changing Light at Sandover,* the poet intersperses his verse with the dictation he and his lover David Jackson take through a Ouija board from the chatty dead. The spirit visitors include several poets and novelists but only one literary critic, Marius Bewley, who is summoned by Merrill's "Where's Marius?"

> MY DEAR JAMES Is there an Athenian
> Club where you can get a drink and read
> The underground newspapers? O INDEED
> PLATO & WYSTAN ARE ITS CO-CHAIRPERSONS
> And Chester's Luca, still under Plato's wing?
> LUCA! CUT MY LACE THAT THAT THAT THING
> ROAMING HEAVEN LIKE A VAST STEAMROOM.[2]

Bewley, Merrill's charmingly catty guide to the homosexual afterlife, was while living known in gay circles for the parties he hosted, occasionally dressed in a cardinal's robe, at the Staten Island home he shared with his lover, an illustrator who reportedly hid penises in his pictures for children's books.[3] It was in the context of this camp demimonde that Merrill and Bewley became friends in the early 1950s.[4]

Among academics, however, Bewley was best known for his book *The Eccentric Design* (1959), an exploration of symbolism in the American novel. In that study, Bewley argues that symbolism, unlike the more conventional genre of allegory, is the startling infusion of the extraordinary into everyday life and therefore represents and engenders an instantaneous, unexpected, and vulnerable epiphany. Bewley's account of symbolism and allegory reverses that proposed by Richard Chase, in which allegory brings unsettling *beyondness* to the quotidian while symbolism bears the burden of conventional meanings. Though the terminology is inverted, what is significant for both critics is a similar outcome to literary form: the creation of a hopeful "world elsewhere" that corrects and renews social conventions in order to make a figurative place hospitable to the outcasts from Cold War America. Both critics describe literature as a forum in which explicit articulation of a text's ideals in content is matched by a circulation of sensation between text and reader that can generate the hopefulness necessary to initiate and continue the work of making imaginative realms. How and why literary form became a bracketed space within Cold War discourse, a "world" operating apart from social "reality," is the subject of this chapter.

Despite Bewley's antipathy to the genre, allegory may be the best way to understand his appearance in Merrill's poem. Auden's "co-chairperson" in the spiritual men's club is the original allegorist, Plato. Merrill's joining of the poet Auden and the allegorist Plato suggests that Merrill is offering an allegory *about* symbolism. I argued in the second chapter that Plato's Allegory of the Cave is a meta-allegory about the filtering of "reality" through images that may be interpreted, but never as transparent signifiers of a "meaning" apart from the reader's speculative constructions. Understood in this way, Merrill's poem is an allegory, in which symbols figure forth the afterlife, the quintessential shadowy world, which is knowable only *through* those symbols and hence is reliant for its shape on the reader's accumulation and shaping of projections into an imagined—but necessarily elusive—whole. That Merrill maintains the illusion of authenticity through the Ouija board, promising direct communication through the displaced form of letters, draws attention to our desire to find a directly accessible actuality beyond what remains symbolic form, first in the alphabet and then in the poem itself.

Merrill makes explicit, moreover, a connection that, I argued in my discussion of Richard Chase, could remain only implicit in Chase's use of allegory: the relationship between literary form and gay life, particularly as it was lived during the Cold War. Leaving aside the question of whether Plato's desire for Alcibiades justifies calling him "gay," Merrill's coupling of Plato and Auden, joining allegory and symbolism, at the same time makes the heavenly men's club they supervise a distinctly queer space. Literary form thus becomes simultaneous with a gay world in ways that fit the needs of gay life as it emerged in the context of the post–World War II "return to normalcy," when homosexuals found themselves figured as a disguised and predatory force scarcely less threatening to the American "way of life" than the Soviet Union.[5] To be against Joseph McCarthy, the senator once said, was to be either "a communist or a cocksucker."[6] Arthur Schlesinger Jr. described communism as "something secret, sweaty, and furtive like nothing so much, in the phrase of one wise observer of modern Russia, as homosexuals in a boy's school," while a 1950 Senate report entitled *Employment of Homosexuals and Other Sex Perverts in Government* claimed that "one homosexual can pollute a government office."[7] In that era, gay life, as I argued in the second chapter, *became* allegory, relying on signs that surface and vanish, accruing meaning only for those "in the know." The symbolic nature of gesture, tone, and location provided protection and communication, disguise and visibility. That paradox, intrinsic to allegorical reading, was literally policed by state homophobia, but it also, I have suggested, gave rise to the subcultural world of Cold War queer life. The irony is that men like McCarthy, believing that they could peer through seemingly insignificant surfaces to discover the subversive truth hidden beneath, missed the ways their efforts to create symbols only to discard them helped *create* gay life as the pure surface of symbolic form.

When the critic was himself gay, that thing to be revealed and denounced, the symbolic nature of gay life animated theories of literary form. For critics like Bewley, allegory and symbolism perform the relationship between meaning and text, reality and shadow, object and subject of observation. Those critics did not merely refuse the concept of a hidden meaning, a shameful displacement of the secret life of the closet, in favor of an elusively communicative surface, however. Rather, gay critics conceived of a speculative and idealistic *excess* of the literary surface, a reimagining of the confining space of alienation into a new realm of infinitely imaginative possibility. That realm, when given literary form, becomes what Chase calls "allegory" and Bewley terms "symbolism."

The first function of symbolism is to disguise, a service that suggests that literature, despite what I claim earlier, is for Bewley a surface obscuring a hidden truth. Indeed, protective masks were a way of life for many gay men and lesbians in Cold War America. At the same time, the mask may reflect as well as disguise, becoming in effect a mirror that turns back on them viewers' suspicious intrusions. For Bewley, symbolism, a mask that reflects another's desire, functions not only as self-protection, saying in shadows what cannot be spoken outright, but also as the refusal of suspicion. Reflecting this simultaneity of disguise and the epistemology of suspicion, Bewley titled a collection of his critical essays *Masks and Mirrors*.

The first essay in that volume, originally published in 1949 and titled "The Mask of John Donne," examines the conjuncture of symbolism and same-sex eroticism. In that essay, Bewley turns the hermeneutics of suspicion against heterosexuality, taking up Donne's love poems addressed to Elizabeth Drury, only to disparage them as halfhearted distractions from Donne's deeper interests. Where other critics saw erotic declarations, Bewley discerns a tonal dissonance that reveals Donne's lack of interest in sex. For Bewley, Donne's poetry demonstrates a "mood of cynicism in sexual matters"; he writes that "even when he appears to be most serious in his love poems, a sense of the hopelessness or feebleness of the experience frequently causes him to magnify it."[8] Although in Donne's love poems "the urgency behind them is expressed in sexual terms, the force is not concentrated there."[9] With characteristic wit, Bewley states that Donne's love poems "do not possess the object as much as they claw at it," and he concludes, "The real vigor of this poem arises from feelings that are ultimately beyond the realm of sex."[10] In previous criticism of Donne's poetry, Bewley contends, a heterosexist bias led critics to take surface content at face value, to see nothing on the surface but narrative statement, to read, in other words, mask as reality. Without such a bias, Bewley, alert to tonal undercurrents and the protective cover of what *appears* to be heterosexual love, recognizes the passionless sex of Donne's poetry as a subterfuge, just as it would have been for mid-century homosexuals sensitive to those attempting to pass as straight, a situation discernible only by those able to interpret the tone that belies appearances. Donne's less astute readers, "condemning Donne for a lapse of sincerity, or a failure of candor," were unable to understand the necessity of symbolic indirection, which far from a "failure" is Donne's exemplary modeling of how to create a public facade compelling enough that onlookers mistake self-protection for verisimilitude.[11] Masking is more than a form of the closet, however; it is also, for Bewley, a refusal of the suspicious gaze of either critics or state agents. As Bewley observes, "Donne's mask of impersonality is always so well maintained that it is difficult ever to penetrate it."[12] This difficulty generates the perspicuity of those who, like Donne, understand the need to disguise and protect a living passion that, if revealed directly, would result in persecution: "We may say that those 'who know they have one [a "rich soul"]'" persevere despite real or potential banishment.[13]

Understood as a necessary masking, then, Donne's lovers, Bewley insists, "light up the meaning but do not contribute to its substance."[14] The "substance" behind Donne's sexual content, Bewley says, was religious. Donne's poetry "may be read in a double, or even a triple, sense," Bewley writes, arguing that Donne's performance of frustrated sexual longing was a cover for his interest in Catholicism under the persecutory religious institutions of Elizabethan Anglicanism.[15] He reports that Donne "might have felt an overpowering compulsion to make such a concealed confession of his views about the world he lived in, and his relations with it."[16] Donne's masks were necessary, Bewley claims, for one who strove "to make his way in the world, without at the same time betraying his conscience and integrity more than absolutely necessary. The world being what it was in those days," Bewley observes with apparent empathy, "this was a tall order."[17] Bewley's empathy is also clear when he observes that the "peculiar difficulties" facing those who seek to avoid or survive persecution "have been paralleled in ours only on the political level, and even there, only during comparatively brief intervals of intensified suspicion and witch-hunting."[18] Bewley's, like Donne's, "was not a day for indiscretions and revelations."[19]

While his assertion of religion as the real meaning underlying a heterosexual cover seems to brush aside literary surface in favor of a more significant depth, Bewley's focus on ritual in the struggle between Catholicism and Anglicanism in Donne's world suggests otherwise. Meaning's depth resurfaces as ritual form, its symbolic surface being the only place where spirit is knowable. "The opening lines of *The First Anniversary* make it clear," Bewley writes, "that what we have to deal with is not a particular person, but an abstraction—a symbol of what at one moment appears to be the soul's interior awareness of its own spiritual possibilities, and a moment later, the objectification of those possibilities in terms of a theology."[20] Although the (sexual) body of Donne's content gives way to the (spiritual) interior of its "substance," that interior becomes evident only through the return of the body in ritual performance. The sexual tension between the poems' lovers—like the tension between heaven and earth or spirit and theology—can, Bewley insists, be "consummated and fulfilled only if they resort to their bodies."[21] In this account, Bewley's transformation of the sexual body into symbol does more than obscure or disguise; it produces "abstraction," an excess that transcends both surface and depth.

That "excess" soon becomes another layer of meaning, although one discernible neither in nor on a text but in the imaginative investment of readers. And that investment, for Bewley, comes from the combination of masking, mirroring, and ritual performance known particularly to gay men and lesbians. Paradoxically, given that he begins by turning Donne's heterosexual content into something metaphysical, the "third sense" he refers to in Donne's love poems may be once again sex, although of a decidedly nonheterosexual kind. Bewley hints at a sexuality that, beyond the animal urges that he associates with heterosexuality in Donne's poetry, represents "a function and fulfillment of his humanity."[22] To mask protectively is not, Bewley argues, to suppress "a kind of hot-breathed, almost repellant, intimacy" that "manages to get under the skin of impersonality"[23] and animates Donne's "tortured, theatrical, and perversely sincere"[24] qualities. Rather, behind the mask of passionless heterosexuality lies a faith banished from institutions and subject to persecution (the theological level of Donne's symbolism), yet surviving because of an animating series of affects, desires, and strategies. Claiming that Donne's "feelings," discerned through a doubly displaced symbolism, "are very like our own,"[25] Bewley seems to claim universality for not-quite-masked affects. Perhaps the audience he addresses with that "our" is more specific, however. For the hot-breathed and nervous feelings Bewley describes in Donne might characterize as well homosexuals at midcentury: "They make their appearances . . . and they retire—only to come forward again," visible only to the knowing who are sensitive to "the casual" and "the accidental."[26] For them, symbolism is not the surface or the depth but something more invested and inventive. And when Bewley, separating himself from other critics, invents from Donne's poetry the experience of both masking and mirroring, he becomes one of those readers who live as well as interpret symbolism.

My reading, like Bewley's, involves speculation, but whenever one reads symbols speculation is the point. Symbolism was, for Bewley, what I have called a practice of hope, deeply connected to dissatisfaction with claims to represent a singular authoritative truth, and to an awareness that below the surface lies not a truer truth but perpetual opportunity to speculate about what truth might look like from other perspectives and different epistemological methods. Symbolism is not simply content or form, then, but a way of reading, the result of which is not the satisfaction and finality of meaning but an invitation to imagine hopefully. Symbolism awakens a will to meaning that never rests. It is the holding open of an unending space where, as in Plato's cave, reality appears as shadows that, representing semblance infused with desire, become more ideal than the real they reflect and alter. Bewley's interpretation of Donne is animated, I believe, by an ideal of struggling faith, the inventive opportunity stretching beyond the real, resulting in "the revitalization of a language that was on the point of growing tired."[27] That is what makes symbolism, for Merrill and for Bewley, a queer practice of hope.

Speculation is essential to a symbolic experience because it turns the *is* into *not-yet*, a sensation that, for Bewley, is akin to revelation. That experience, in the context of symbolism, is not an unveiling from within but an active participation on the part of the reader, a practice rather than a passive reception. That practice was discouraged, in the 1950s, by an emerging technocracy that insisted on a clear opposition between rational empiricism and what was cast as the dreamy impracticality of the humanities. Science, presented as an objective and therefore apolitical mode of thought, ontologically distinct from the subjective, variable, and fanciful methodologies taken up by the humanities, gave a veneer of objectivity to what might otherwise have appeared a paranoid spread of suspicion. When McCarthy looked for communists, he went for writers, literary scholars, and movie directors. When the governments of the United States and the USSR sought to ground their superiority in irrefutably objective evidence, they turned to aeronautics and nuclear technology. The popular science fiction of the period divided the oxymoron of that genre name into a battle between nefarious "aliens" (this term for extraterrestrial life was first coined by the science fiction writer John Wood Campbell in 1953) and heroic scientists, the latter always victorious over the flawed logic of irrational enemies. Such logics of absolute opposition were plausible in a culture organized around the Manichaean divide between the Soviet Union and the United States, and its domestic corollaries in the antagonisms of treachery/loyalty, homosexual/heterosexual, or simply good/evil.

Such divisions were anathema, however, to critics like Bewley and the man who was his primary influence, Charles Feidelson. In *Symbolism and American Literature* (1953), Feidelson examines the battle American Romantic writers waged against Cartesian dualism. Romantics opposed the division of the world into matter and mind, a partition that, in Feidelson's view, "made the world safe for science."[28] Observing that the division of mind and matter quickly transformed into a distinction between what is and is not culturally relevant, Feidelson contends that scientific empiricism "held that the given materials of knowledge are atomistic sensations, passively received and variously combined by the intellect."[29] For Feidelson, "the fullness of subjective life" became science's constitutive other, the creative world Feidelson calls the "unreal."[30] Science, for Feidelson, conceives of itself as objective, rule-bound, and politically neutral, a set of values seen as essential to a well-functioning society. The consequence is a conformity that appears voluntary yet is irresistible, circumscribing, "in Hume's words, the 'creative power of the mind.'"[31] Feidelson's critique of scientific objectivity and the social conformity it naturalized had its corollary in his discussion of literary genre. Allegory is, for him, where conventionality finds its literary expression. In Feidelson's account, allegory is "safe because it perceive[s] the conventional distinction between thought and things and because it depend[s] on a conventional order whose point of arrangement was easily defined."[32] Where "symbolism leads to an inconclusive luxuriance of meaning," Feidelson asserts, "allegory imposes the pat moral and the simplified character";[33] accepting conventional relationships between ideas and things, the allegorist "needs not inquire whether either sphere is 'real' or whether reality consists in their interaction."[34]

Interaction is not, however, the same as synthesis, for Feidelson saw the binary logic underlying dialectics as the epistemological equivalent of the divisions insisted upon by science (objective/subjective) and by allegory (thought/things). Although synthesis would seem to resolve that binary logic, Feidelson believed the former requires its perpetuation of the latter, producing new contrasts to give purportedly fixed meaning to the dialectical product. Although dialecticism "aims at reuniting strands of thought that logic itself had separated," it "can only partially counteract the apparent disputatiousness of logical method."[35] As Feidelson writes, "Each reconciling statement excludes far more than it entails; once the opposition becomes explicit, new reconciliation is necessary; and dialectic proceeds through wider and wider generalizations. In the very act of resolving an opposition, it must always respect the law of opposition, the 'either-or' of logic."[36] Rejecting dialectics as a "divisiveness of logic" that believes it "can define a word only as meaning *this, not that*,"[37] Feidelson, sounding very much like Derrida, advocates for a different epistemological framework in which the process of meaning making "is endless, for each resolution contains within itself the possibility of a new conflict."[38] That deferral of meaning finds its literary form in symbolism, for, as Feidelson states, "In symbolism no 'either-or' can arise."[39]

Because of that absence, symbolism, in Feidelson's account, corrects science's purposeful destruction, the misleading assurances of allegory, and the misplaced aspirations of dialectics. For Feidelson, symbolism comprises "an act of faith in a unity which is prior to logical exclusion and which appears in the human capacity to entertain contradictory propositions."[40] This is not the "unity" of dialectical synthesis—a false coherence that constitutively requires continued division—but a unity of mimetic signifier, affective response, and something akin to "meaning" but without the conventionality of preexisting interpretive codes or the stasis of empirically notable presence. As R. W. B. Lewis puts it in his review of *The Symbolic Tradition*, "The knower, the known and the knowledge . . . dance in consort; and the dance is reality."[41] Symbolism, in other words, refuses the hard distinction between what Feidelson calls "absolute materialism and absolute idealism," which in the sciences "are not only opposed, but actually contradict one another."[42] Symbolism makes that contradiction clear, highlighting "the tension between the infinity of symbolic aspiration and the conclusiveness which the objective work entails."[43] In so doing, symbolism takes the "queer leap from fact as fact to fact as meaning."[44] Operating as an epistemology in which "absolute dualism is abandoned," symbolism ensures that "there is no longer any question of subjective expression or objective description." Rather, symbolism ensures that the "real" world "is known in symbolic form; to know is to symbolize in one way or another."[45] Turning symbolism into an epistemology in this way, Feidelson makes it a form of critique through which "literature supersedes, manipulates, and recasts logical structure,"[46] serving "to overthrow conventional reality by dissolving all rational order."[47]

The critique Feidelson imagines involves the simultaneous presence of materiality and idealism—something close to the nonhuman agencies theorized by contemporary theorists such as William Connolly, Bruno Latour, and Jane Bennett—that makes for symbols.[48] As Feidelson writes, "Literature renders the ideas and the thing as interdependent factors in a creative movement of experience."[49] The unsettling simultaneity of mind and matter, speculation and empiricism, is found not in the text's "meaning" but in "the endless becoming of reality"[50] resulting from the uncanny revelation of the *otherwiseness* always there to be experienced in the knowable. As Feidelson puts his case, "All things can become significant in the 'unexpected glimpse' which removes them from the customary world,"[51] since "the moment of imagination is a state of becoming."[52] That moment is found, according to Feidelson, in symbolic literature, which makes apparent "the relationship of the imagination to *any* fact."[53] "Instead of describing reality," Feidelson succinctly asserts, "a poem is a realization,"[54] an invitation to revelatory sensation that changes perspective and awakens invention. Releasing consciousness from the certainties of science and the predictability of allegory, symbolism "is humanism, but a critical humanism."[55] Even more, the critique carried out by symbolism, refusing the division of the real and the unreal, allowing the latter to suffuse the former, becomes a visionary hopefulness, giving literature its "visionary forms."[56] Admonition and vision, acuity and idealism, are no more dividable for Feidelson than are mind and matter; their simultaneity is what he calls symbolism.

To exemplify his ideas, Feidelson cites Hester Prynne's first appearance on the scaffold in *The Scarlet Letter*. Standing before the Puritan ministers who believe they have imprisoned her in allegory—the letter *A* she wears on her chest conveying a fixed significance inscribed in the dominant logic of the Law—Hester seems to have little choice but to accept that "this hostile society and its judgment upon her are 'her realities.'"[57] Looking down at the symbol, however, Hester experiences a revelation, understanding that "the scaffold of the pillory was a point of view," and one wholly different from that of her judges.[58] Hester becomes a symbol, not in the way intended by her Puritan judges, but in the sense of critical vision described by Feidelson. She "establish[es] 'a neutral territory, somewhere between the real world and fairy-land, where the Actual and the Imaginary may meet, and each imbue itself with the nature of the other.'"[59] That infusion of each into the other takes place in the perspective of those whose dispositions grow from the experience of exclusion. "The world thus illuminated," Feidelson writes, "is at once physical and ideal. At its center are human beings who perceive the world by wearing the symbol in mind and body."[60] To wear the symbol on one's body is, on one level, exactly what the stigmatizing categories of deviance seek to accomplish. By moving from supposedly hidden depths to the surface, however, symbols open to the play of language, productive of what Feidelson calls "the 'changed attitude of the ego.'"[61]

The example of Hester Prynne suggests that symbolic perspective is not open to just anyone but is the domain of "the unconventional, the novel, the disorderly," those drawn to "the attraction of inverted values— the extreme form of that anticonventional impulse which is inherent in symbolism."[62] Following Poe, Feidelson calls this anticonventionality "perversity," which Poe defined as "'a perpetual inclination, in the teeth of our best judgment, to violate that which is *Law*, merely because we understand it to be such.'"[63] Considered "abnormal from the standpoint of reason,"[64] perversity allows those who see symbolically to sustain "a precarious life, fostering the mutual criticism of reason and imagination and a provisional trust in both."[65] As the following section will show, for those who followed Feidelson in his analysis of symbolism, the disorderly and novel perspective he refers to became the purview of queers.

Expanding Feidelson's theory of symbolism to offer an account of the rise of American literature, in *The Eccentric Design: Form in the Classic American Novel*, Bewley maintains that American authors, caught between the idealistic promises and materialistic degradation of democracy, turned the former into an "inner reality" that struggles continually with a conservative and profit-driven society.[66] Recognizing that the private individualism involved in interiority is a betrayal of democratic promise, however, those writers responded to the material conditions of their society with literary depictions of symbolic action. Even more than in their plots, American authors showed the tensions characteristic of American culture through literary form, where symbolism, for Bewley as for Feidelson, disrupts convention and allows for more idealistic, less prescribed social imaginaries. And like Feidelson, Bewley argues that symbolism is primarily "concerned with the ultimate problem of determining and evaluating the nature of reality itself."[67]

Though Bewley's ideas follow Feidelson's, however, he introduces two significant innovations in his analysis of symbolism, both indicative of the intensification of Cold War social dynamics during the 1950s. First, he reframes Feidelson's analysis of symbolism as a challenge to the nation itself. Second, he concentrates on symbolism as a form of personification in ways that bring him close to psychology. For Feidelson, symbolism remains a more or less linguistic phenomenon. Bewley's "real," in contrast, focuses on the lived consequences of those linguistic constructions. Whereas for Feidelson symbolism performs a deferral of the real akin to deconstruction, Bewley takes symbolism back into the sphere of human events, giving it a historical as well as a linguistic impact.

Bewley's exploration of symbolism as a means of social action begins, however, as it did for Feidelson, with literary form. The first chapter of *The Eccentric Design* is titled "The Question of Form." In that chapter, after acknowledging that form "is an elusive, even frightening, word," Bewley adopts British critic Herbert Read's definition: "'form is the natural effect of the poet's integrity.'"[68] With that claim, Bewley draws critical attention not to "'the life of form'" but to "'the form of life,'" which "results from emotions and ideas coming together in various combinations in the moulds provided by the conventions and manners of a given society."[69] In that way, an author "meets and resolves those problems that form the medium in which he lives his intellectual and emotional life."[70]

Literature brings ideals into the realm of human action and, inversely, turns depictions of the material world into representatives of ideal counterrealities that cannot be anticipated through conventional precedents. Literary symbolism is "related to the objective world in which the authors lived," but rather than being determined by their contexts, literary symbols express "moral judgment on that world."[71] In setting forth his concept of literature, furthermore, Bewley is clear that it operates not only on the material conditions of "the objective world" but also on the consciousness of the author and the reader. Literature, for Bewley, is an evacuation of selfhood shaped by social conventions and a reshaping of selves through an altered relationality that connects authors to readers. Even a literary text "having no symbolic ambitions"—his example is J. Hector St. John de Crèvecoeur's *Letters from an American Farmer* (1782)—"can slip the leash of the external limitations imposed by the objective data it describes, and rising to a high imaginative level, live in the mind with essentially symbolic life which is intrinsically related to the facts it records."[72] By extension, the power to "slip the leash" extends to readers, whose engagement with symbolism allows their creativity to transform social convention. For writers like Hawthorne, symbolism brings the "inner sphere of reality" into the outside world, making ideals more historically grounded and history more ideally oriented. In Bewley's reading, Hawthorne "projects the inner moral . . . travail *outward* into a world of external symbols where its significance continues to exist for the imagination apart from the protagonist in whom it had its local origin."[73] Literary symbolism transforms "reality" idealistically, a practice of hope the crux of which is the author's "inner reality."[74]

That phrase—"inner reality"—marks Bewley's poignantly enigmatic response to the Cold War. Most immediately, it removes artists from a spatial realm figured as national. In contrast to the contest between the United States and the Soviet Union, which exaggerated national divisions and demanded loyalty pledges from those living not only within the geopolitical boundaries of those countries but throughout the world, "inner reality" provides a "world elsewhere," in Richard Poirier's phrase, that belongs to no country. That non-space is, at the same time, a laboratory and an archive, allowing for other relational possibilities grounded in *opposition to* as well as retreat from the "reality" of a nationalized world. When the geopolitical realities of nationalism betray the principles undergirding nationhood (whether the liberty promised by America or the socialism of the Soviet Union), those ideals find a safe haven in an "inner reality" where, released from the binds of social imperatives, they take unexpected and enhanced form.

If Bewley's "inner reality" functions like the idealistic space of Richard Chase's mythic "withdrawal," unlike Chase, Bewley understood "return"—the second stage of Chase's mythic structure in which ideals infuse and transform social "reality"—not as the content of literary myth but as its form. When the idealism of an author's "inner reality" returns to the material conditions governing literary conventions, the results are formal idiosyncrasies (the "eccentricity" of Bewley's title). Bewley uses various names for those unconventional manifestations—"form," "design"—but his most frequent is "style." Unlike form, style is difficult to discern, a slippery presence that provokes the reader to conjecture rather than to rely on categorical certainty inspired by, to take one example, genre. Style is palpable and yet immaterial, like "inner reality" itself. It signifies individuality in an author, and yet one that is collectively known. Style, in other words, is the "open secret" of literary expression. And as the phrase "open secret" suggests, "inner reality" combines the idea of a protective and idealistic space-which-is-no-space with style to produce an "eccentric design" analogous to gay life in the late 1950s. The gay demimonde—operating in worlds within worlds ("ghettos") that were always mobile (shifting contingently under the pressure of persecution), recognizable through style, and comprising alternative relationships that implicitly critique the normality of the "American way of life"—operates *as* symbols. And symbols, conversely, function queerly.

The following section explores these implications of the "inner reality" proposed in *The Eccentric Design* as a mode of literary analysis that simultaneously condemns Cold War nationalism and twists its professed ideals into a queer countersociality, a form of world making that demonstrates the double nature of critique. Symbolism, in Bewley's treatment, not only becomes a practice of hope, the mutual constitution of critique and idealism, but also shows how the shape and the content of symbols function as oppositional thought. The imaginative eccentricity of literary form, at least as much as the stories authors tell, is what brings people to literature, not just as an escape from everyday life but as the expression of a world differently configured. That, I believe, was

Bewley's point, and it represents the last stage of a development from the socialist critics of the 1930s, who espoused political ideals rather than writing literary criticism, to those of the late 1950s and early 1960s, who were more innovative and daring in their interpretations than they were in their explicit political positions. The turn to literary form was not, I contend, a turn *away* from politics but their relocation. In turning away from form in order to find "politics" and "ideology" expressed in the content of literature or, worse, in an external reality that constitutes the "meaning" of literature, subsequent critics overlook an important site of social commentary and, more important, of reconstructive idealism. What critics like Bewley show us is that when these come together in literary form and are perceivable to readers, then criticism becomes a true practice of hope.

A British scholar living in the United States, Bewley wrote *The Eccentric Design*, he says in the preface, to answer critics who panned his earlier study, *The Complex Fate*, for its national disloyalty. Significantly, they disagreed only about to *which* nation he was unfaithful. Bewley defends himself against the reviewer for "an American weekly widely known for its crisp sophistication, if not urbanity," who condemned *The Complex Fate* for "betraying the United States for the United Kingdom out of snobbery and general servility."[75] In another weekly, this one known for its "wilted politics," Bewley was accused of insulting Britain in favor of an America First program.[76] Tossed back and forth across the Atlantic, Bewley insists, "my interest is still in literature, not passports."[77]

Although Bewley was perceived as being opposed to both British and American nationalism, his antipathy was directed most explicitly toward the latter. American literature reveals, Bewley contends, "the terrible emptiness and solitude of the American sensibility, forced back upon itself in utter isolation, with no theology or faith, no sense of intimacy with the European past and present to impart significance to its own dissenting forms, and with a growing distrust of its own democratic credo."[78] He is particularly critical of Hawthorne, whose "compulsive affirmation of American positives, particularly in the political sense," became "a nervous necessity in that degree in which he found it difficult to cast aside his dissatisfactions with . . . that society that, as an American, he wished to believe in."[79] In Hawthorne, Bewley finds "the tension between isolation and social sympathy" that he believes is intrinsic to American nationalism, with its "conflict between democratic faith and despair."[80] Contesting Allen Tate's claim that American authors found their subject in the story of "progressive self-discovery for the nation," Bewley comments, "Perhaps he is thinking more of the surface of American life than of the more inaccessible problem and conflicts" manifest in the "tensions and inner struggles"[81] of American authors and their characters. Although he speaks of the literature he studies as "American," Bewley claims that nationalism is not "a matter simply of planting the American flag in easily marked out territories."[82] If literature conveys something "American," that designation comes from "the levels below patriotic and personal expediency, below jingoism, below a nostalgic interest in need of folklore and history, below the preachments and parables of literary axe-grinders and demagogues."[83]

Bewley saw the dangers of American nationalism as intrinsically tied to capitalism. Observing that "the American Constitution was an instrument capable of being seriously perverted by those in power,"[84] Bewley, echoing the 1930s critics, condemns the "powerful body of vested interests which tended to identify the good of the country with their private prosperity,"[85] thereby "cloak[ing] its self-interest in patriotic language."[86] Throughout *The Eccentric Design*, Bewley not only brings economics to the critique of nationalism (where, today, it is too often missing) but also turns the two principal Cold War American rationales, capitalism and nationalism, against one another. Bewley is nostalgic for a nineteenth-century economy in which the United States was dependent on Great Britain's superior trade apparatus. That dependence brought to the United States a transatlantic identity as well as gentility that, albeit snobbish, conferred cultural sophistication. In the twentieth century, however, as Britain became more reliant on the United States, American "'men of property' (who are no longer 'men of talents') . . . have no literary preferences at all. Modern literature means as little to them as modern England. No doubt if they ever read books they would prefer something in the realistic line, stressing the hard facts and 'spiritual' dynamism of America."[87]

The divisions attendant on capitalist nationalism—between pragmatism and idealism, greed and fellow feeling, violence and equality—produced a literary struggle that, for Bewley, found paradigmatic form in the novels of James Fenimore Cooper, particularly in *The Deerslayer*'s contest between Natty Bumppo and Hurry Harry March. Personifying the divide between the possible realization of America's proclaimed political ideals and the economic realities that render them cynical at best, "Harry is an indication of how things *will* be, Deerslayer of how they *might* have been."[88] The moral struggle between the two represents, for Bewley, the battle waged in Cooper's "inner reality" between "a highly developed and refined moral consciousness" and "the shock of a brutal necessity";[89] Cooper, Bewley writes, "never forgets that Hurry's scalping practices are legally sanctioned and encouraged by the government under which Deerslayer also lives."[90] Natty's subsequent "flight before the advance of American civilization," Bewley claims, "is virtually a moral judgment on it."[91] Bewley insists that "the real subject of *The Bravo* is the way a financial aristocracy in a republic keeps itself in power."[92] He reports that "Cooper takes us into the inner workings of the secret police and spy systems; shows us the way mutual mistrust is implanted in the various classes; the way that the state forces services and confessions from its victims by alternate threats and promises of rewards."[93] The betrayal of ideals takes place behind "the state's perpetual incantatory praise of its own justice and liberality,"[94] and the ruling powers are swift to punish dissent. Bewley quotes the novel: "'They will pardon complaints against all but their justice. This is too true to be forgiven.'"[95]

Despite the bad odds facing an idealist like Natty, however, Cooper, in Bewley's account, did not give up hope. In Cooper's time, Bewley, describing what in the introduction to this study I identify as Ernesto Laclau's concept of democracy as an empty signifier, writes, "the word 'democracy' had not yet become the slightly obnoxious shibboleth that it is today. It was still possible to investigate its claims seriously and critically. It did not induce narcosis, but an imaginative intensity that stimulated creative effort."[96] For Bewley, Natty Bumppo represents a humanity that works *against* national belonging; instead, Cooper identifies his hero with a tolerant universal humanism that "is nothing more than intelligent and sensitive understanding—perception deep enough to find the substantial likeness under the shadows of division."[97] Building on what Bewley calls "Deerslayer's vision,"[98] later American authors such as Hawthorne and Henry James could evaluate "the moral action and outlook of men, not primarily as citizens, but as private human beings."[99] That outlook extends beyond privacy, however, for symbolism expresses "the magnetic chain of humanity envisaged on a transatlantic scale."[100]

The struggle between Natty and Harry over the fate of democracy is, for Bewley, an allegory of the fate of idealism during the Cold War, as his references to spies, secret police, self-congratulatory rectitude, mutual mistrust, and forced confessions suggest. At moments, the connection between Cooper's day and Bewley's becomes explicit, as when the critic calls Harry Marsh "the artistic progenitor of Senator McCarran's racial ideal."[101] Here Bewley likens Cooper's villain to the Nevada senator and anticommunist crusader who in 1952 sponsored the McCarran-Walter Act, setting quotas on immigration into the United States. Bewley's reference to McCarran, in turn, takes him back to Cooper, in whose day the Alien and Sedition Acts sponsored by John Adams made possible the deportation of "aliens" deemed dangerous, as they were under McCarran's own Internal Security Act of 1950. Where Cooper was "concerned with threats to democracy that are from abuse of its own nature,"[102] political literature in Bewley's era, repeating the government's ethos of suspicion, "largely concerns itself with the threat to democracies from the outside."[103] More than suspicion, however, Bewley blames conformity for the death of democracy in Cold War America. Writing that "the type of American democrat [Cooper] looked forward to has failed to develop," Bewley laments that "levelers and Babbitts have multiplied."[104] The key to the power of politicians like McCarthy and McCarran's was their ability to produce paranoia, a capacity that relied on their authority to name truth claims as "fact." The reification of "reality" in the name of facticity had three disastrous consequences. First, it gave a purportedly empirical existence to a nonexistent enemy, provoking citizens to distrust manifest meanings in a self-fulfilling search for "truths" said to lurk behind appearances. Such assertions of fact gave a phantasmatic shape to what remained invisible, ensuring perpetual cycles of suspicion and anxiety when the object of suspicion failed to materialize. Second, such assertions of fact forestalled the debate that acknowledged speculation would occasion, conferring empirical inevitability on what might otherwise be open to other interpretations. Finally—and this was what concerned Bewley most—assertions of fact made an enemy of the aspirational imagination. The rhetoric of "protection" that orchestrated Cold War paranoia relied on a conservative impulse that turned imaginative alternatives into threats. Here communist rhetorics of a revolution-to-come served to justify imperatives for stasis represented by McCarthyism.

The first step in refusing the regime of fact, Bewley believed, is to refute reality claims that function as pledges of allegiance to social conventions. Nineteenth-century American literature offers compelling models for that refusal. Living in what Bewley characterizes as "a society whose democratic dogma and practice left little scope for the exceptional individual incapable of being leveled down to the common denominator, or of finding an acceptable corner in the Jacksonian version of reality,"[105] Americans experienced a sense of deprivation: "the sense of being without certain kinds of reality that men ought to have: the sense that there is a world of abstract ideas and ideals, and a world of bitter fact, but no society or tradition or orthodoxy in which the two worlds can interact and qualify each other."[106] It was this absence that authors filled by generating an internal space, an "inner reality," that stood as a counterreality, a place where, withdrawn from the realm of "bitter facts" authorized by consensus, they could imaginatively develop ideals in a disenchanted age. The division of inner from outer reality is, for Bewley, what characterizes American literature, which, in its form if not its content, constitutes a site apart from "a society in which the abstract idea and the concrete fact could find little common ground for creative interaction."[107] The American author, in Bewley's account, takes refuge in the literary form that becomes the only place where "the original American artist" can "confront starkly his own emotional and spiritual needs which his art" becomes "the means of comprehending and analyzing."[108]

At the same time, however, this withdrawal from reality carries dangers. Bewley believed that an extreme withdrawal into "inner reality" poisons all but the best of Hawthorne's work and, insofar as Melville threatens at times to take refuge in a self-created metaphysics, almost destroys his writings as well. The greatest danger is in the failure to achieve balance, a failure that mars *The Great Gatsby*. Although Gatsby is aware of the cruel "realities" of everyday material life, he also has a sense of the superior reality "that hovers somewhere out of sight in this nearly ruined American dream."[109] Too bound to material life to achieve that superior reality, Gatsby swings to the opposite extreme, believing in an ideal that torments because he fails to ground it in "the tangible forms of his world, and relate it to the logic of history."[110] For Bewley the best literature comes from the movements between inner and outer reality. Although Cooper's fiction is concerned with "the tangible reality of *things*,"[111] it also possesses "significant intuitions into the moral nature of reality."[112] That "moral nature" comprises the idealism suffusing the materials of everyday life. Bewley imagines this introduction of ideals into the supposedly real world in terms of heroic action; it is the transition from ideals into actions—what Bewley describes as "the shifting grounds of action from the world of the imagination to the world of profit"[113]—that, he writes, keeps the American novel rooted in the real without tying it to the inevitable and the banal. The middle ground between ideals and reality is the metaphysical equivalent of the cosmopolitanism that Bewley admired in Henry James, who "searched through his fictions for a reality that is poised in suspension among the multiple possibilities that Europe and America offer him, but which is really the property of neither."[114] In Bewley's reading, "James's international theme provided him with a double-edged instrument which could cut out a more subtle version of reality."[115] The reality-without-nationalism Bewley saw in James is the world made from symbolism, which transforms "the provincial, local, and native, into a more spacious, humane, and comprehensive reality."[116]

James was also, not coincidentally, a master of style. Bewley seems to follow Oscar Wilde's principle that "in matters of grave importance, style, not sincerity, is the vital thing."[117] Style, for Wilde, signified the love that dare not speak its name but nevertheless insists on leaving its signature. It is the author's insistence on being present in a context that demands his or her effacement. In literary terms, it is a ubiquitous consistency of manner that animates the atmosphere in which characters live and plots unwind, an overarching force running through objects and people animated by something intrinsic to but larger than themselves. Like symbolism, style is the relay between the visible and the imminent. And just as symbols mark readers' desire for a larger significance, style suggests their yearning to see a surface take life, animated by an author's personal flourish that turns out not to be personal at all, but part of a lexicon of gestures known—if not acknowledged—before the encounter. Intimate and codified, style is in the eye of the beholder. Style is, in short, the text's open secret, insincere in its deliberateness and superficiality, but the trace of matters the authors yearn to create new language for only to find themselves proscribed by formal and social convention.

More than a literary matter, however, Wilde's style was what marked him as a sodomite. In Bewley's day, too, homosexuality was discernible in the performance of a distinctive style or pose, associated with the unnecessary flourishes of hairdressers, interior decorators, and painters, musicians, and writers. Such stereotypes became a means for mutual recognition among gay men denied more forthright forms of public address. Functioning between the articulated and the prohibited, public denigration and subcultural production, style was dangerous but also integral to the aesthetic education essential to the world-making capacity for wonder.

The title of Bewley's book *The Eccentric Design* calls up these associations. Eccentricity—literally a position outside the center—challenged the cultural conformity of the 1950s with an affirmative rubric that often served as a euphemism for homosexuality. For Bewley the literary concept of "eccentric design" named the distortion of fictional conventions by their encounter with an author's "inner reality," becoming the trace of a negotiation between the real and the ideal. But a design is also an intention, a plan of action. An eccentric design is, therefore, a queer stratagem. Bewley's opening page quotes Lionel Trilling's observation that American authors "have not turned their minds to society," because "the reality they sought was only tangential to society."[118] Whereas Trilling meant to suggest that writers such as Hawthorne and Melville had little interest in social mores, Bewley turned "tangential" to "eccentric," introducing his thesis that the American novelist "discovered his great alternative in symbolism."[119] The "point of tangency," for mathematicians, is infinitely small. To be tangential to society, then, is to occupy a place the infinite tininess of which correlates to the rapidity with which it expands into an alternative trajectory. What is sacrificed in the author's role as reporter of the status quo is gained in his or her work as critic or visionary. To live—or write—tangentially, then, is to propose an "eccentric design" as an alternative to convention. It is, to put it another way, to achieve what Richard Poirier described as "an eccentricity of defiance."[120]

Gay men had good reasons to defy American social norms in the era of the Cold War. In 1953, President Dwight Eisenhower's Executive Order 10450 authorized purges of homosexuals from government employment as part of a broader crusade led by the likes of J. Edgar Hoover, Roy Cohn, and Joseph McCarthy. Homosexuals were portrayed, like communists, as secretive and devious, characterizations that left gay men and lesbians vulnerable to arrest, beatings, unemployment, and loneliness. Literary criticism in that period could become an intellectual corollary to gay-bashing, as when Henry Bamford Parkes, in a 1949 article on Poe, Melville, and Hawthorne in *Partisan Review*, complains that a "normal and healthy sexuality is . . . conspicuously absent . . . from almost the whole of nineteenth-century literature." Poe and Melville, in particular, Parkes claims, "cross the borders of the abnormal," representing "an apparent element of homosexuality." Their deviance paled beside the sexual abnormality of the twentieth century, however. Parkes concludes that the literary "social misfits" of the nineteenth century were harbingers of the even more perverted writers of Parkes's day, whose "maladjustment" was "very likely to fit with the general pattern defined by the writers of a hundred years ago."[121] Two years before Parkes's essay appeared, the U.S. Congress convened the House Un-American Activities Committee, and in 1948, Alfred Kinsey published *Sexual Behavior in the Human Male*. Although differing in intent, Parkes, HUAC, and Kinsey shared the assumption that "abnormal" sexuality is simultaneously everywhere and exotic, quotidian and threatening, discernible and unseen.

In these circumstances, it is not surprising that Bewley turned in his discussion of symbolism to issues of secrecy, suffering, and fellowship. A decade after Leslie Fiedler's 1948 claim that interracial homosexuality is the emotional core of American fiction,[122] Bewley agreed that the "great loves in American literature are between Ishmael and Queequeg, Natty and Chingachgook, Huck and Jim, even perhaps Gatsby and Nick Carraway."[123] Bewley was not content, however, with Fielder's two-dimensional understanding of homosexuality; instead, being gay in Cold War America, he was more nuanced about the *experience* of homosexual life, about the causes and costs of secrecy, and about how symbolism embraces secrecy and turns it into an idealistic critique arising from suffering but generative of new social formations. In his discussions of nineteenth-century literature, Bewley shows how secrecy destroys the spirit of those who hide; more destructive, however, are the corrosive effects it has on the kind of functional democracy Bewley idealized in his discussions of symbolism. In the case of Arthur Dimmesdale, the sinning minister of *The Scarlet Letter* whose secret shame becomes his downfall, "the original sexual transgression is almost lost sight of, while the actual guilt springs from the festering concealment that poisons the whole context of human relationships."[124] The central image of Hawthorne's story "The Minister's Black Veil," Bewley says, "symbolizes that distrust and suspicion which is the motivation of concealment."[125] Despite his frustration and anger with those who conceal, he was more often compassionate, perhaps because of the paradox faced in his own day by gay men, forced by social stigma into privacy yet compelled into public through rituals of shameful confession. Bewley recognizes this paradox as endemic to disenchanted democracy, which "practically condemns isolation while it makes, on a social level, anything but isolation undesirable."[126] Secrecy, Bewley warns, "separates men from each other, depriving them of sympathy, love, and understanding."[127]

Bewley's theory of symbolism is, then, a response to secrecy and its devastating consequences. Symbols, giving "hidden" meaning a familiar surface, release what is secret into common life but not as the confession of an already-discerned sin. Rather, symbols bring forth what is hidden without making it, in any certain sense, knowable. They encourage in readers an appreciation of the indeterminacy and inexhaustibility of meaning. More to the point, symbols, as Bewley conceives of them, awaken readers' sense of style, a capacity to find oblique significance in the commonplace and then to recognize that act of "finding" as an imposition of an oblique perspective on the blank page of the ordinary. Symbols encourage the recognition of shared style, not common essence, among readers, and out of that recognition arises the possibility of social connection based on disposition, contingent, fleeting but nevertheless sustaining. In the context of symbolic reading, secrecy is not the opposite of democratic participation but the beginning of an emergent counterdemocracy, a human connection arising from a queer epistemology at once oblique, tangential, speculative, critical, and imaginative. Understood this way, secrecy is potentially something more than shameful self-destruction; it is the basis of a "magnetic chain of humanity," "a current of sympathy."[128] While a man's inner reality might mean that "his perception of reality will be unshared, imprisoned within himself," there is the possibility that, through symbolism, "a deeply shared sense of emotional and spiritual communion" might allow men "to communicate what they see and feel and hear, and external reality will not be imprisoned, in the form of sense perception, in them."[129] The connection between inner realities is not the utopian camaraderie of Whitman or the Over-Soul of Emerson but a shared experience of suffering and vulnerability. "It is because each suffered . . . privately in his unique way," Bewley writes of the nineteenth-century authors he interprets, "that we sometimes lose sight of how they also suffered . . . in common."[130] The fellow feeling born from suffering is more than an idyllic escape from the conditions of already-existing social relations; it is, in its imaginative idealism, a reproach to and critique of "the surrounding social medium, that intolerable element."[131] What Bewley writes of Hawthorne can be read as his own manifesto: "His interest is focused on an analysis of the barriers which arise between human spirits in a conventional society when its code has been transgressed, and of the poisons that are generated because of those barriers."[132] That critique is a form of queer idealism, in which suffering generates "a speculative turn of mind . . . to a degree not often recognized today."[133]

A fellowship made from suffering, easy to overlook, releasing from "the horror of the imprisoned or isolated identity"[134] into a "we" who share a "resemblance," all of which can be suggested only "tangentially": Bewley's description of the "eccentric design" of symbols in American literature sounds something like queer subculture in the 1950s. There is a way in which literary studies in the United States during the Cold War was itself a gay subculture, by which I mean that homosexuality was for many of the foundational critics of that field—Newton Arvin, F. O. Matthiessen, Richard Chase, Leslie Fiedler, Marius Bewley, and Richard Poirier, among others—the defining feature of American literature, the source of its hopeful idealism and its incisive critique. Those critics used literary analysis to express an idealism that was linked with same-sex intimacy, sometimes explicitly with homosexuality. Several named as a significant influence D. H. Lawrence, whose *Studies in Classic American Literature* (1923) famously divided the nineteenth-century canon between propriety and passion, especially the unconscious drives of homosexuality. Although Lawrence enthusiastically sided with passion, he was also capable of virulent homophobia. Cold War era literature scholars, however, cast transgressive sexuality as a powerful antidote to what Matthiessen called the "mechanization" of modern society that threatens the "wholeness" of man and leads to the "neurotic strain" in modern life.[135] Arvin centered his reading of Melville, as the previous chapter showed, on a "strong, deflected sexuality," unashamed and sometimes orgiastic," that marks Melville's obsession with "that easy, youthful, irresponsible, bachelor association with his own sex."[136] Melville's "unappeased, perhaps unappeasable, but never quite abandoned reaching out for the perfect mutuality of an ideal friendship,"[137] Arvin asserts, brought forth "all that was visionary, enthusiastic, and illusory in the romantic habit of mind."[138] Chase attributed Romanticism to the "extreme experiences" characteristic of those who live "radical forms of alienation, contradiction, and disorder" necessary for the development of the "blissful, idyllic, erotic attachment to life and to one's comrades."[139] And Poirier identified the power to make worlds "elsewhere" as a characteristic of "the sexually irregular."[140]

Where many midcentury critics saw queer idealism in the content of nineteenth-century literature, however, Bewley diverged from his colleagues by finding it in literary form. That difference does not indicate Bewley's turning away from social engagement but, instead, his experimentation with ways to bring readers into a queer world not through description but through sensations aroused by symbolism. Given this difference, Bewley found his exemplar not in Melville, as Chase and Arvin had, but in Hawthorne's most sensuous symbolist, Clifford Pyncheon from *The House of the Seven Gables*. Having moved, like many gay men in Bewley's day, from wrongful imprisonment to the limited circle of others who, in Hawthorne's words, gnash their teeth on the law, Clifford "endeavors to break down the barriers that keep him isolated from men."[141] Watching humanity pass below his upper-story window, Clifford blows soap bubbles that float among passersby on the street. In Bewley's reading, the bubbles induce wonder as they reflect symbolically the ephemeral but transcendent enchantment already discernible—but only obliquely—within everyday life for those prepared to read idealistically what others see only as trivial or broken. The profound critique in Hawthorne's work, for Bewley, comes in "those soap-bubbles, with the big world depicted, in hues bright as imagination, on the nothing of the surface."[142] Bewley was not naive in his endorsement of idealism, any more than Hawthorne was in creating the damaged character of Clifford. The ideals informing symbolism are forged through pain and determination. It is that pain, however, that grants the power "to sustain the magnetic chain of humanity in unbroken integrity, or make it whole again."[143]

When symbols open up a reflective space in the closed surface of reason or convention, they reveal an aspiration that is also a speculative disposition, suggesting a not-yetness that gestures beyond the is-ness of painful realities. Symbols protect and disguise. They are at once familiar, quotidian, transgressive, and even erotic. Symbols become, for Bewley as for Feidelson, a deconstructive denial of the truth claims of convention. But above all, symbols, as Clifford shows, are a hopeful phenomenon. Unlike popular nineteenth-century entertainments, which, in Richard Chase's view, gave "not a sense of wonder and excitement, but a reassurance that no wonders really existed,"[144] symbolism, as Clifford demonstrates, with its conviction that objects (and people) have a mystical *something* that gives them more than predictable significance, endows them with a sense that the physical and the metaphysical exist in a dynamic simultaneity. In understanding symbolism as what Bruno Latour, using differently a word that would have been familiar to mid-century gay men, calls a "fairy position,"[145] I mean to offer, then, an alternative to paranoid, deep, symptomatic, or suspicious readings, one that is dispositional rather than programmatic, based not on description or fact but on speculation and idealism, what Deleuze calls "a state of mystical contemplation."[146] That state is, in the work of Marius Bewley, a world of symbols, the interpretation of which is a queer practice of hope.

Although his hopeful reading involves replacing the external world—the realm of "reality" with its explicit political positions—with what he calls "aesthetic reality,"[147] for Bewley reading symbolically does have consequences outside the text in the form of what Feidelson calls a "habit of perception."[148] The change consequent on symbolic reading, for Feidelson, occurs in the reader's consciousness, since "perception effectually 'opens' an imaginative reality."[149] The effect of romances by Hawthorne and Melville is "not so much to impose a new form on the world as to adopt a new stance in which the world takes on new shapes."[150] The goal of criticism oriented toward symbolic perception is not to prescribe a particular course of action or belief (a mode of instruction oriented toward those predisposed to agree) but, addressing the disposition of consciousness, to encourage an imaginative openness to possibilities of *otherwise*-ness that, being flexible and contingent, may take multiple and unpredictable forms.

This ideal of a criticism oriented toward literature's potential to alter consciousness was most explicitly and imaginatively developed during the Cold War by Richard Poirier, the Marius Bewley Professor of English at Rutgers University, where, with James Merrill, he organized the Marius Bewley Prize for literary study. By 1966, when Poirier published *A World Elsewhere: The Place of Style in American Literature*, the Cold War had entered a new phase. Direct nuclear antagonism between the governments of the United States and the Soviet Union had given way to interrelated forms of indirect conflict: proxy wars in what became known as the Third World and, at the same time, increasingly visible dissent within the United States from antiwar protests, youth culture, and the civil rights and feminist movements. In *A World Elsewhere*, Poirier integrates these movements and their rhetoric of "consciousness" into Bewley's theories of symbolism and literary style. In that conjoining, however, Poirier's criticism allies itself more closely with the "altered states of consciousness" (a phrase coined by Arnold Ludwig in the year *A World Elsewhere* was published)[151] associated with the drug culture than with more overtly activist forms of consciousness-raising that directly challenged oppressive systems and forms of bad faith identified by Kathie Sarachild's lecture "A Program for Feminist Consciousness Raising" (1968): "Romantic fantasies, utopian thinking and other forms of confusing present reality with what one wishes reality to be." In fact, Poirier privileges precisely those phenomena as modes of world making. As he writes of the American literature analyzed in *A World Elsewhere*, "There is less a tendency to criticize existing environments—for that one would read Howells or Sinclair Lewis—than an effort to displace them."[152] Romantic novels, for Poirier, are "designed to make the reader feel that his ordinary world has been acknowledged, even exhaustively, only to be dispensed with as a source of moral or psychological standards. They are written so as finally not to be translatable into those standards, and their extravagances of language are an exultation in the exercise of consciousness momentarily set free."[153] American literature represents for Poirier "a struggle to create through language an environment in which the inner consciousness of the hero-poet can freely express itself, an environment in which he can sound publicly what he privately is."[154]

The aspect of literary language most important to Poirier is style, which becomes the register of consciousness across a range of symbols, dictions, forms, and other aesthetic effects. As was the case with Bewley, style in Poirier's handling could be described as queer, at once elusive and declarative, palpable and evanescent. Although literary style marks a mode of expression observable across a writer's body of work, for Poirier and Bewley, it is a social phenomenon as well, pulling simultaneously in the direction of the tangible and the evanescent, the personal and the collective. Style, in other words, is symbolism written on the body, a mode of perception, the outer limit of available expression: in short, the literary version of consciousness. Poirier describes style as arising from the friction between shared language and inexpressible experience, language giving temporary form to experience, thus rendering it sharable, experience preventing that form from solidifying into conventional meanings that would end imaginative transformation. Style works the way Feidelson describes the operations of symbols, but, as Bewley knew, style, being the trace of embodied experience, represents the push and pull of social belonging and individual psychology, what allows the world to shape the individual consciousness and, conversely, what makes the latter a force of transformative unsettling in the former. For Poirier, the "tension between the writer's commitment to visionary possibilities and his obligations to certain conventions of expression that tend to frustrate those possibilities, to call them into question," is manifest in literary style, showing "the degree to which visionary experience has to confirm itself within the antagonistic realities of daily life and within the literary artifacts that have shaped those realities."[155] Although that confirmation usually fails, a "world elsewhere" hospitable to free consciousness persists in "the possibilities of a new style" that can "release hitherto unexpressed dimensions of the self into space where it would encounter none of the antagonistic social systems which stifle it in the more enclosed and cultivated spaces of England and of English books."[156] Celebrating "the strangeness of American fiction,"[157] Poirier insists, "Not God, nor religion, not reality, history, or nature, but style is its only authority."[158] Literature comprises "a style filled with an agitated desire to make a world in which tensions and polarities are fully developed and then resolved,"[159] since "only language can create the liberated place."[160] Literary styles "create environments radically different from those supported by economic, political, and social systems,"[161] because only style exists "in a continually fluid state, continually transforming itself into new and mysterious forms."[162]

By locating the socially transformative power of literature in style, Poirier finds a text's "politics" neither in its content nor in a "meaning" that lies below or beyond the surface but rather in that surface itself. In this, Poirier anticipates recent critical turns toward "surface reading" but with an important difference: practitioners of surface or descriptive reading endorse a turn, in the words of Stephen Best and Sharon Marcus, to "what has almost become taboo in literary studies: objectivity, validity, truth."[163] The turn toward objectivity and trust in facts, derived from the social sciences with which some of its practitioners explicitly identify, allies "surface reading" with "suspicious" interpretations, in which analytic acuity is measured by the seriousness with which ideological abstractions are figured as historical truths.[164] Poirier, in contrast, opposes critics' "marked failure to give requisite attention to the demanding styles by which these writers create an imaginary environment that excludes the standards of that 'real' one to which most critics subscribe."[165] Rejecting that critical fetish, Poirier turns literary style into a form of what Giles Deleuze calls "disavowal," which "suspends belief in and neutralizes the given in such a way that a new horizon opens up beyond the given and in place of it." Disavowal challenges "the validity of existing reality in order to create a pure ideal reality."[166] For Poirier, American Romanticism is an extended disavowal, its representative authors having found that "there is nothing within the real world, or in the systems which dominate it, that can possibly satisfy their aspirations."[167] That disavowal occurs through the "very discomforting agitations of style,"[168] which overcomes reality claims that for Poirier, as for Feidelson and Bewley, are naturalizations of structures of power and threats to the imaginative capacity to conceive worlds organized otherwise. Only criticism attuned to what Poirier calls "oddity,"[169] in which "reality" is "antagonistically received,"[170] can be "a direct challenge to those who believe in the fixed realities of our physical environment or our moral life."[171] Truth claims are anathema to literary style, which allows readers, in Hawthorne's words, to "'lessen those iron fetters, which we call truth and reality, and make ourselves even partially sensible what prisoners we are.'"[172]

For most literary critics, the era when changing "consciousness" seemed an effective means of social transformation may have given way in the decades after A World Elsewhere to the more referential literary politics of New Historicism (which maintained more wit and whimsy than most austere versions of critique today). Yet something like Poirier's commitment to literary style as a social disavowal continued beyond the Age of Aquarius and still holds out the possibility for a productive methodological combination of critique and imaginative idealism—of hope—even in the wake of New Historicism, New Americanism, and other forms of ideology critique. In 1998, for example, Sacvan Bercovitch, a figure closely associated with New Historicism, arrived at the familiar conclusion that critique is necessary to reveal what, echoing Poirier, he calls "systems," or "the rules that frame the rhetorics of culture."[173] Having articulated the continuing need for critique, however, Bercovitch asserts that the critique of systems should coincide with literature's power of transvaluation, through which systemic abstractions "may in time become specific points of departure, perhaps points from which to reconceive the game at large. So reconceived, the game of culture, while systemic at any given moment, remains universally subject to intervention."[174] Such interventions Bercovitch calls

> the as-if world we enter . . . through a willing suspension of disbelief, allowing for the temporary dissolution of commonsense barriers between fancy and hard fact, so that even events that are empirically impossible may become a means of conveying what's humanly probable. We might conceive of literature in this sense as a test of the cultural work of the imagination. The as-if text proves its worth by heightening our understanding of the world as we know it.[175]

Understood this way, literature becomes, for Bercovitch, echoing Poirier, Bewley, and Feidelson, "a temporary, ludic *resistance* to received modes of explanation—to the disciplinary frameworks, the structures of belief, within which we learned those hard facts in the first place."[176] As Poirier put it two decades earlier, "The extraordinary dislocations of our fixed ideas of reality that occur while we read" occasion "the suspension and then the redirection of our way of seeing things and of feeling them."[177] Anticipating Bercovitch, Poirier made literature the source of what, following Hegel, he calls freedom, which "is a creation not of political institutions but of consciousness,"[178] stirring readers to "create a world in which consciousness might be free to explore its powers and affinities."[179] In championing literature's power to create an "as-if world"—akin, I would argue, to the anticipatory illuminations Ernst Bloch calls hope—Bercovitch approaches Poirier's concept of the relationship between freedom and the "world elsewhere" of literature.

There are, of course, dangers in allowing transformation to stop with literary consciousness-changing. Poirier knew this. In *A World Elsewhere* he criticizes authors who insist on the purity of an uncompromised vision too easily sustained in literature. Poirier worries that too much faith in the purity of literature's "idealistic effort to free the heroes' and the readers' consciousness from . . . conventional moralities"[180] can foreclose compromise with existing social conditions and frustrate the imaginative transformations literature seeks to enable. When American authors saw their heroes as prisoners of convention, Poirier recognizes their own culpability as jailers. British authors such as Jane Austen and Charles Dickens, Poirier writes, offer their characters options for compromise, allowing them to find a social niche without entirely abandoning their peculiarities or principles. If characters in American literature are stifled, it is often because of their stubborn insistence on remaining outsiders possessing only pure ideals. In this critique, too, Poirier anticipates Bercovitch, who in his classic study *The American Jeremiad* (1978) criticizes American literature's support of the rigidly pure ideals promoted in America's overly flattering self-portraits. In the guise of social critique, the jeremiad structure of much American literature, inveighing against the failure of ideals in a flawed world, implies that ideals can be realized in a pure form, beyond the contamination of human fallibility and compromise. On that level of purity, ideals lose their power of hopeful transformation, since without the compromise and complex complicities social engagements involve, "politics," in Poirier's day as today, must ultimately remain bounded by the covers of a book.

By 1998, Bercovitch, like Poirier in his critique of fettering reality, was moving beyond the belief that ideals have a self-evident political orientation and predetermined consequence, an assumption characteristic of the closed-system totalities of Cold War melancholy. For Poirier, ideals—impure, dependent on use for the determination of consequences, irreducible to material conditions that would exhaust desire and therefore suspend the growth of consciousness—are *meant* to fail, that failure being the drive that turns freedom into a practice, not a promise. Moving from his focus on the jeremiad to his belief in the "as-if world," Bercovitch forges another link in what this book has identified as a chain of transformations reaching from the progressive politics of the 1930s to the study of aesthetic form in the 1950s and beyond. What is maintained through those transformations is the faith in literature—and literary criticism—as a means of social change that does not rely on the dispositional orientation of critiquiness but rests on the wonder-generating powers of "the marvelous and eccentric vitality of American writing (and one often feels of American life)" that "has been pacified or explicated away by commentators."[181] That Bercovitch, a pioneer of New Historicist critique, moved after the end of the Cold War to something akin to what I have called a practice of hope suggests that, if we work to supplant routine forms of suspicion with a sincere investigation into critique's diverse resources, there are imaginative ways for criticism to move beyond its melancholic identification with state epistemologies and the hermeneutics of suspicion they engendered. Neither Bercovitch nor Poirier calls for an end to critique; on the contrary, both were well aware of the "fetters" of economic, social, and political conditions that require constant analysis and condemnation. But after that, what? For Poirier, the answer was a reconstructive engagement with hope: with ideals by which worlds can be ordered differently and with the imagination to envision how those worlds might be brought into being, even if piecemeal and in compromised forms.

In disenchanted times, Poirier knew that criticism should not answer to the demands of social realism, despite the need for social critique, but must enact the ongoing dissatisfaction that prevents truth claims from being mistaken for imperatives. It may be hard to accept that as the basis of criticism today, when, as Cindy Weinstein and Christopher Looby observe, "For many years the predominant approach in American literary studies, as in many other sectors of the academic humanities, was a politically engaged historicism," in which aesthetics were "consciously dismissed (although never, to be sure, successfully avoided) as a matter of minor importance, trivial distraction, or accidental detail."[182] The critical phrase in their account of the fate of aesthetics in the age of New Historicism is, for me, the parenthetical "although never . . . successfully." I have argued in this chapter that the disparagement of aesthetics was countered, and belief in the world-making capacities of symbolism and style maintained, throughout the Cold War and beyond by critics such as Feidelson, Bewley, and Poirier. They made criticism into practices of hope, giving it a radical pedagogical mission.

Asserting that the "classic American writers try through style temporarily to free the hero (and the reader) from systems, to free them from the pressures of time, ideology, economics, and from the social forces which are ultimately the undoing of American heroes and quite often of their creators,"[183] Poirier—linking texts and readers—makes apparent his pedagogical investment in literary (and literary critical) worlds elsewhere. The danger of both suspicious and surface readings that insist on the objective discernment of the critic is that they conclude the interpretive act with the *critic's* reading, essentially rendering unnecessary other readers, either of the primary text or of its criticism. Poirier insists, however, on the suspension of the facticity of meaning, thereby including the reader—*any* reader—in an imaginative process of extending, rather than exhausting, the imaginative work of literature. Without such collaborations there is no change in consciousness, and without changed consciousness, what are politics except an exercise of will or, even worse, the critiquiness that comes from preaching to the choir?

To return to the queer hypothesis with which this chapter began, I would assert that American literary criticism has maintained, despite the odds, its faith in world making, in the study of literature as a practice of hope rather than as the production of disenchantment tales. The usable past I have offered here owes everything to gay men and lesbians like Rourke, Matthiessen, Arvin, Bewley, and Poirier, to those like Chase and Feidelson who explored the power of "myth and symbols" to reimagine the world from the perspective of the "sexually irregular," and to those today who keep faith with literature in a cynical age. For all of these, literature was and is "a kind of defense against moralistic and sociological judgments and presuppositions, judgments that society is always ready to make of its members."[184]

But literature offers more than protection. In a passage from *The Changing Light at Sandover* preceding the one with which I began this chapter, Merrill asks, "Is that you, Marius," and there, like a blasé bachelor uncle, perhaps dressed in liturgical vestments and cocktail in hand, is Bewley, ready to be a stereotype if that means becoming a symbol.

> COME & GONE MY DEAR
> PLATO SAYS ATHENS WAS AT BEST HALF QUEER
> What's Plato *like*? O YOU KNOW TATTLETALE GRAY
> NIGHTGOWN OFF ONE SHOULDER DECLASSE,
> TO QUOTE MM A GAY, TO QUOTE CK.[185]

Bringing together symbolism (Marianne Moore's cameo as MM is significant) and style, Merrill's world, unlike Plato's, is more than half queer—as full of the wit, irony, direct rebukes, and charming idiosyncrasies as are the pages of *The Eccentric Design* and *A World Elsewhere*, which perform as well as describe style's enlivening effects. The result of those effects is what Poirier admired in the "mythic character" of Jay Gatsby, "something commensurate to his capacity to wonder."[186] For a reader whose consciousness is open to "imagination," Poirier exhorts, "the moments of delight are especially vivid because they are grasped with a sort of astonishment at their availability."[187] He is writing here of Henry James's novel *The Ambassadors*, but he might be speaking of literature in general. Could the description apply to literary criticism? It may be hard to accept such an aspiration in our own times, when disenchantment is so highly valued. But although it has, like Bewley's ghost, come and gone, hopefulness persists, just waiting to be summoned.

NOTES

INTRODUCTION

1 Bennett, *Enchantment of Modern Life*, 3.
2 Chase, *Herman Melville*, 301.
3 For versions of "postcritique" analysis, see Best and Marcus, 1–21; Castronovo and Glimp; Felski, "Context Stinks!," 573–591; and Love, 371–391. See especially the collection *Critique and Postcritique.*
4 Fleissner, 700.
5 Adorno, 12.
6 Felski, "Context Stinks!"
7 Ahmed, 197.
8 Matthiessen, *American Renaissance*, 372.
9 Bentley, 147.
10 Best and Marcus, 16.
11 Ibid., 17.
12 Guillory, 475.
13 "Joyful Revolt: A Conversation with Julia Kristeva," in Zournazi, 75.
14 "Hope, Passion, Politics: A Conversation with Chantal Mouffe and Ernesto Laclau," in Zournazi, 127.
15 Ibid.
16 Ibid., 146.
17 Ibid., 147–148.
18 Ibid., 130.
19 Ibid., 124.
20 Ibid., 128.
21 Ibid., 129.
22 Saldívar, 595.
23 "The Rest of the World: A Conversation with Gayatri Spivak," in Zournazi, 173.
24 Bloch, *Literary Essays*, 340.
25 Solnit, 5.
26 Ibid., 4–5.
27 Bloch, *Utopian Function of Art and Literature*, 50.
28 "A Carnival of the Senses: A Conversation with Michael Taussig," in Zournazi, 54.
29 Ibid.
30 Arvin, *Whitman*, 160.

31 Emerson, "Circles," in *Selected Essays*, 225.

32 Ibid., 232.

33 Arvin, *Whitman*, 184.

34 Bennett, *Enchantment of Modern Life*, 28.

35 Ibid., 140.

36 Lewis, *American Adam*, 339.

37 Arvin, *American Pantheon*, 14.

38 Ibid., xvi.

39 Chase, *Herman Melville*, vi.

40 On critical mood, see Felski and Fraiman, v–xiii.

41 Gaddis, 32.

42 Pease, *New American Exceptionalism*.

43 Latour, "Why Has Critique Run Out of Steam?," 225–240.

44 Bennett, *Enchantment of Modern Life*, 156.

45 Foucault describes askesis as the "task of testing oneself, examining oneself, monitoring oneself in a series of clearly defined exercises" central to "the truth concerning what one is, what one does, and what one is capable of doing," with the ultimate goal of "enjoyment without desire and without disturbance." *History of Sexuality*, 68.

46 Bennett, *Enchantment of Modern Life*, 157.

47 Latour, "Why Has Critique Run Out of Steam?"

48 Kaul, 5–6.

49 Ibid., 7.

50 Ibid., 5.

51 Ibid., 43.

52 Ibid., 318.

53 Ibid., 313.

54 Ibid., 306.

55 Ibid., 317.

56 Ibid., vii.

57 Ibid.

58 Ibid., 7.

59 Ibid., 312.

60 Ibid., 9.

61 Ibid., 5.

62 Ibid., 311.

63 Ibid., 309.

64 Ibid., 320.

65 Ibid., 321.

66 Ibid., 311.

67 Ibid., 321.

68 Ibid., 4.

69 Frankel, 115.

70 Trilling, *Liberal Imagination*, 220, 260.

71 Lewis, *American Adam*, 196.

72 Ibid., 9.

73 Mumford, xxi.

74 Ibid., xxviii.

75 Ibid., xxviii–xxix.

76 Ibid., xxix.

77 Ibid.

78 Arvin, *American Pantheon*, 330.

79 James, *American Civilization*, 38, 30, 36.

80 Ibid., 31.

81 Mumford, x.

82 Lewis, *American Adam*, 196.

83 James, *Mariners, Renegades and Castaways*, 115.

84 James, *Black Jacobins*, 265.

85 For a fuller discussion of this passage from James and its implications for how we understand imagination as a revolutionary force, see my "Revolution Is a Fiction," 397–418.

86 Lewis, *American Adam*, 1.

87 Ibid.

88 Ibid.

89 Ibid., 4.

90 Ibid., 2.

91 Ibid., 1–2.

92 Ibid., 3.

93 Parrington, xiii.

94 Ibid., 436.

95 Lawrence, 151, 82.

96 Matthiessen, *American Renaissance*, 518; Arvin, *Herman Melville*, 181, 99.

97 Mumford, xix.

98 Ibid., ix.

99 Chase, *American Novel and Its Tradition*, 1–2.

100 Ibid., 19, 107.

101 Poirier, 7.

102 Ibid.

103 Trilling, *Liberal Imagination*, xv.

104 Ibid., 92.

105 Lewis, *American Adam*, 196.

106 Ibid., 195–196.

107 Ibid., 10.

108 Ibid., 9.

109 Mumford, xiii.

110 "Carnival of the Senses," 48.

111 Latour, "Why Has Critique Run Out of Steam?," 248.

112 Felski, "Suspicious Minds," 218.

113 Lewis, *American Adam*, 9–10.

114 Arvin, *American Pantheon*, 31.

115 Brooks, 339.

116 Arvin, *American Pantheon*, 14.

CHAPTER 1. NATION

1 Latour, "Why Has Critique Run Out of Steam?," 225–248.

2 Ibid., 227.

3 Sedgwick, *Touching Feeling*, 113.

4 Latour, "Why Has Critique Run Out of Steam?," 229.

5 Sedgwick, *Touching Feeling*, 117.

6 Latour, "Why Has Critique Run Out of Steam?," 228.

7 Ibid., 229.

8 Ibid.

9 Ibid., 229, 243.

10 Ibid., 229–230.

11 Ibid., 225.

12 Ibid., 230.

13 Ibid., 243.

14 Ibid., 247.

15 On "the hermeneutics of suspicion," see Ricouer. On the Cold War context for critical suspiciousness, see Sieber.

16 Michaels and Pease; Bercovitch, *Reconstructing American Literary History*; Bercovitch and Jehlen; Tompkins; Reynolds, *Beneath the American Renaissance*.

17 On the New Americanism and suspicious critique, see Fleissner, 699–717. See also Wiegman, 385–407.

18 Pease, "*Moby Dick* and the Cold War," 155.

19 Pease, *Visionary Compacts*, 47.

20 Ibid., 10, 47.

21 Ibid., 47, 48

22 Ibid., 6, 7.

23 Michaels, 177–178.

24 Ibid., 178.

25 Ibid., 177.

26 Ibid.

27 Ibid., 178.

28 Pease, *New American Exceptionalism*, 1–2.

29 Ibid., 6.

30 Ibid., 22.

31 Ibid., 27.

32 Ibid., 27–28.

33 Ibid., 11.

34 Hicks, *I Like America*, 3–4.

35 Ibid., 3.

36 Perhaps Hicks perceived early that, as historian Thomas Ferguson has shown, the leaders in Franklin Delano Roosevelt and Harry S. Truman's administrations were also the representatives of "capital-intensive industries, investment banks, and internationally oriented commercial banks." Bringing high capital into the running of government (and vice versa), those men were, as John Fousek argues, "able to project their own values and beliefs into a dominant position in the nation's public life and largely to set the terms of public discussion concerning 'America's world role.'" Quoted in Fousek, 10.

37 Hicks, *I Like America*, 3.

38 Ibid., 3–4.

39 Ibid., 5.

40 Ibid.

41 Ibid.

42 Berlant, 37.

43 Ibid., 38.

44 Ibid.

45 Ibid., 41.

46 Ibid., 40.

47 Hicks, *I Like America*, 5.

48 Trachtenberg, 124.

49 Ibid.

50 "Hope, Passion, Politics," 146.

51 Ibid., 147–148.

52 Ibid., 130.

53 Berlant, 41.

54 Gruez, 21.

55 Hicks, *I Like America*, 211–212.

56 Berlant, 41–42.

57 Ibid., 42.

58 Dean, 18.

59 Berlant, 42.

60 Hicks, *I Like America*, 48.

61 Ibid., 135.

62 For a description of American communists and nationalism, see Caren Irr.

63 Hicks, *I Like America*, 141.

64 Ibid.

65 Ibid., 212.

66 Ibid., 105.

67 Ibid., 104.

68 Ibid., 136.

69 Ibid., 138.

70 Ibid., 87.

71 Ibid., 190.

72 Ibid., 111.

73 Ibid., 123.

74 Ibid., 120.

75 Ibid., 123, 120.

76 Ibid., 121.

77 For an account of Hicks's life in Grafton, see Levenson and Natterstad, "Granville Hicks and the Small Town," 95–112.

78 Hicks, *I Like America*, 15.

79 Ibid., 26–27.

80 Ibid., 27.

81 Ibid., 28–29.

82 Observing that "matters of utter simplicity ought to be expoundable with the utmost calmness, with utter freedom from passion," Percy Boynton contends, "Mr. Hicks, on the contrary, though not as explosive and ungenerous as Karl Marx usually was to friends and foes alike, is at least reminiscent of his master." Boynton, 473. F. O. Matthiessen was more sympathetic in his review of *The Great Tradition*, noting that Hicks "has not fallen into . . . facile theorizing, but has gained a mastery of his subject by very wide reading, and has reflected penetratingly what he has read" (223). Matthiessen goes on to say, however, that despite having "a good deal of both respect and sympathy for Mr. Hicks's political position," he nevertheless finds that Hicks appears "to draw such a close analogy between politics and literature as to blur the essential distinctions between them" (232). Matthiessen, "Great Tradition," 223–234.

83 Matthiessen, "Great Tradition," 223.

84 Ibid., 228.

85 Ibid., 230.

86 Hicks, *I Like America*, 6, 93.

87 See LeBlanc and Davenport.

88 Brooks, 340.

89 Ibid., 339, 340.

90 Mumford, xxix, xxiv.

91 Rourke, *Roots of American Culture*, 48.

92 Ibid., 295.

93 See Doss.

94 Rourke, *Roots of American Culture*, 45.

95 Ibid., 48.

96 Ibid., 45.

97 Ibid., 55.

98 Ibid., 24.

99 Ibid., 52.

100 Ibid., 55.
101 Ibid., 12.
102 Ibid., 16.
103 Ibid., 15.
104 Ibid., 50, 54.
105 Ibid., 290, 291.
106 Ibid., 20, 22.
107 Ibid., 16–17.
108 Ibid., 51.
109 Ibid., 26.
110 Ibid., 19, 55, 56.
111 Beckwith, 222–223.
112 Rourke, *Roots of American Culture*, 193.
113 Ibid., 162–164.
114 Ibid., 182.
115 Ibid., 15.
116 Ibid., 161, 177–178, 181.
117 Ibid., 87.
118 Ibid., 112.
119 Ibid., 76.
120 Ibid., 79, 82.
121 Ibid., ix–x.
122 Ibid., 73, 74, 75.
123 Ibid., 269–270.
124 Ibid., 271.
125 Ibid., 274.
126 Ibid., 27, 58.
127 Trachtenberg, 223.
128 Rourke, *Roots of American Culture*, 196, 197.
129 Ibid., 282.
130 Ibid., 26, 50.
131 Ibid., 244, 280.
132 Writing that "approaching the commonplace and the familiar as if it were strange and enigmatic is to melt its protective stonelike armature, to reveal the provisional and arbitrary character of all human construction," Trachtenberg extols Rourke's appreciation of "capriciousness, eccentricity, and extravagance," all of which represent a "straying from the ordered, regular, or usual course of conduct, decorum, or propriety" (220). Whereas modern "criticism subjects all that exists to the corrosive power of reason in the hope of solving the riddle, defeating the enigma, capturing and holding the vagaries under the glass of analysis and deconstruction" (221), Trachtenberg writes, Rourke, honoring the fluidity and variety of local cultures that render the nation unstable and ever-changing, "pledged herself to the goals of democratic cultural criticism" (332).

133 Kazin, "Irreducible Element," 259–260, quoted in Trachtenberg, 223. See also Rourke, "Miss Rourke Replies to Mr. Blair," 207–210. In that essay, Rourke reports that the roots of American humor are not in realism but in fantasy (207).

134 Rourke, *Roots of American Culture*, 248.

135 Ibid., 240, 296.

136 Ibid., 250.

137 Ibid., 239, 240, 241.

138 Ibid., 243.

139 On the sales of *I Like America*, see Levenson and Natterstad, *Granville Hicks*, 100–101. See also Lamont.

140 Hicks, *Where We Came Out*, 7.

141 Ibid.

142 Ibid., 9–10.

143 Ibid., 239.

144 Ibid., 241, 249.

145 Ibid., 249.

146 Ibid., 248, 249.

147 Ibid., 241.

148 On the details of Hicks's appearance before the House Un-American Activities Committee, see O'Neill, 85–86. See also Fisher, 544.

149 Hicks, *Where We Came Out*, 3.

150 Irr, 25.

151 Hicks, *Where We Came Out*, 12.

152 Ibid.

153 Ibid., 13.

154 Ibid.

155 Ibid., 245.

156 Ibid., 7.

157 Hicks, *Great Tradition*, 328.

158 Ibid., 329.

159 Kaplan, 141–147; Marx, 118–134.

160 Kaplan, 141.

161 Ibid., 142.

162 Ibid., 142.

163 Ibid., 146.

164 Marx, 127.

165 Ibid., 128–129.

166 Ibid., 127.

167 Ibid., 129.

168 Ibid., 120.

169 Ibid., 130.

170 Kaplan, 146.

171 Ibid.

172 Hicks, *Great Tradition*, 329.

173 Hicks, *Where We Came Out*, 246.

174 Ibid.

175 Arvin, *American Pantheon*, 24.

176 Irr, 26.

177 Hicks, *Great Tradition*, 214.

178 Hicks, "On Attitudes and Ideas," 126.

179 Ibid., 127.

180 Hicks, *I Like America*, 215.

CHAPTER 2. LIBERALISM

1 Richard Chase to Newton Arvin, February 15, 1950.

2 Chase, letter to Newton Arvin.

3 Ibid.

4 Chase, *Herman Melville*, v.

5 Ibid.

6 Sparks, 530.

7 Chase, *Herman Melville*, 292.

8 Ibid., vi.

9 Ibid., 64.

10 Chase, "Progressive Hawthorne," 97.

11 Ibid., 100.

12 Ibid., 97.

13 Ibid.

14 Ibid., 98.

15 Ibid.

16 Chase, *Herman Melville*, v.

17 Ibid., 5.

18 Ibid., 283.

19 Barrett, "What Is the 'Liberal' Mind?," 331.

20 Arvin, Davis, and Aaron, 221.

21 Ibid., 222.

22 Ibid., 221.

23 Ibid.

24 Ibid.

25 Barrett, "What Is the 'Liberal' Mind?," 331, 333.

26 Ibid., 333.

27 Barrett, "What Is the 'Liberal' Mind?," 331.

28 Chase, *Herman Melville*, 63.

29 Ibid., 22.

30 Ibid., 65.

31 Chase, "Liberalism and Literature," 649.

32 Ibid., 652.

33 Trilling, "A Rejoinder to Mr. Barrett," 656.
34 Ibid.
35 Ibid., 657.
36 Ibid.
37 Murphy.
38 McGann, x.
39 Ibid., 13.
40 Ibid., 23.
41 Ibid., 26.
42 Ibid., 27.
43 Ibid., 23.
44 Ibid., 29.
45 Ibid., 28.
46 Ibid., 3.
47 Ibid., 28.
48 Ibid., 11.
49 Ibid., 30.
50 Ibid., 1.
51 Chase followed the lead of his thesis adviser and Columbia colleague Lionel Trilling. In the early 1930s, Trilling had belonged to the Communist Party's National Committee for the Defense of Political Prisoners and identified himself with the anti-Stalinist, Trotskyite circle of *Partisan Review* writers. As growing disillusionment broke the unity of the communist "front" in New York, however, Trilling left Trotsky for Freud. In works such as his landmark book *The Liberal Imagination* (1950), Trilling popularized the "darker" Freud of *Beyond the Pleasure Principle* and *Civilization and Its Discontents* to create a psychologically complex—often unsavory and self-destructive—picture of the individual psyche and of social relations. Despite Trilling's less than sanguine depiction of "personality," however, his work suggests the ways New Liberalism, rather than wholly abandoning a previous generation's utopian politics, translated them into the cultural terms of early Cold War America. In a period of heavily regulated social conformity, Trilling showed how social conventions function as a restrictive superego, suppressing libidinal instincts and making nonnormativity necessary to psychic and social health. As universities underwent unprecedented social diversification that rendered a one-size-fits-all political philosophy impractical, Trilling placed individual comprehension and resolve at the heart of social responsibility, allowing politics an adaptability foreclosed by externally imposed dogma. Trilling may have interiorized politics, then, but he also made them more inventive and participatory. The resemblances are striking between Trilling's theories of personality and 1960s activists' faith in consciousness-raising, as a means for developing "moral imagination," rejecting repressive law through the release of libidinal energies, beliefs that led to the 1968 antiwar uprising at Columbia, where both Trilling and Chase were teaching.

52 Chase, letter to Newton Arvin.
53 Ibid.
54 Chase, *Herman Melville*, vii.
55 Ibid., viii.
56 Ibid., 135.
57 Ibid., 81.
58 Ibid., 101.
59 Chase, letter to Newton Arvin.
60 Chase, *Herman Melville*, 140.
61 Ibid.
62 Ibid., 257.
63 Ibid., 276.
64 Chase, "Melville's Confidence Man," 137, 138.
65 Ibid., 138.
66 Ibid.
67 Ibid., 127.
68 Chase, *Herman Melville*, 207, 208.
69 Chase, "Melville's Confidence Man," 138.
70 Chase, *Herman Melville*, 55.
71 Ibid., 283.
72 Ibid., vii.
73 Ibid., 121.
74 Ibid., 4.
75 Ibid.
76 Ibid., viii.
77 Ibid., 143.
78 Ibid., 283.
79 Ibid., x.
80 Ibid., 152.
81 Ibid., x.
82 Rahv, 732.
83 Kazin, "On Melville as Scripture," 67, 69.
84 Ibid., 68, 74.
85 Ibid., 75.
86 Hayford, 129–131.
87 Kazin, "On Melville as Scripture," 68.
88 Benjamin, 229.
89 Ibid., 164.
90 Copeland and Struck, 4.
91 Ibid., 5–6.
92 Benjamin, 226.
93 Copeland and Struck, 6.
94 Chase, *American Novel and Its Tradition*, 19, 107.

95 Fineman, 46–66.

96 Ibid., 60.

97 Ibid., 48.

98 See, for instance, Bérubé; Chauncey; and D'Emilio.

99 "Richard Volney Chase Memorial," *Plymouth Record*, August 20, 1940, http://www.findagrave.com.

100 Hayford, 131.

101 Chase, *Walt Whitman Reconsidered*.

102 Ibid., 9–10.

103 Ibid., 18.

104 Ibid., 44.

105 Ibid., 52–53.

106 Ibid., 79.

107 Ibid., 51.

108 Ibid., 81.

109 Ibid., 51.

110 Ibid., 56.

111 Ibid., 43.

112 Ibid., 124.

113 Sparks, 525.

114 Ibid., 526.

115 Ibid., 530.

116 Chase, *Walt Whitman Reconsidered*, 35.

117 Ibid., 43.

118 Ibid.

119 Ibid., 48.

120 Ibid., 62.

121 Ibid., 76.

122 Ibid., 34.

123 Ibid., 45.

124 Ibid., 114.

125 Ibid., 114–115.

126 Ibid., 116.

127 Ibid., 39–40.

128 Ibid., 43.

129 Ibid., 17.

130 Ibid., 39.

131 Ibid., 82.

132 Ibid., 80.

133 Ibid., 18.

134 Aaron, 99–110.

135 Ibid., 101.

136 Ibid., 99.

137 Ibid., 104.

138 Ibid., 105.

139 Ibid., 105–106.

140 Ibid., 108.

141 Ibid.

142 Ibid., 109.

143 Ibid., 102.

144 Ibid., 100.

145 Leslie Fiedler to Richard Chase, January 30, 1949.

146 Chase, *Herman Melville*, 302.

147 Ibid.

CHAPTER 3. HUMANISM

1 Arvin, "The House of Pain: Emerson and the Tragic Sense," in *American Pantheon*, 31.

2 Ibid., 38.

3 Ibid.

4 Fromm, ix.

5 Arvin, "House of Pain," 19.

6 Arvin, *Whitman*, 274.

7 Aaron and Schendler, "Introduction," in *American Pantheon*, xvii.

8 Arvin writes of Augustine, "'Evil has no positive nature,' he says in *The City of God*; but the loss of good has received the name 'evil.'" Like the Neoplatonists, Augustine saw evil "as a rejection or refusal of the Good, not as an ultimate and independent essence in itself." Good could be distinguished from evil, Arvin believed, only "by distinguishing between what is real to the intellect and what is real to the conscience—real, that is, in the conduct of life itself." Arvin, "House of Pain," 30.

9 Ibid., 20.

10 Ibid., 21.

11 Ibid., 20.

12 Arvin, "Brooks's Life of Emerson," in *American Pantheon*, 13.

13 Arvin, "House of Pain," 26.

14 Foucault, *Discipline and Punish*.

15 On the relationship of wonder and the unexpected in everyday life, see Bennett, *Enchantment of Modern Life*.

16 Arvin, "The House of Pain: Emerson and the Tragic Sense" originally appeared in the *Hudson Review* 12, no. 1 (Spring 1950). The page numbers here refer to the reprinted essay in *American Pantheon*.

17 Arvin, "Brooks's Life of Emerson," 12.

18 Ibid.

19 Arvin, "The Usableness of Howells," in *American Pantheon*, 134.

20 Arvin, "Brooks's Life of Emerson," 12, 11.

21 Ibid., 13.
22 Ibid.
23 Ibid., 15.
24 Ibid., 13.
25 Ibid., 18, 13.
26 Arvin, "Whitman's Individualism," in *American Pantheon*, 43.
27 Ibid., 46–47.
28 Ibid., 43.
29 Arvin, "Brooks's Life of Emerson," 13–14.
30 Arvin, *American Pantheon*, xvii.
31 Arvin, "House of Pain," 18, 27.
32 Ibid., 23.
33 Ibid., 25.
34 Ibid., 23.
35 Ibid.
36 Ibid.
37 Ibid., 36.
38 Ibid., 32.
39 Ibid., 36, 27.
40 William James, 83.
41 Ibid., 85.
42 Ibid.
43 Ibid., 144–145.
44 Ibid., 51.
45 Ibid., 140, 88.
46 Ibid., 134.
47 Ibid., 88.
48 Ibid., 32, 142.
49 Ibid., 89, 136, 144.
50 Arvin, "Brooks's Life of Emerson," 13.
51 Arvin, "House of Pain," 17.
52 Ibid., 27.
53 Arvin, "Usableness of Howells," 134.
54 Ibid.
55 Ibid., 129.
56 Ibid., 132.
57 Arvin, "House of Pain," 36.
58 Arvin, "Usableness of Howells," 133.
59 Arvin, "Brooks's Life of Emerson," 14.
60 Arvin, "Letters of Henry Adams," in *American Pantheon*, 217.
61 For the details of Arvin's biography, see Werth.
62 Martin, "Newton Arvin," 290. "It would be a good thing," Andrew Delbanco writes in his review of Werth's biography, "if *The Scarlet Professor* were to open

the way to a more general reappraisal of the pioneer generation of American literary scholars to which Arvin belonged." Delbanco asserts, "Far from being the restrictive canonizers they are sometimes made out to be, they were critics—and Arvin will hold his place among them—who discovered a capacious literature that does not flinch before the full range of human experience. As this book reminds us, the freedom imagined by the American writers whom these critics discovered was sometimes too much for America to bear" (73). Delbanco, 64–73. Although both Martin and Delbanco call for closer attention to Arvin's criticism, both focus primarily on the critic's biography.

63 Delbanco, 67.

64 "The Whitman biography," Robert K. Martin reports, "is an attempt to work out, through the writing of another life, the meaning of Arvin's own life and his commitment to a practice of literary criticism that is engaged and contestatory," particularly about homosexuality and its relation to politics. Martin, "Newton Arvin," 308.

65 Arvin, *Herman Melville*, 55.

66 Arvin, *Whitman*, 161.

67 Arvin, *Herman Melville*, 44.

68 Arvin, *Hawthorne*, 76–77.

69 Ibid., 91.

70 Newfield, 29–62.

71 Arvin, *Hawthorne*, 59.

72 Ibid., 62.

73 "I call its way of life an ethics," Michael Warner writes, "not only because it is understood as a better kind of self-relation, but because it is the premise of the special kind of sociability that holds queer culture together. A relation to others, in these contexts, begins in an acknowledgment of all that is most abject and least reputable in oneself. Shame is bedrock. Queers can be abusive, insulting, and vile toward one another, but because abjection is understood to be the shared condition, they also know how to communicate through such camaraderie a moving and unexpected form of generosity" (35).

74 Arvin, *Hawthorne*, 61.

75 Ibid., 40.

76 Ibid., 15.

77 Berlant and Warner describe queer world making as requiring "the development of kinds of intimacy that bear no necessary relation to domestic space, to kinship, to the couple form, to property, or to the nation" (558).

78 Arvin, *Hawthorne*, 11.

79 Ibid., 58.

80 On the construction of a queer counterpublic around Hester, see my "Genealogy of a Democratic Crush," 201–204.

81 Arvin, *Hawthorne*, 37.

82 Ibid., 275.

83 Ibid., 39.
84 Ibid., 207.
85 Ibid., 67.
86 Ibid.
87 Ibid., 202.
88 For a critique of queer theory's abhorrence of the ordinary, see Martin, "Extraordinary Homosexuals and the Fear of Being Ordinary," 100–125.
89 Arvin, *Hawthorne*, 202.
90 Ibid., 203–204.
91 Ibid., 203.
92 Ibid., 204.
93 Ibid., 202.
94 Ibid.
95 Ibid., 67.
96 Ibid., 185.
97 Ibid., 204.
98 Ibid.
99 Ibid., 17.
100 Ibid., 206.
101 Ibid., 65.
102 Arvin, *American Pantheon*, xvi.
103 Arvin, *Hawthorne*, 182.
104 Ibid.
105 Ibid., 183.
106 Arvin journal entry, January 6, 1962, quoted in Martin, "Newton Arvin," 291.
107 Quoted in Arvin, *Whitman*, 1.
108 Ibid., 4.
109 Ibid., 4–5.
110 Ibid., 273–274.
111 Ibid., 2–3.
112 Ibid., 88.
113 Ibid., 90, 91.
114 Ibid., 92.
115 Ibid., 105.
116 Ibid., 116.
117 Ibid., 263.
118 Ibid., 118.
119 Ibid., 111.
120 Ibid., 109.
121 Ibid., 170.
122 Ibid., 144.
123 Ibid., 284.
124 Ibid., 262.

125 Ibid., 76.
126 Ibid., 256.
127 Ibid., 176.
128 Ibid., 214.
129 Ibid., 5.
130 Ibid., 170.
131 Ibid.
132 Ibid., 29.
133 Ibid., 12–13.
134 Ibid., 176.
135 Ibid., 115.
136 Ibid., 113.
137 Ibid., 177.
138 Ibid., 182.
139 Ibid., 251–252.
140 Ibid., 41.
141 Ibid., 187.
142 Ibid., 160.
143 Ibid., 184.
144 Ibid., 233–234.
145 Ibid., 161.
146 Ibid., 234.
147 Ibid., 270.
148 Ibid., 207.
149 Ibid.
150 Ibid., 276.
151 Ibid., 277.
152 Ibid., 276–277.
153 Ibid., 252.
154 Ibid., 282.
155 Ibid., 262.
156 Ibid., 273.
157 Ibid., 263.
158 Ibid., 279.
159 Ibid.
160 Ibid., 288.
161 Ibid., 275.
162 Ibid., 281.
163 Ibid., 140.
164 Ibid., 220.
165 Ibid., 200.
166 Ibid., 221.
167 Ibid., 224.

168 Ibid., 252.
169 Arvin, *Herman Melville*, 181.
170 Ibid., 191.
171 Ibid., 107.
172 Ibid., 98.
173 Ibid., 34.
174 Ibid., 30.
175 Ibid., 7.
176 Ibid., 96–97.
177 Ibid., 35.
178 Ibid., 88.
179 Ibid.
180 Ibid., 37.
181 Ibid., 77.
182 Ibid., 10.
183 Ibid., 128.
184 Ibid., 57.
185 Ibid., 256.
186 Ibid., 203.
187 Ibid., 129.
188 Ibid., 128.
189 Ibid., 131.
190 Ibid., 181.
191 Ibid., 176.
192 Ibid., 178–179.
193 Ibid., 178.
194 Ibid., 44.
195 Ibid., 174.
196 Ibid., 182.
197 Ibid., 287.
198 Ibid., 97.
199 Ibid., 282.
200 Ibid., 294.
201 Ibid., 257.
202 Ibid., 287.
203 Ibid., 281.
204 Arvin, *Whitman*, 2.
205 Arvin, *American Pantheon*, xvi.
206 Arvin, *Whitman*, 283.
207 Ibid., 2.
208 In his introduction to *Socialist Humanism*, for instance, Erich Fromm writes, "Today, more than ever, we find concepts like freedom, socialism, humanism, and God used in an alienated, purely ideological way, regardless of who uses them.

What is real in them is the word, the sound, not a genuine experience of what the word is supposed to indicate. The contributors [to the collection of essays] are concerned with the *reality* of human existence, and hence are critical of ideology; they constantly question whether an idea expresses the idea or hides it" (xi–xii).

209 Arvin never quite lost his identification with Socialism. As late as 1961, he wrote in his journal, "I belong on the left, the far left, as much as I ever did. The enemy has assumed a somewhat different guise, but he is still there, and always will be, and the struggle is unremitting." Quoted in Martin, "Newton Arvin," 297.

210 Arvin, "House of Pain," 29.

211 Arvin, "Grounds of Literary Judgment," 41.

212 Ibid.

213 Ibid., 46.

214 Ibid., 36.

215 Ibid., 7.

216 Ibid.

217 Ibid., 14–15.

218 Ibid., 12.

219 Ibid., 52.

220 Ibid., 54.

221 Ibid., 54–55.

222 Ibid., 3.

223 Ibid., 55–56.

224 Ibid., 6.

225 Ibid., 6, 7.

226 Ibid., 34.

227 Thompson, 24.

228 Ibid.

229 Arvin, *Longfellow*, 74.

230 Ibid., 324.

231 Ibid., 322.

232 Ibid., 323.

233 Ibid., 324.

234 Ibid.

235 Ibid., 325.

236 Ibid., 324.

237 Ibid., 325.

238 Ibid., 47.

239 Ibid., 326.

240 Best and Marcus, 2.

241 Ibid., 19.

242 Arvin, *Longfellow*, 46–47.

243 Ibid., 67.

244 Ibid., 49.

245 Ibid., 67.

246 Ibid., 68.

247 Ibid., 67.

248 Ibid., 67–68.

249 Ibid., 67.

250 Ibid., 326.

251 Ibid., 314.

252 Martin, *Hero, Captain, and Stranger*

CHAPTER 4. SYMBOLISM

1 Brooks, 340.

2 Merrill, *Changing Light at Sandover*, 305.

3 On the penises in Gary Mackenzie's illustrations, see Cookley. On Bewley's parties, see Thomas.

4 Bewley reviewed Merrill's *Country of a Thousand Years of Peace* for *Partisan Review* in 1959, at which point they were already friends. See Hammer, 271. Merrill and Bewley had an extensive correspondence, starting in 1952. James Merrill Papers.

5 See Johnson. See also Sherry.

6 Quoted in Micklethwait and Woodbridge, 45.

7 Quoted in Whitefield, 43, 44.

8 Bewley, *Masks and Mirrors*, 25.

9 Ibid., 26.

10 Ibid., 26, 27.

11 Ibid., 15.

12 Ibid., 26.

13 Ibid., 36.

14 Ibid., 10.

15 Ibid., 42.

16 Ibid., 47.

17 Ibid., 18.

18 Ibid., 15.

19 Ibid., 47.

20 Ibid., 35.

21 Ibid., 12.

22 Ibid., 10.

23 Ibid., 26.

24 Ibid., 47.

25 Ibid., 48.

26 Ibid., 47.

27 Ibid., 16.

28 Feidelson, 110.

29 Ibid.

30 Ibid.
31 Ibid.
32 Ibid., 15.
33 Ibid.
34 Ibid., 8.
35 Ibid., 67.
36 Ibid., 69.
37 Ibid., 68.
38 Ibid. On the relationship between Feidelson and Derridean deconstruction, see Foley, 44–64.
39 Feidelson, 69.
40 Ibid., 68.
41 Lewis, "Literature and Things," 308.
42 Feidelson, 67.
43 Ibid., 73.
44 Ibid., 77.
45 Ibid., 52.
46 Ibid., 58.
47 Ibid., 26.
48 See, for example, Coole and Frost; Connolly; Bennett, *Vibrant Matter*; and Latour, *We Have Never Been Modern*.
49 Feidelson, 65.
50 Ibid., 18.
51 Ibid., 13.
52 Ibid., 30.
53 Ibid., 8.
54 Ibid., 18.
55 Ibid., 218.
56 Ibid., 30.
57 Ibid., 10.
58 Ibid.
59 Ibid., 7.
60 Ibid., 12.
61 Ibid., 17.
62 Ibid., 14, 15.
63 Ibid., 39.
64 Ibid.
65 Ibid., 74.
66 Bewley uses the phrase "inner reality" (141) as well as "inner sphere" (127) and "inner sphere of reality" (129) repeatedly in his discussion of Hawthorne.
67 Ibid., 122.
68 Ibid., 13.
69 Ibid.

70 Ibid., 16.
71 Ibid., 102.
72 Ibid., 102–103.
73 Ibid., 141.
74 Ibid.
75 Ibid., 9.
76 Ibid.
77 Ibid.
78 Ibid., 215.
79 Ibid., 115.
80 Ibid., 19.
81 Ibid., 17.
82 Ibid., 288.
83 Ibid., 289.
84 Ibid., 50.
85 Ibid., 51.
86 Ibid., 50.
87 Ibid., 10.
88 Ibid., 96.
89 Ibid., 98.
90 Ibid.
91 Ibid., 111.
92 Ibid., 58.
93 Ibid., 59.
94 Ibid.
95 Ibid.
96 Ibid., 23.
97 Ibid., 97.
98 Ibid., 98.
99 Ibid., 186.
100 Ibid., 232.
101 Ibid., 94.
102 Ibid., 47.
103 Ibid.
104 Ibid., 68.
105 Ibid., 138.
106 Ibid., 17.
107 Ibid., 18.
108 Ibid., 19.
109 Ibid., 275.
110 Ibid.
111 Ibid., 92.
112 Ibid., 76.

113 Ibid., 54.

114 Ibid., 221.

115 Ibid., 223.

116 Ibid., 221.

117 Wilde, 289.

118 Bewley, *Eccentric Design*, 13.

119 Ibid., 14.

120 Poirier, 5.

121 Parkes, 157–165.

122 Fiedler, "Come Back to the Raft Ag'in, Huck Honey," 664–671.

123 Bewley, *Eccentric Design*, 240.

124 Ibid., 166.

125 Ibid., 133.

126 Ibid., 131.

127 Ibid., 134.

128 Ibid., 127.

129 Ibid., 132.

130 Ibid., 18.

131 Ibid., 174.

132 Ibid.

133 Ibid., 167.

134 Ibid., 131.

135 Matthiessen, 518.

136 Arvin, *Herman Melville*, 10, 57.

137 Ibid., 256, 263.

138 Ibid., 203.

139 Chase, *American Novel and Its Tradition*, 107.

140 Poirier, 7.

141 Bewley, *Eccentric Design*, 181.

142 Ibid.

143 Ibid., 182.

144 Chase, *Herman Melville*, 76.

145 Latour, "Why Has Critique Run Out of Steam?," 237.

146 Deleuze, 32, 33.

147 Feidelson, 14.

148 Ibid., 7.

149 Ibid., 9.

150 Ibid., 27.

151 Ludwig, 225.

152 Poirier, 6.

153 Ibid., 7.

154 Ibid., 35.

155 Ibid., 91–92.

156 Ibid., 39–40.
157 Ibid., 9.
158 Ibid., 17.
159 Ibid., xxii.
160 Ibid., 5.
161 Ibid., 16.
162 Ibid., 22.
163 Best and Marcus, 17.
164 For a fuller discussion of this shared investment in fact or what I call "soft critique," see my "Revolution Is a Fiction," 397–418.
165 Poirier, 7.
166 Deleuze, 31–33, 35.
167 Poirier, 5.
168 Ibid., xx.
169 Ibid., 70.
170 Ibid.
171 Ibid., 142.
172 Ibid., 92.
173 Bercovitch, "The Function of the Literary," 84.
174 Ibid.
175 Ibid., 70.
176 Ibid.
177 Poirier, 84.
178 Ibid., 4.
179 Ibid., xxi.
180 Ibid., 35.
181 Bercovitch, *American Jeremiad*, xx.
182 Weinstein and Looby, 5.
183 Poirier, 5.
184 Ibid., 152.
185 Merrill, *Changing Light at Sandover*, 158.
186 Poirier, 52.
187 Ibid., 136–137.

REFERENCES

Aaron, Daniel. "Conservatism, Old and New." *American Quarterly* 6, no. 2 (Summer 1954): 99–110.

Adorno, Theodor. "Something's Missing: A Discussion between Ernst Bloch and Theodor W. Adorno on the Contradictions of Utopian Longing." In Ernst Bloch, *The Utopian Function of Art and Literature: Selected Essays*, translated by Jack Zipes and Frank Mecklenburg, 1–17. Cambridge, MA: MIT Press, 1988.

Ahmed, Sara. *The Promise of Happiness*. Durham, NC: Duke University Press, 2010.

Anderson, Benedict. *Imagined Communities: Reflections on the Origin and Spread of Nationalism*. New York: Verso, 2006.

Anker, Elizabeth, and Rita Felski, eds. *Critique and Postcritique*. Durham, NC: Duke University Press, 2017.

Arvin, Newton. *American Pantheon*. Edited by Daniel Aaron and Sylvan Schendler. New York: Delacorte Press, 1966.

———. "The Grounds of Literary Judgment." Unpublished typescript, 1952. Sophia Smith Collection and College Archives. Neilson Library, Smith College, Northampton, MA.

———. *Hawthorne*. Boston: Little, Brown, 1929.

———. *Herman Melville*. New York: Grove Press, 2002.

———. *Longfellow: His Life and Work*. Boston: Atlantic-Little, 1962.

———. *Whitman*. New York: Macmillan, 1938.

Arvin, Newton, Richard Gorham Davis, and Daniel Aaron. "Liberalism and Confusion." *Partisan Review* 16, no. 2 (February 1949): 220–222.

Barrett, William. "Art, Aristocracy, and Reason." *Partisan Review* 6, no. 6 (June 1949): 658–665.

———. "What Is the 'Liberal' Mind?" *Partisan Review* 16, no. 3 (March 1949): 331–336.

Beckwith, Martha. "Review." *Journal of American Folklore* 56, no. 221 (1943): 222–223.

Benjamin, Walter. *The Origin of German Tragic Drama*. London: Verso, 1998.

Bennett, Jane. *The Enchantment of Modern Life: Attachments, Crossings, and Ethics*. Princeton, NJ: Princeton University Press, 2001.

———. *Vibrant Matter: A Political Ecology of Things*. Durham, NC: Duke University Press, 2010.

Bentley, Nancy. "Introduction." *J19: The Journal of Nineteenth-Century Americanists* 1, no. 1 (Spring 2013): 147–153.

Bercovitch, Sacvan. *The American Jeremiad*. Madison: University of Wisconsin Press, 1978.

———. "The Function of the Literary in a Time of Cultural Studies." In *Culture and the Problem of the Disciplines*, edited by John Carlos Rowe, 69–86. New York: Columbia University Press, 1998.

———, ed. *Reconstructing American Literary History*. Cambridge, MA: Harvard University Press, 1996.

Bercovitch, Sacvan, and Myra Jehlen, eds. *Ideology and Classic American Literature*. New York: Cambridge University Press, 1996.

Berlant, Lauren. "Citizenship." In *Keywords for American Cultural Studies*, edited by Bruce Burgett and Glenn Hendler, 37–41. New York: New York University Press, 2007.

Berlant, Lauren, and Michael Warner. "Sex in Public." *Critical Inquiry* 24, no. 2 (Winter 1998): 547–566.

Bérubé, Allan. *Coming Out under Fire: The History of Gay Men and Women in World War II*. New York: Free Press, 1990.

Best, Stephen, and Sharon Marcus. "Surface Reading: An Introduction." *Representations* 108, no. 1 (Fall 2009): 1–21.

Bewley, Marius. *The Eccentric Design: Form in the Classic American Novel*. New York: Columbia University Press, 1959.

———. *Masks and Mirrors: Essays on English and American Literature from Donne to Eliot, from Cooper to Wallace Stevens*. London: Chatto and Windus, 1970.

Bloch, Ernst. *Literary Essays*. Stanford, CA: Stanford University Press, 1998.

———. *The Utopian Function of Art and Literature: Selected Essays*. Translated by Jack Zipes and Frank Mecklenburg. Cambridge, MA: MIT Press, 1988.

Boynton, Percy. "Review." *International Journal of Ethics* 44, no. 4 (1934): 471–474.

Brooks, Van Wyck. "On Creating a Usable Past." *Dial: A Semi-monthly Journal of Literary Criticism, Discussion, and Information* 64, no. 7 (April 1918): 337–341.

Calverton, V. F. *The Liberation of American Literature*. New York: C. Scribner's and Sons, 1932.

Castiglia, Christopher. "Genealogy of a Democratic Crush." In *Materializing Democracy: Toward a Revitalized Cultural Politics*, edited by Russ Castronovo and Dana D. Nelson, 195–217. Durham, NC: Duke University Press, 2002.

———. "Revolution Is a Fiction: The Way We Read (Early American Literature) Now." *Early American Literature* 51, no. 2 (2016): 397–418.

Castronovo, Russ, and David Glimp. "After Critique." *English Language Notes* 51, no. 2 (Fall/Winter 2013): 45–60.

Chase, Richard. *The American Novel and Its Tradition*. Baltimore: Johns Hopkins University Press, 1957.

———. "Dissent on Billy Budd." *Partisan Review* 15, no. 11 (November 1948): 1212–1218.

———. *Herman Melville: A Critical Study*. 1949. Reprint, New York: Hafner, 1971.

———. Letter to Newton Arvin, February 15, 1950. Richard Volney Chase Papers. Butler Library, Columbia University, New York.

———. "Liberalism and Literature." *Partisan Review* 6, no. 6 (June 1949): 649–653.

———. "Melville's Confidence Man." *Kenyon Review* 11, no. 1 (Winter 1949): 122–140.

———. "The Progressive Hawthorne." *Partisan Review* 16, no. 1 (January 1949): 96–99.

———. *Walt Whitman Reconsidered*. New York: William Sloane Associates, 1955.

Chauncey, George. *Gay New York: Gender, Urban Culture, and the Making of the Gay Male World, 1890–1940*. New York: Basic Books, 1995.

Connolly, William E. *Processes, Neoliberal Fantasies, and Democratic Activism*. Durham, NC: Duke University Press, 2013.

Cookley, William Lee. "What to Do until the Poet Comes, Part One." *Keep the Lights On*, December 20, 2011. http://keepthelightsonfilm.

Coole, Diana, and Samantha Frost, eds. *New Materialisms: Ontology, Agency, and Politics*. Durham, NC: Duke University Press, 2010.

Copeland, Rita, and Peter T. Struck. *The Cambridge Companion to Allegory*. New York: Cambridge University Press, 2010.

Dean, Jodi. *Democracy and Other Neoliberal Fantasies: Communicative Capitalism and Left Politics*. Durham, NC: Duke University Press, 2009.

Delbanco, Andrew. "On Newton Arvin." *Raritan* 21, no. 4 (Spring 2002): 64–73.

Deleuze, Gilles. *Masochism: Coldness and Cruelty*. New York: Zone Books, 1991.

D'Emilio, John. *Sexual Politics, Sexual Communities: The Making of a Homosexual Minority in the United States, 1940–1970*. Chicago: University of Chicago Press, 1983.

Doss, Erika. *Benton, Pollock, and the Politics of Modernism from Regionalism to Abstract Expressionism*. Chicago: University of Chicago Press, 1995.

Emerson, Ralph Waldo. *Emerson: Essays and Lectures*. Edited by Joel Porte. New York: Library of America, 1983.

———. *Selected Essays*. Edited by Larzer Ziff. New York: Viking, 1982.

Feidelson, Charles. *Symbolism and American Literature*. Chicago: University of Chicago Press, 1953.

Felski, Rita. "Context Stinks!" *New Literary History* 42, no. 4 (Autumn 2011): 573–591.

———. "Suspicious Minds." *Poetics Today* 32, no. 2 (Summer 2011): 215–234.

Felski, Rita, and Susan Fraiman, eds. "In the Mood." *New Literary History* 43, no. 3 (Summer 2012): v–xiii.

Fiedler, Leslie. "Come Back to the Raft Ag'in, Huck Honey." *Partisan Review* 15, no. 6 (June 1948): 664–671.

———. Letter to Richard Chase, January 30, 1949. Richard Volney Chase Papers. Butler Library, Columbia University, New York.

Fineman, Joel. "The Structure of Allegorical Desire." *October* 12 (Spring 1980): 46–66.

Fisher, Louis. "Mr. Hicks and the Liberals." *New Republic*, April 1945, 544.

Fleissner, Jennifer. "Historicism Blues." *American Literary History* 25, no. 4 (Fall 2013): 699–717.

Foley, Barbara. "From New Criticism to Deconstruction: The Example of Charles Feidelson's *Symbolism and American Literature*." *American Quarterly* 36, no. 1 (Spring 1984): 44–64.

Foucault, Michel. *Discipline and Punish: The Birth of the Prison*. New York: Vintage, 1979.

———. *The History of Sexuality*. Vol. 3, *The Care of the Self*. New York: Vintage, 1986.

Fousek, John. *To Lead the Free World: American Nationalism and the Cultural Roots of the Cold War*. Chapel Hill: University of North Carolina Press, 2000.

Frankel, Matthew Cordova. "Tattoo Art: The Composition of Text, Voice, and Race in Melville's Moby-Dick." *ESQ* 53, no. 2 (2007): 114–147.

Fromm, Erich, ed. *Socialist Humanism*. Garden City, NY: Doubleday, 1966.

Gaddis, John Lewis. *The Cold War: A New History*. New York: Penguin, 2006.

Gruez, Kirsten Silva. "America." In *Keywords for American Cultural Studies*, edited by Bruce Burgett and Glenn Hendler, 16–21. New York: New York University Press, 2007.

Guillory, John. "The Sokal Affair and the History of Criticism." *Critical Inquiry* 28, no. 2 (Winter 2002): 470–508.

Hammer, Langston. *James Merrill: Life and Art*. New York: Knopf, 2015.

Hayford, Harrison. "Review." *Modern Language Notes* 66, no. 2 (February 1951): 129–131.

Hicks, Granville. *The Great Tradition: An Interpretation of American Literature*. New York: International Press, 1933.

———. *I Like America*. New York: Modern Age Books, 1938.

———. "On Attitudes and Ideas." *Partisan Review* 14, no. 1 (January/February 1947): 117–129.

———. *Small Town*. 1946. Reprint, New York: Fordham University Press, 2004.

———. *Where We Came Out*. London: Victor Gollancz, 1954.

Irr, Caren. *The Suburb of Dissent: Cultural Politics in the United States and Canada in the 1930s*. Durham, NC: Duke University Press, 1998.

James, C. L. R. *American Civilization*. Oxford: Blackwell, 1992.

———. *The Black Jacobins: Toussaint L'Ouverture and the San Domingo Revolution*. New York: Vintage, 1989.

———. *Mariners, Renegades and Castaways: The Story of Herman Melville and the World We Live In*. Hanover, NH: University Press of New England.

James, William. *The Varieties of Religious Experience: A Study in Human Nature*. 1902. Reprint, New York: Penguin, 1982.

Johnson, David K. *The Lavender Scare: The Cold War Persecution of Gays and Lesbians in the Federal Government*. Chicago: University of Chicago Press, 2006.

Kaplan, Amy. "A Call for a Truce." *American Literary History* 17, no. 1 (Spring 2005): 141–147.

Kaul, A. N. *The American Vision: Actual and Ideal Society in Nineteenth-Century Fiction*. New Haven, CT: Yale University Press, 1963.

Kazin, Alfred. "The Irreducible Element." *New Republic*, August 1942, 259–260.

———. "On Melville as Scripture." *Partisan Review* 17, no. 1 (January 1950): 69–77.

Lamont, Corliss. "I Like America by Granville Hicks; Hope in America by John Strachey." *Science and Society* 3, no. 2 (1939): 251–254.

Latour, Bruno. *We Have Never Been Modern*. Cambridge, MA: Harvard University Press, 2013.

———. "Why Has Critique Run Out of Steam? From Matters of Fact to Matters of Concern." *Critical Inquiry* 30, no. 2 (2004): 225–248.

Lawrence, D. H. *Studies in Classic American Literature*. New York: Thomas Seltzer, 1923.

LeBlanc, Paul, and Tim Davenport, eds. *The "American Exceptionalism" of Jay Lovestone and His Comrades, 1929–1940: Dissident Marxism in the United States*. Leiden: Brill, 2015.

Levenson, Leah, and Jerry Natterstad. *Granville Hicks: The Intellectual in Mass Society*. Philadelphia: Temple University Press, 1993.

———. "Granville Hicks and the Small Town." *Syracuse University Library Associates Courier* 20, no. 2 (1985): 95–112.

Levine, Robert S. *Dislocating Race and Nation: Episodes in Nineteenth-Century Literary Nationalism*. Chapel Hill: University of North Carolina Press, 2008.

Lewis, R. W. B. *American Adam: Innocence, Tragedy, and Tradition in the Nineteenth Century*. Chicago: University of Chicago Press, 1955.

———. "Literature and Things." *Hudson Review* 7, no. 2 (Spring 1954): 308–311.

Love, Heather. "Close but Not Deep: Literary Ethics and the Descriptive Turn." *New Literary History* 41, no. 2 (Spring 2010): 371–391.

Ludwig, Arnold M. "Altered States of Consciousness." *Archives of General Psychiatry* 15, no. 3 (September 1966): 225–234.

Martin, Biddy. "Extraordinary Homosexuals and the Fear of Being Ordinary." *Differences* 6, nos. 2–3 (Summer/Fall 1994): 100–125.

Martin, Robert K. *Hero, Captain, and Stranger: Male Friendship, Social Critique, and Literary Form in the Sea Novels of Herman Melville*. Chapel Hill: University of North Carolina Press, 1986.

———. "Newton Arvin: Literary Critic and Lewd Person." *American Literary History* 16, no. 2 (Summer 2004): 290–317.

Marx, Leo. "On Recovering the 'Ur' Theory of American Studies." *American Literary History* 17, no. 1 (Spring 2005): 118–134.

Matthiessen, F. O. *American Renaissance: Art and Expression in the Age of Emerson and Whitman*. New York: Oxford University Press, 1968.

———. "The Great Tradition: A Counter-statement." *New England Quarterly* 7, no. 2 (1934): 223–234.

McGann, Jerome J. *The Romantic Ideology: A Critical Investigation*. Chicago: University of Chicago Press, 1983.

Merrill, James. *The Changing Light at Sandover*. New York: Macmillan, 1982.

———. James Merrill Papers. Special Collections and Archives, Washington University Libraries, Washington University. St. Louis, MO.

Michaels, Walter Benn. "Romance and Real Estate." In *The American Renaissance Reconsidered*, edited by Walter Benn Michaels and Donald E. Pease, 156–182. Baltimore: Johns Hopkins University Press, 1985.

Michaels, Walter Benn, and Donald E. Pease, eds. *The American Renaissance Reconsidered*. Baltimore: Johns Hopkins University Press, 1985.

Micklethwait, John, and Adrian Woodbridge. *The Right Nation: Conservative Power in America*. New York: Penguin, 2004.

Mumford, Lewis. *The Golden Day: A Study in American Literature and Culture.* Boston: Beacon Hill, 1957.

Murphy, Gretchen. "Ahab as Capitalist, Ahab as Communist: Revising *Moby-Dick* for the Cold War." *Surfaces* 4 (1994). http://www.pum.umontreal.ca.

Newfield, Christopher. "Democracy and Male Homoeroticism." *Yale Journal of Criticism* 6, no. 2 (Fall 1993): 29–62.

O'Neill, William I. *A Better World: The Great Schism: Stalin and the American Intellectuals.* New York: Simon and Schuster, 1982.

Parkes, Henry Bamford. "Poe, Hawthorne, Melville: An Essay in Sociological Criticism." *Partisan Review* 16, no. 2 (February 1949): 157–165.

Parrington, Vernon L. *The Romantic Revolution in America, 1800–1860.* New York: Harcourt Brace Jovanovich, 1955.

Pease, Donald E. "*Moby Dick* and the Cold War." In *The American Renaissance Reconsidered*, edited by Walter Benn Michaels and Donald E. Pease, 113–155. Baltimore: Johns Hopkins University Press, 1985.

———. *The New American Exceptionalism.* Minneapolis: University of Minnesota Press, 2009.

———. *Visionary Compacts: American Renaissance Writers in Cultural Context.* Madison: University of Wisconsin Press, 1987.

Poirier, Richard. *A World Elsewhere: The Place of Style in American Literature.* New York: Oxford University Press, 1966.

Rahv, Philip. "Melville and His Critics." *Partisan Review* 17, no. 7 (September/October 1950): 732–735.

Reynolds, David S. *Beneath the American Renaissance: The Subversive Imagination in the Age of Emerson and Melville.* New York: Knopf, 1988.

Ricouer, Paul. *Freud and Philosophy: An Essay on Interpretation.* New Haven, CT: Yale University Press, 1970.

Rourke, Constance. 1931. *American Humor: A Study of the National Character.* New York: Harcourt Brace Jovanovich, 1959.

———. "Miss Rourke Replies to Mr. Blair." *American Literature* 4, no. 2 (1932): 207–210.

———. *The Roots of American Culture and Other Essays.* Edited by Van Wyck Brooks. Westport, CT: Greenwood Press, 1942.

Saldívar, Ramón. "Historical Fantasy, Speculative Realism, and Postrace Aesthetics in Contemporary American Fiction." *American Literary History* 23, no. 3 (Fall 2011): 574–599.

Sarachild, Kathie. "A Program for Feminist Consciousness Raising." Lecture presented at the First National Women's Liberation Conference, Chicago, IL, November 27, 1968. Accessed November 12, 2015. http://rhetoricalgoddess.wikia.com.

Scott, James. *Weapons of the Weak: Everyday Forms of Peasant Resistance.* New Haven, CT: Yale University Press, 1987.

Sedgwick, Eve Kosofsky. *Shame and Its Sisters: A Silvan Tomkins Reader.* Durham, NC: Duke University Press, 1995.

———. *Touching Feeling: Affect, Pedagogy, Performativity.* Durham, NC: Duke University Press, 2003.

Sherry, Michael. *Gay Artists in Modern American Culture: An Imagined Conspiracy.* Chapel Hill: University of North Carolina Press, 2007.

Sieber, Tobin. *Cold War Criticism and the Politics of Skepticism.* New York: Oxford University Press, 1993.

Solnit, Rebecca. *Hope in the Dark: Untold Histories, Wild Possibilities.* New York: Nation Books, 2005.

Sparks, Clare. *Hunting Captain Ahab: Psychological Warfare and the Melville Revival.* Kent, OH: Kent State University Press, 2006.

Thomas, Inigo. "Bohemian New York." *Slate*, January 31, 2005. http://www.slate.com.

Thompson, Lawrence. "A Tarnished Reputation Reappraised." *New York Times*, May 5, 1963.

Tompkins, Jane. *Sensational Designs: The Cultural Work of American Fiction, 1790–1860.* New York: Oxford University Press, 1986.

Trachtenberg, Alan. "The Ballad in the Street: Listening for the Muffled Strains of a National Culture." *American Scholar* 76, no. 1 (2007): 121–124.

Trilling, Lionel. *The Liberal Imagination.* New York: New York Review Books, 1950.

———. "A Rejoinder to Mr. Barrett." *Partisan Review* 6, no. 6 (June 1949): 653–658.

Warner, Michael. *The Trouble with Normal: Sex, Politics, and the Ethics of Queer Life.* New York: Free Press, 1999.

Weinstein, Cindy, and Christopher Looby. *American Literature's Aesthetic Dimensions.* New York: Columbia University Press, 2012.

Werth, Barry. *The Scarlet Professor: Newton Arvin: A Literary Life Shattered by Scandal.* New York: Anchor, 2001.

Whitefield, Stephen. *The Culture of the Cold War.* Baltimore: Johns Hopkins University Press, 1996.

Wiegman, Robyn. "The Ends of New Americanism." *New Literary History* 42, no. 3 (Summer 2011): 385–407.

Wilde, Oscar. *The Importance of Being Earnest.* 1895. Reprint, New York: Oxford University Press, 2008.

Zournazi, Mary, ed. *Hope: New Philosophies for Change.* New York: Routledge, 2002.

INDEX

Aaron, Daniel, 82, 104–7, 111, 139–40

Abrams, M. H., 84

Adams, Henry, 19, 121

Adorno, Theodor, 2

Ahmed, Sara, 3

aesthetics, 10, 92; contemporary criticism and, 182–83; homosexuality and, 153

allegory, 94; Walter Benjamin on, 94–96; Marius Bewley and, 152; Richard Chase on, 78–99; defined, 94–97; Charles Feidelson on, 158–59; homosexuality and, 96–98, 153–54; idealism and, 92–93, 100; Herman Melville and, 78–80, 87–93; Plato's Allegory of the Cave, 95–96, 98, 152–53; Walt Whitman and, 100; wonder and, 95–96

American exceptionalism, 4, 27, 32, 42, 52–55, 63–64, 69–70; Donald Pease on, 36–38; Constance Rourke on, 62; Stalin on, 53. *See also* nationalism

American studies, 42

Anderson, Benedict, 48

Arvin, Newton, 9, 11, 19, 23, 25, 72; arrest of, 121–22, 144–45, 149–50; and the Cold War, 113, 140–41, 146–47; debate with Richard Chase, 75–78; on Ralph Waldo Emerson, 115–18; and ethical enhancement, 110, 120; on ethics, 127–28; and the Frankfurt School, 111; *Hawthorne*, 122–29; on *Longfellow: His Life and Work*, 144–48; *Herman Melville*, 122–23, 136–40, 174–75; homosexuality and, 114, 123–24, 146–48; on literary judgment, 142–44; on the nature of evil, 197n8; political evolu-tion, 140–41, 203n209; obscurity of, 121; queer humanism and, 110–11, 114, 121, 131, 144, 148, 175; socialism and, 139; on suffering, 111–14, 117, 148; *Whitman*, 122, 129–36, 139–40

Auden, W. H., 151–53

Barrett, William, 82–83, 87

Beckwith, Martha, 59

Benjamin, Walter, 94–96

Bennett, Jane, 1, 9–10, 10–11, 13, 160, 197n15

Bentley, Nancy, 5

Benton, Thomas Hart, 56

Bercovitch, Sacvan, 180–82

Berlant, Lauren, 40–41, 44, 126, 199n77

Best, Stephen, 5, 147, 179

Bewley, Marius, 72; and allegory, 152; appearance in James Merrill's *Chang-ing Light at Sandover*, 151–53, 184: on capitalism, 166–67; on James Fenimore Cooper, 167–68, 170; critique of Cold War America, 164, 168–69; on John Donne, 154–57; on *The Great Gatsby*, 169–70; on Nathaniel Hawthorne, 173, 165–66, 175–76; on Henry James, 170; and "inner reality," 163–65, 169–70, 205n66; and literary form, 162–65, 175; on nationalism, 165–68, 170; sexual sub-culture and, 151, 156–57, 164, 171–73, 174; speculative reading and, 157, 175; style and, 170–73; symbolism and, 152, 162–76

Billings, William, 60

Bloch, Ernst, 111; anticipatory illumina-tions, 95; critique of facts, 9; on disap-pointment, 8; on literature, 9

ABOUT THE AUTHOR

Christopher Castiglia is Distinguished Professor of English and Women's, Gender, and Sexuality Studies at The Pennsylvania State University. He is the author of *Bound and Determined: Captivity, Culture-Crossing, and White Womanhood from Mary Rowlandson to Patty Hearst*; *Interior States: Institutional Consciousness and the Inner Life of Democracy in the Antebellum United States*; and, with Christopher Reed, *If Memory Serves: Gay Men, AIDS, and the Promise of the Queer Past*. He is cofounder of C19: The Society of Nineteenth-Century Americanists and founding co-editor of *J19: The Journal of Nineteenth-Century Americanists*.